GAIA LIGHT
ALESSANDRO COSMELLI

HAVANA BUZZ

TEXT
ABEL FERNÁNDEZ - LARREA

DAMIANI

For Havana

it was a night inside a bus,
a guagua.
the girl was sitting right beside me,
staring at me with her big eyes full of
sky.
i was playing with the bus ticket
(we had bus tickets then, and guaguas),
making a plane with the small piece of
paper.
she stared at me with her big eyes
full of sky,
while i made a plane
out of the paper.
i was chatting with someone,
sort of bragging.
i played with the paper plane and then, careless
left it land upon the back of a seat.
didn't care much about the world around me.
the guagua,
that bus that was part of our everyday life,
like another home,
like a dark street,
like a paper plane.
my stop was near, i walked towards the door,
about to descend from the guagua,
like an angel of despair.
i turned my back for a second,
the big sky ahead in the shape of some eyes.
there was the girl, still staring at me.
in her hands, she held the little piece of paper,
the plane.
she smiled.
the guagua shut its doors and cut my wings.

A guagua named "desire"
Abel Fernández-Larrea

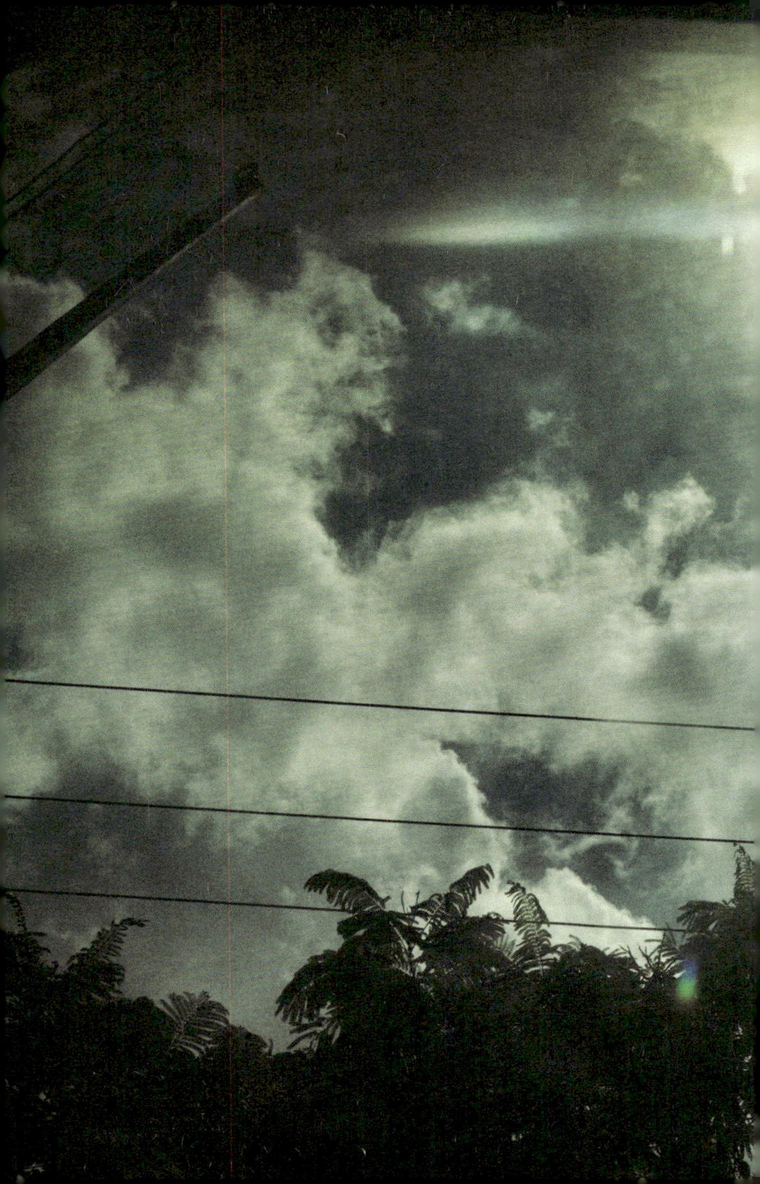

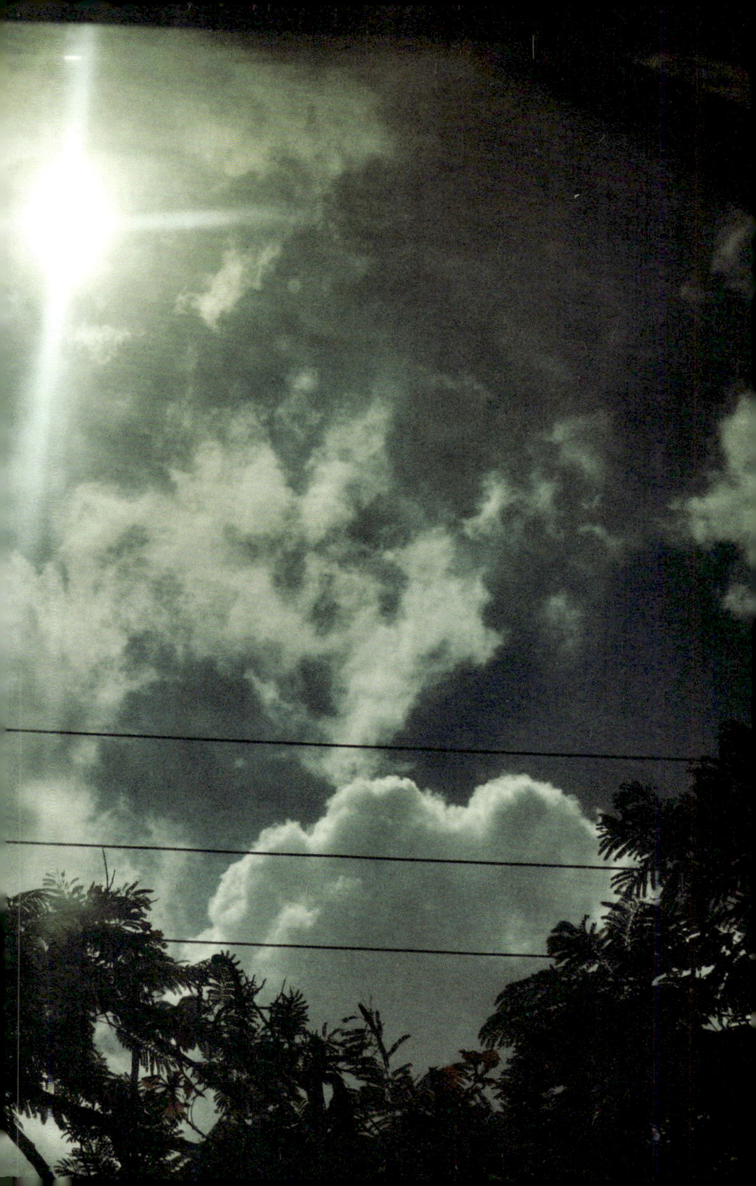

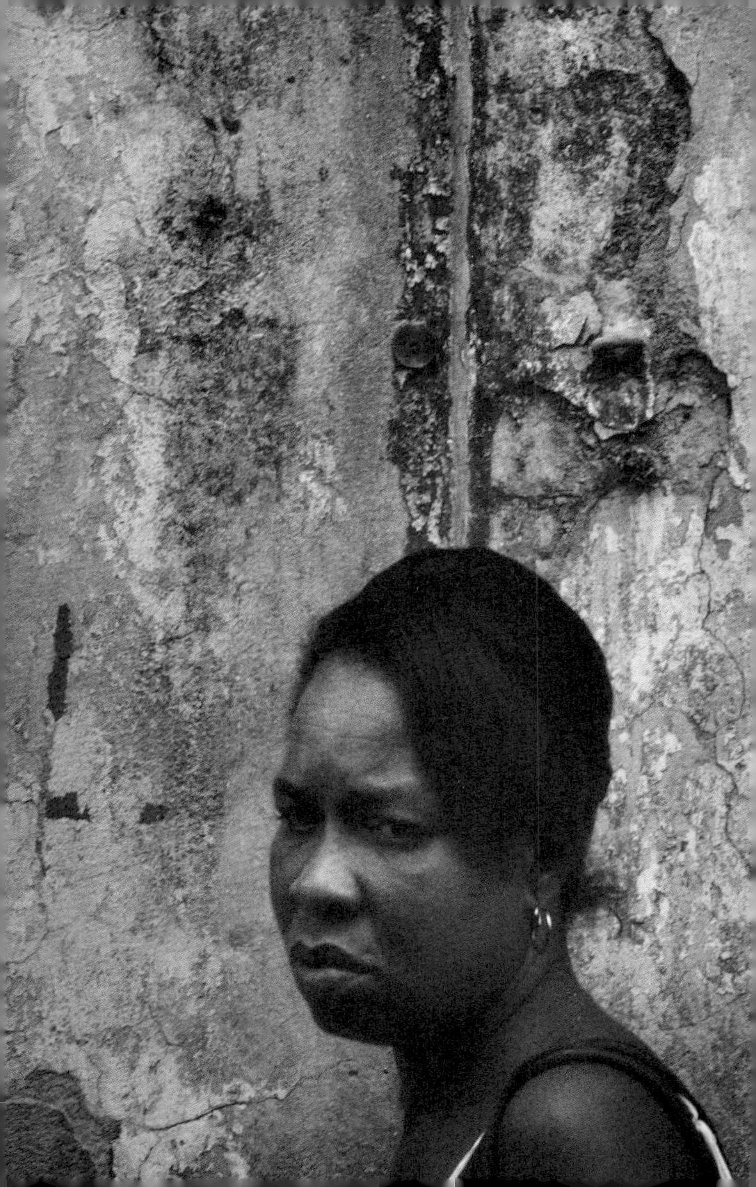

VIVA
RAÚL

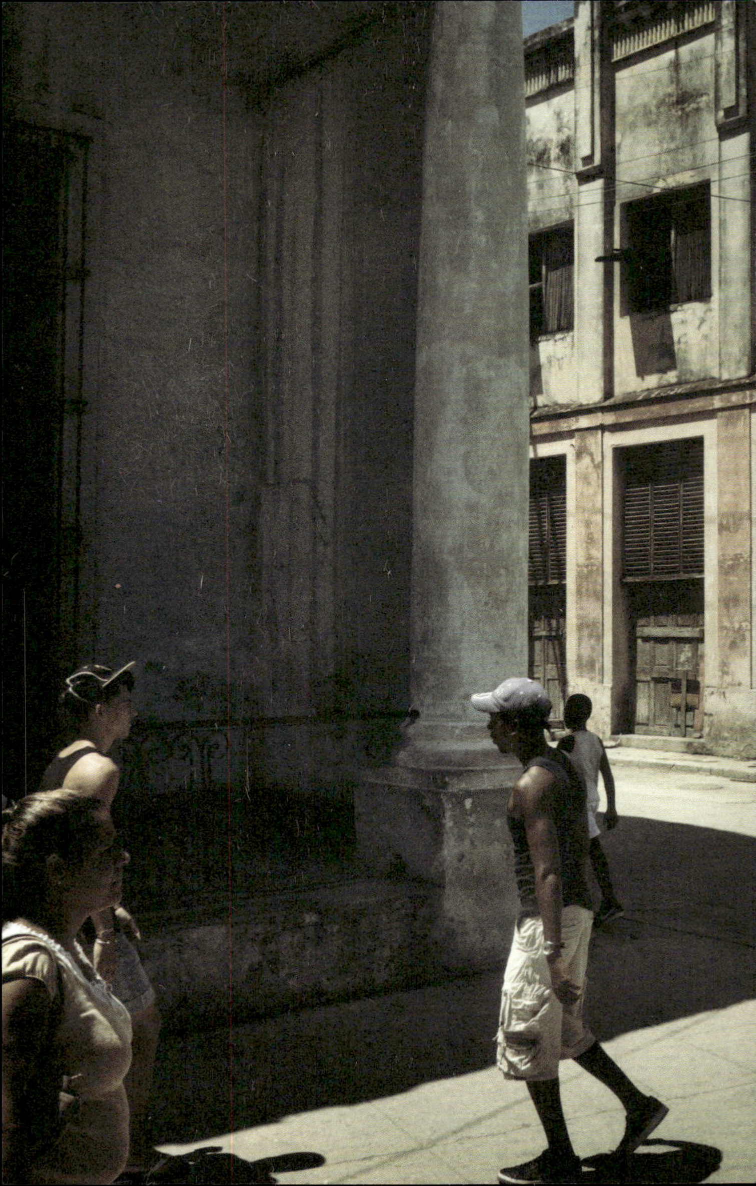

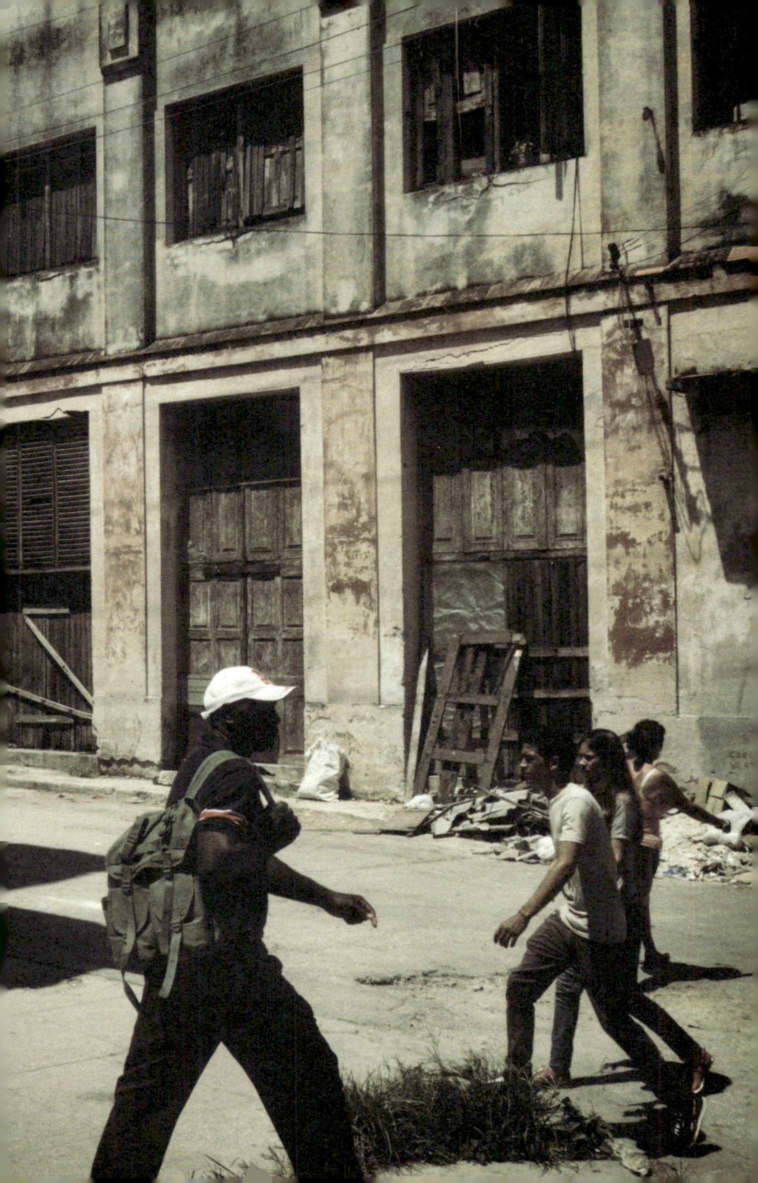

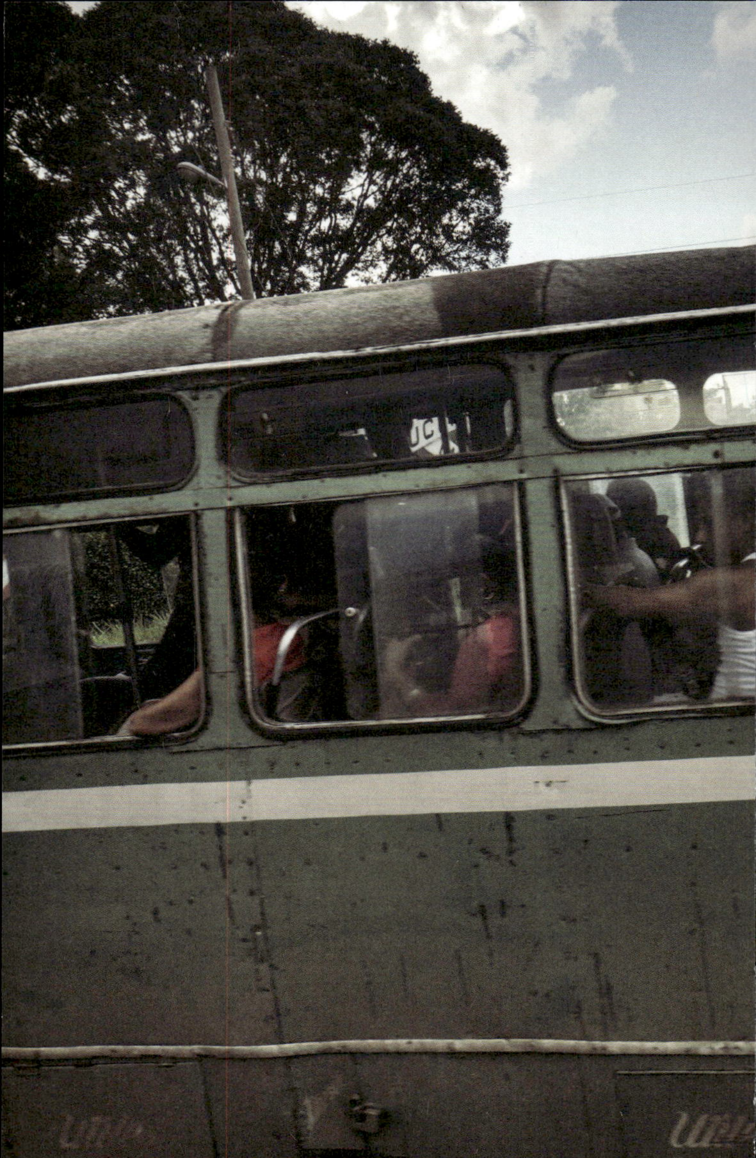

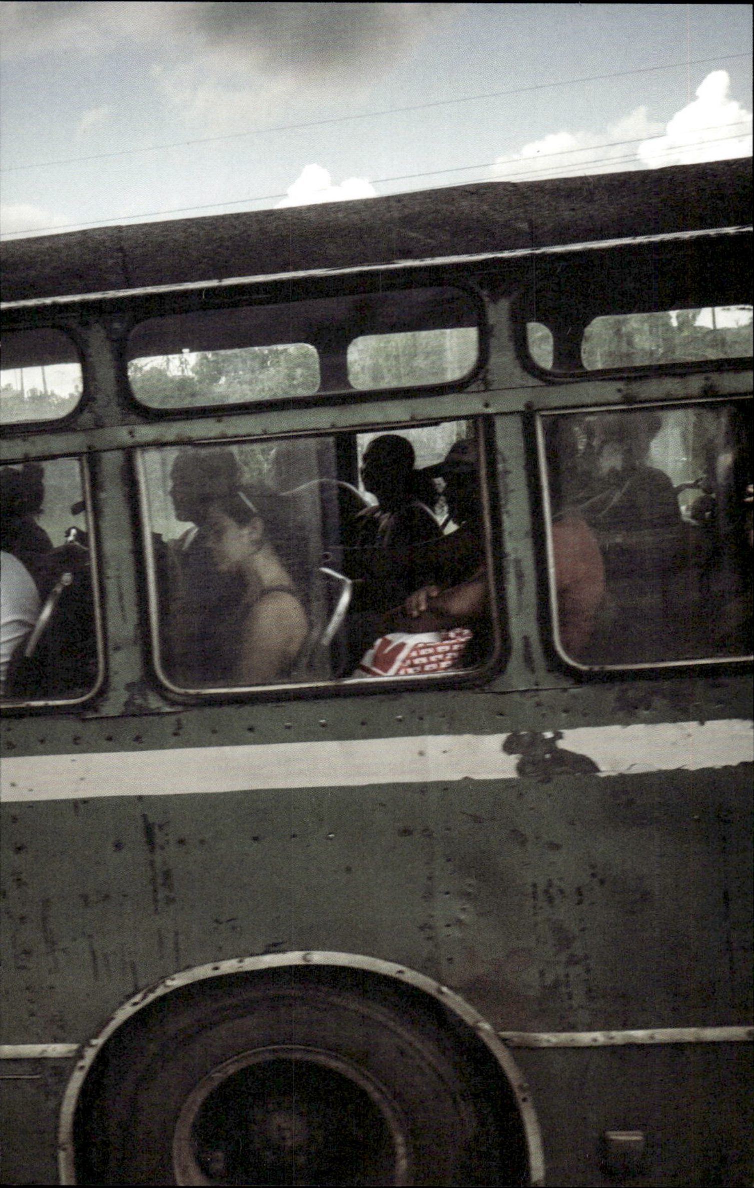

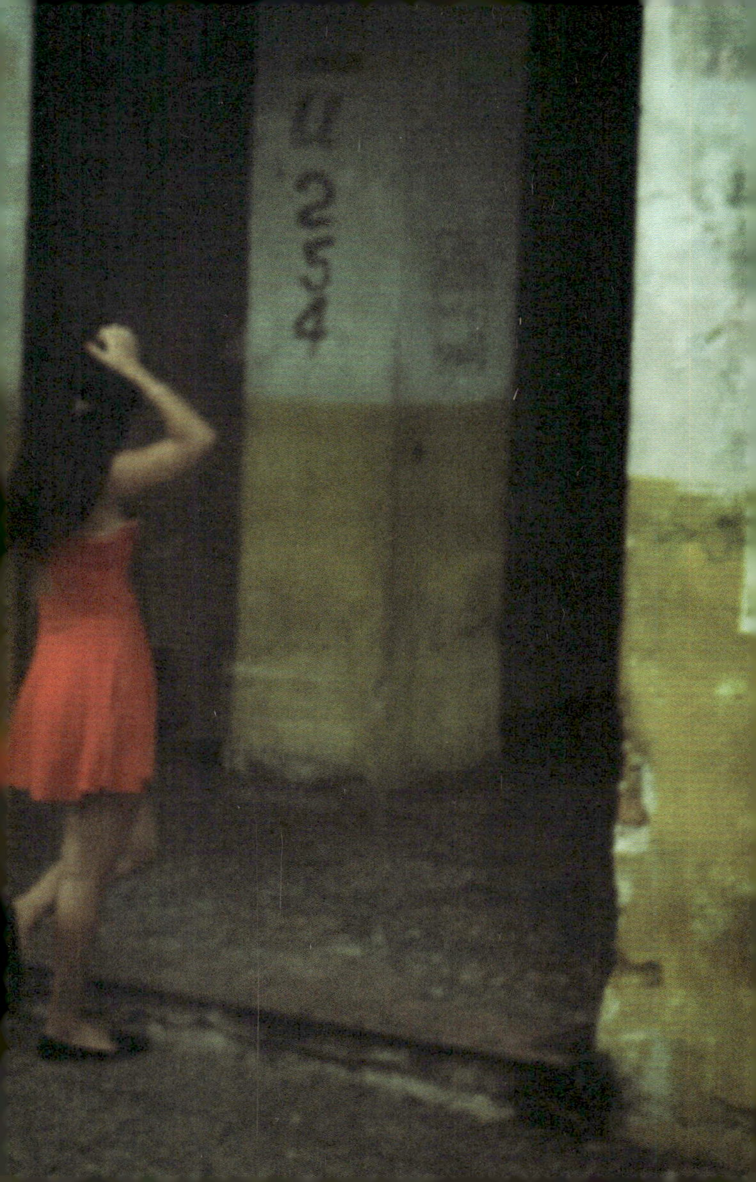

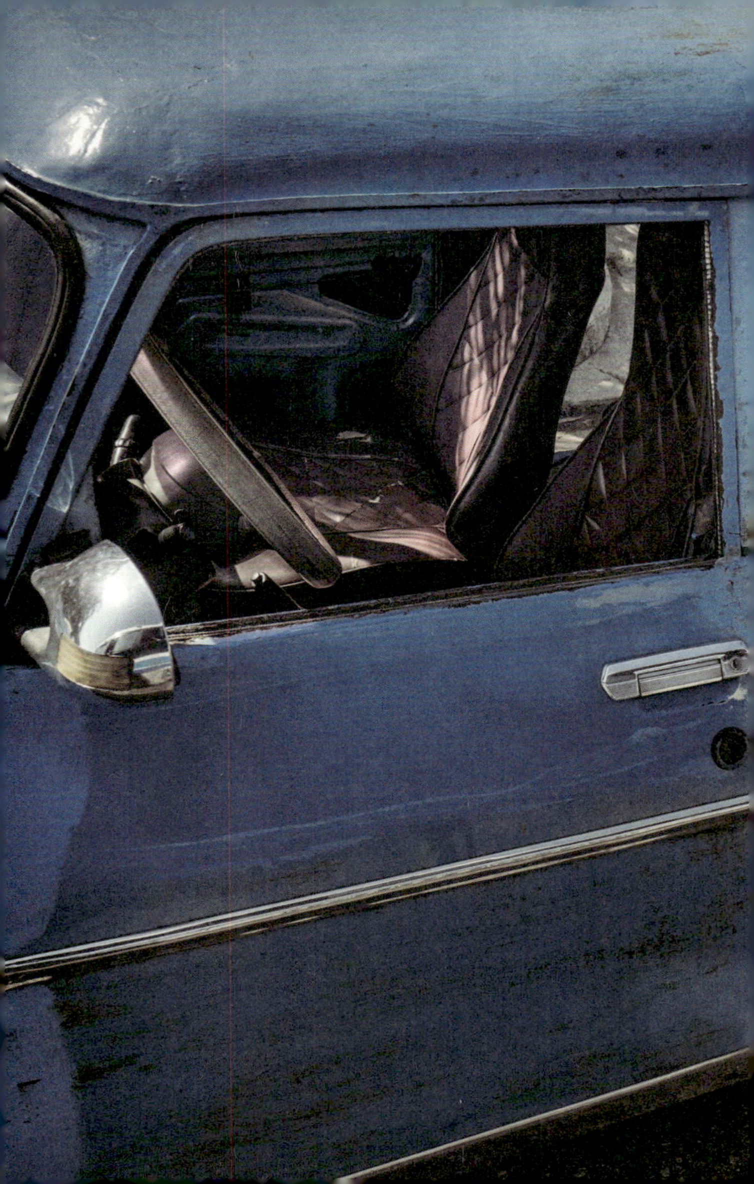

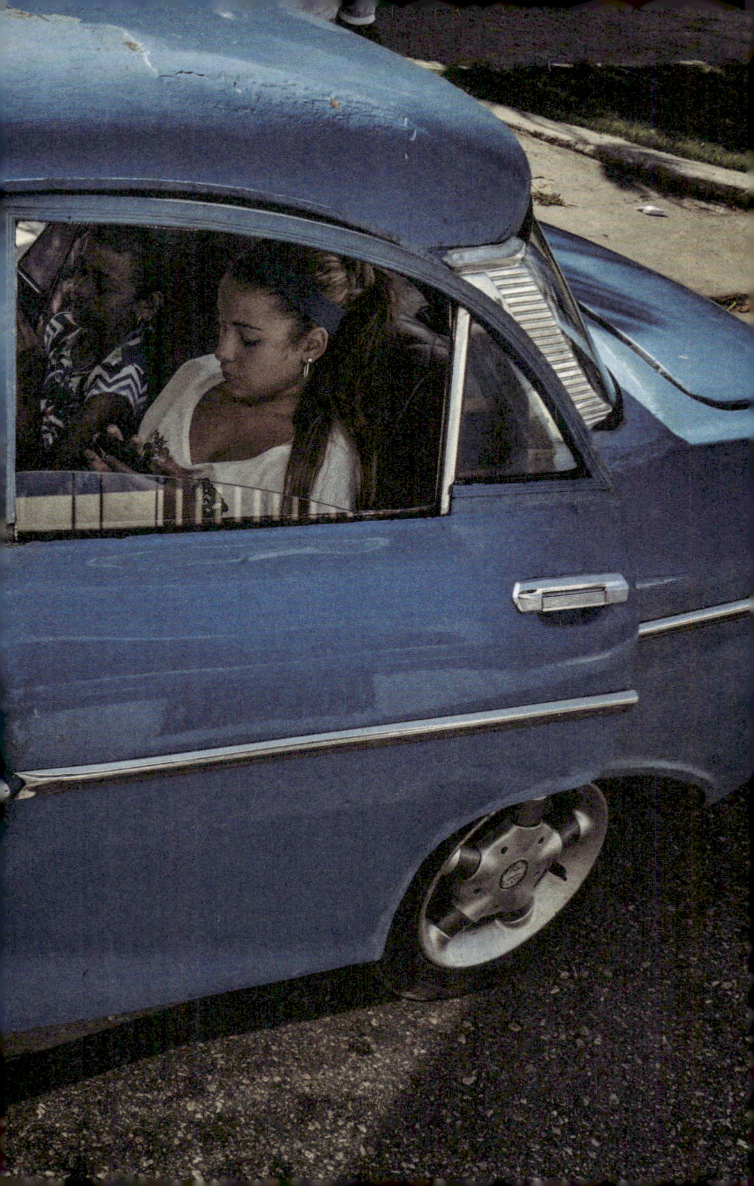

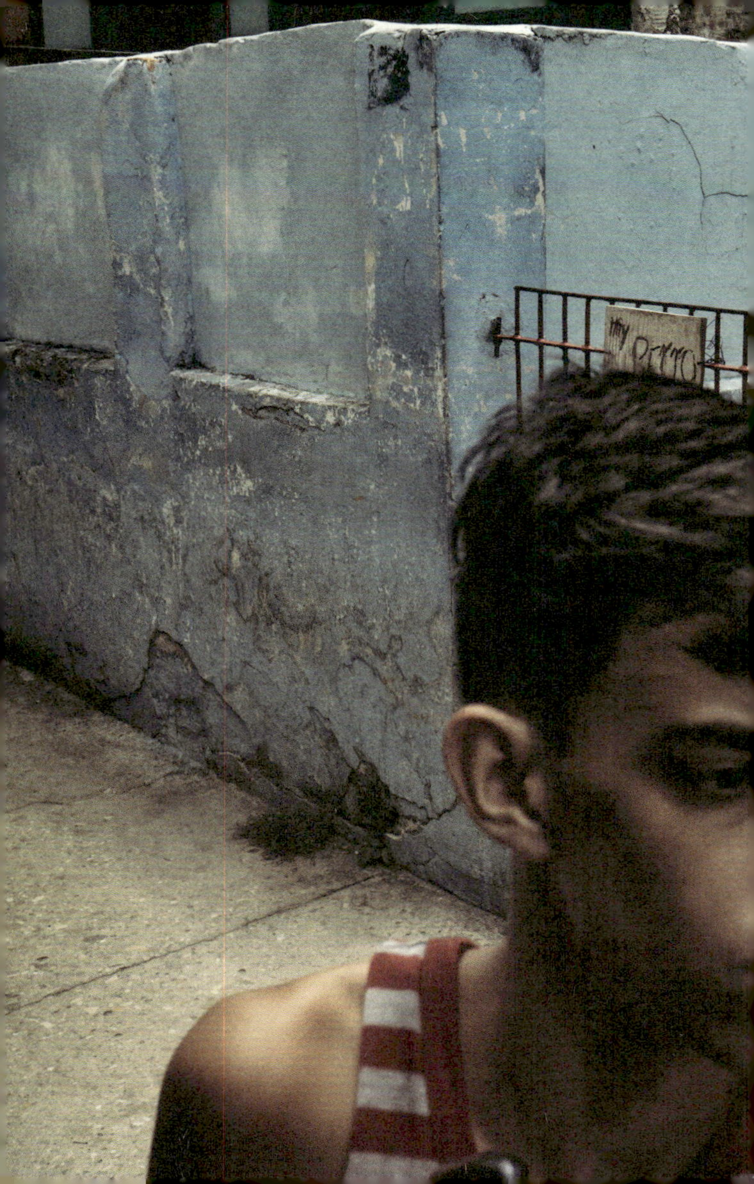

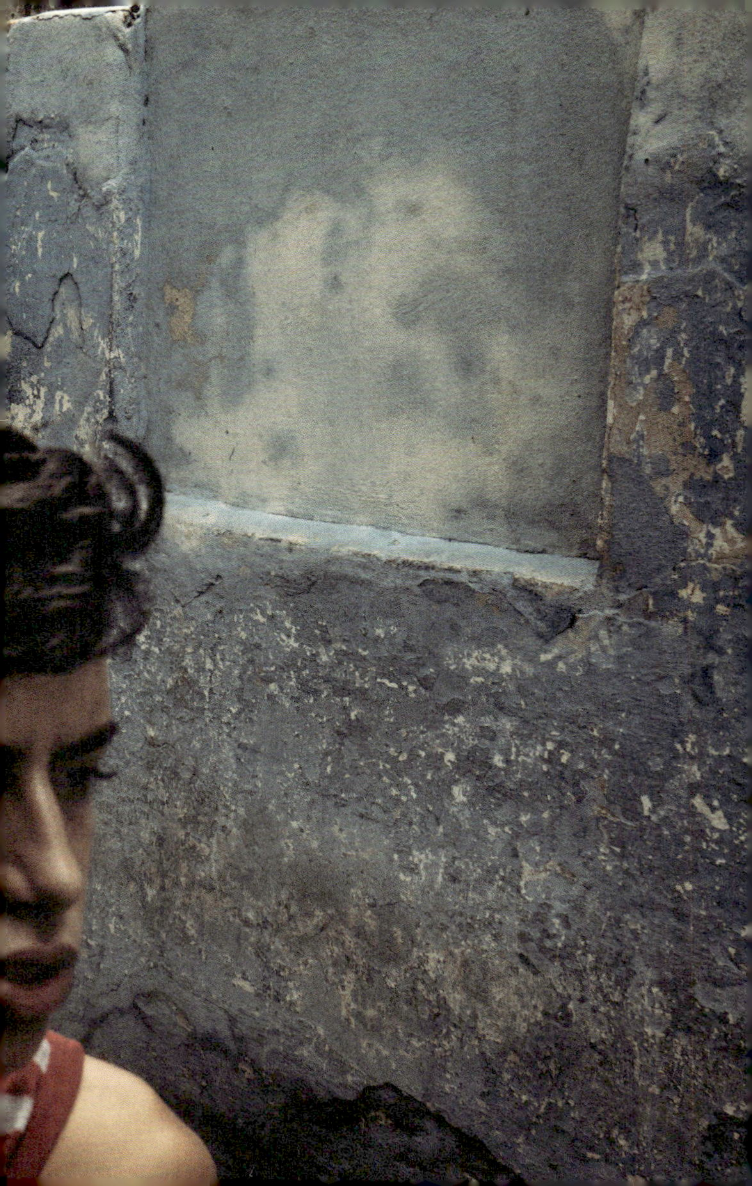

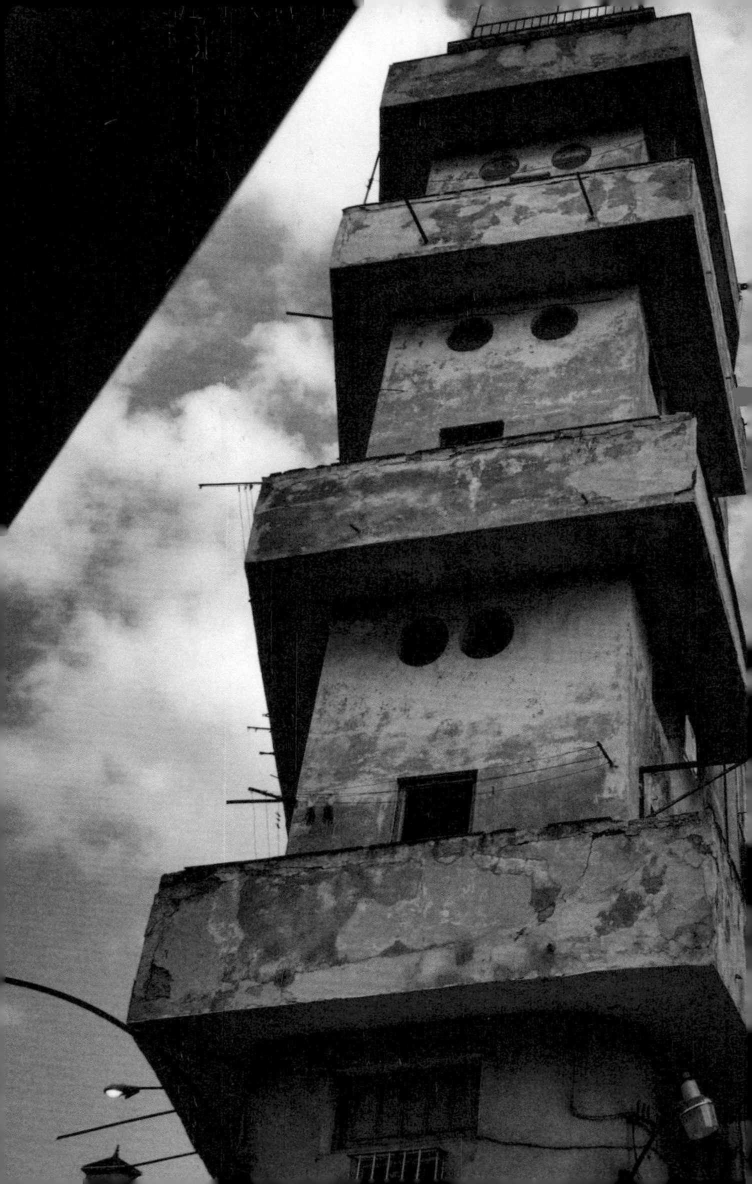

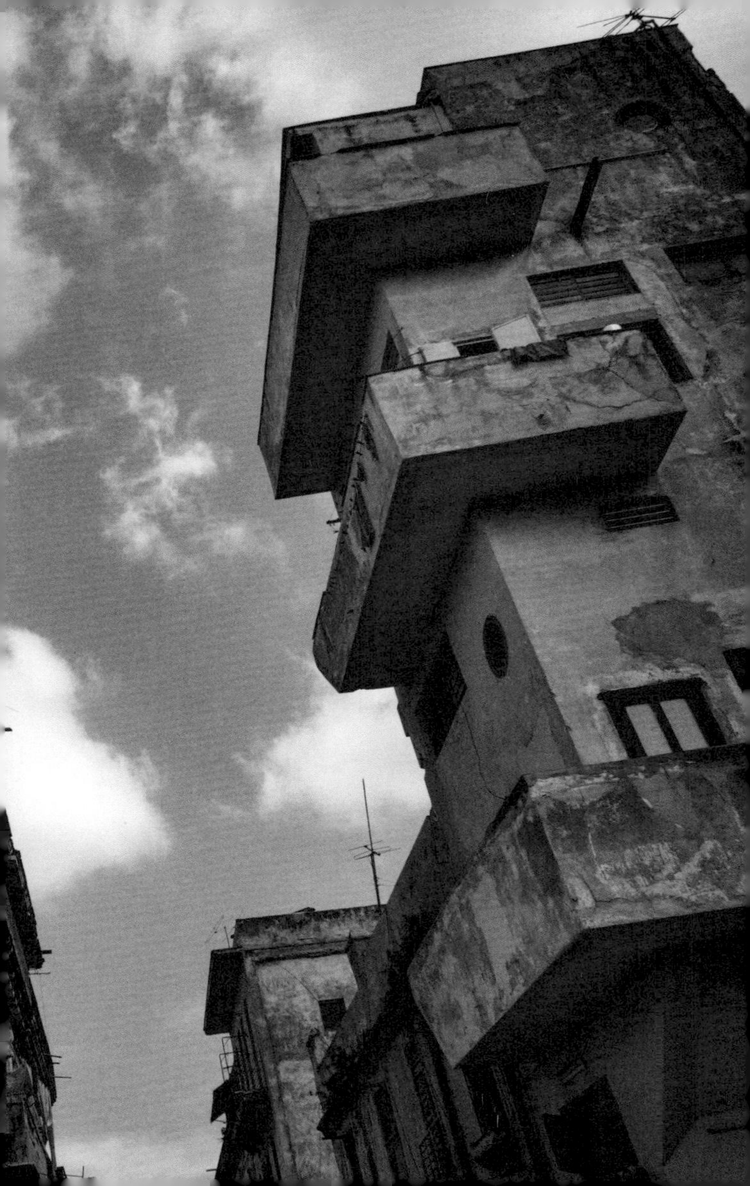

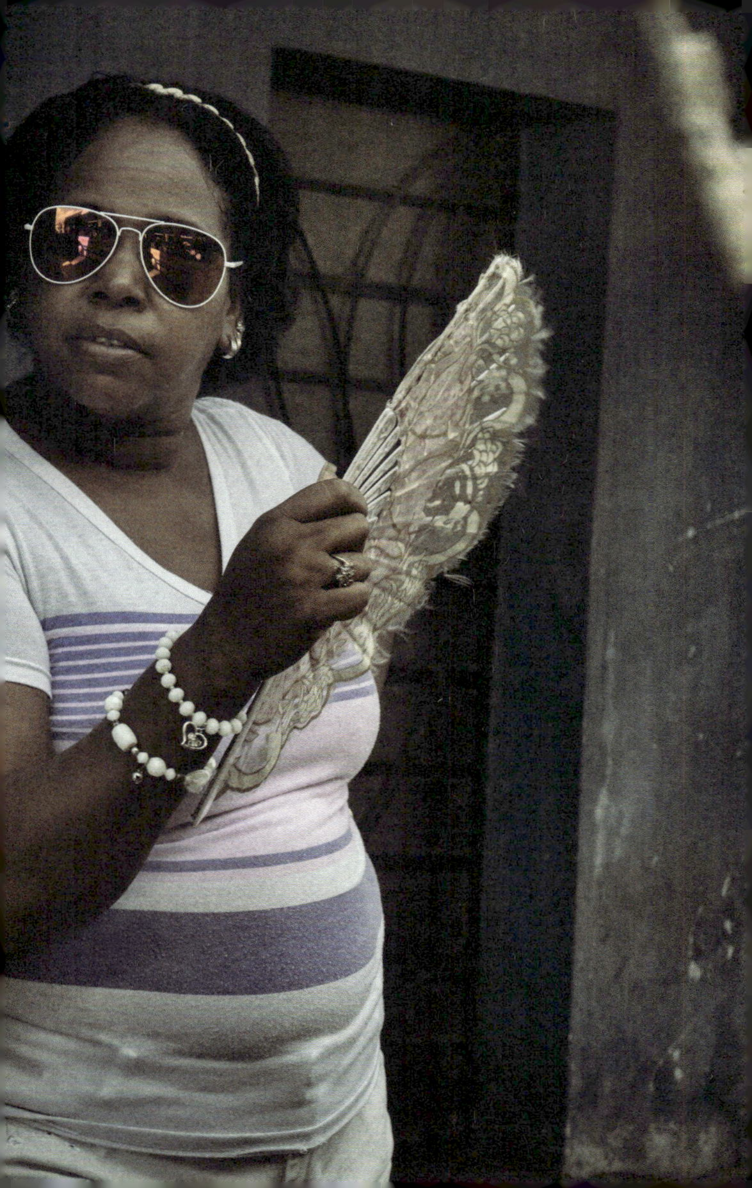

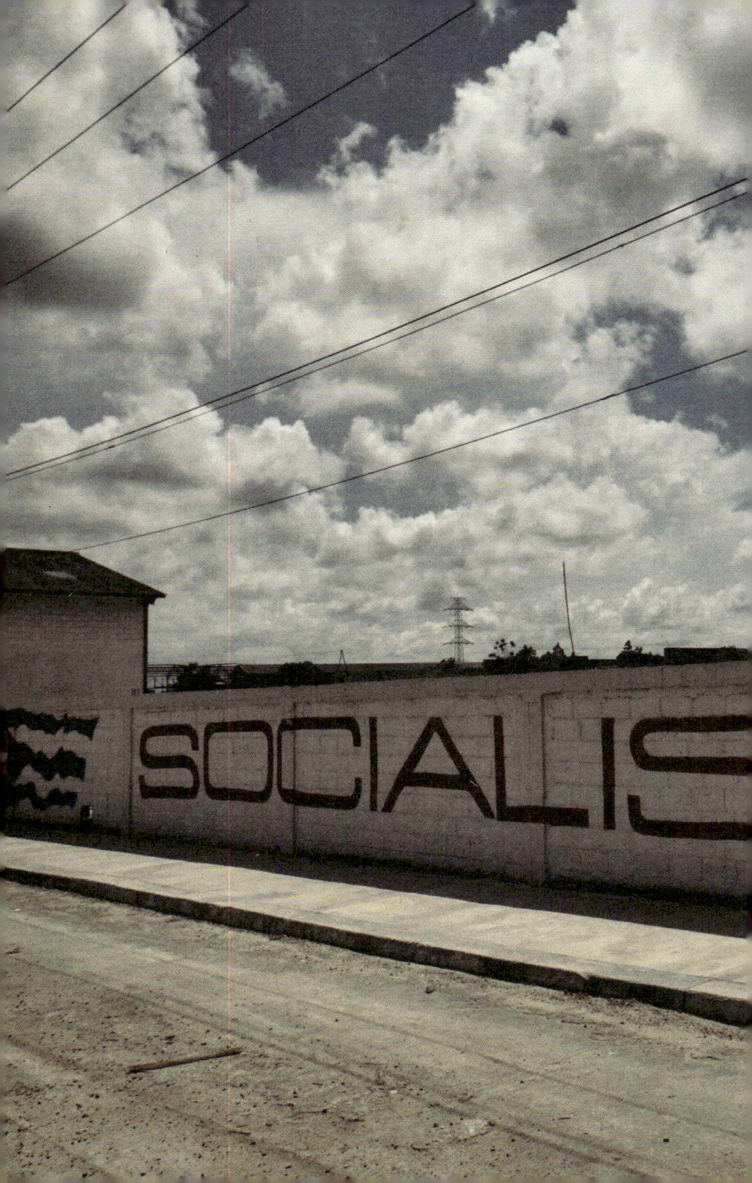
SOCIALIS

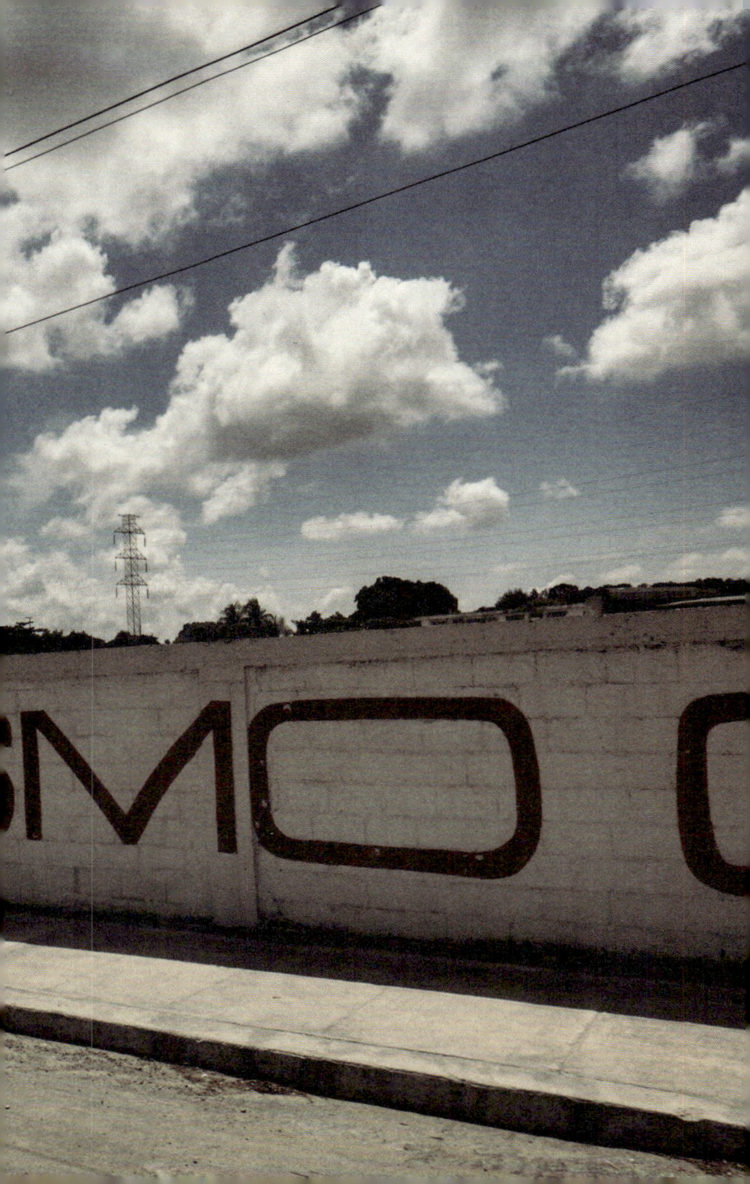
SMO

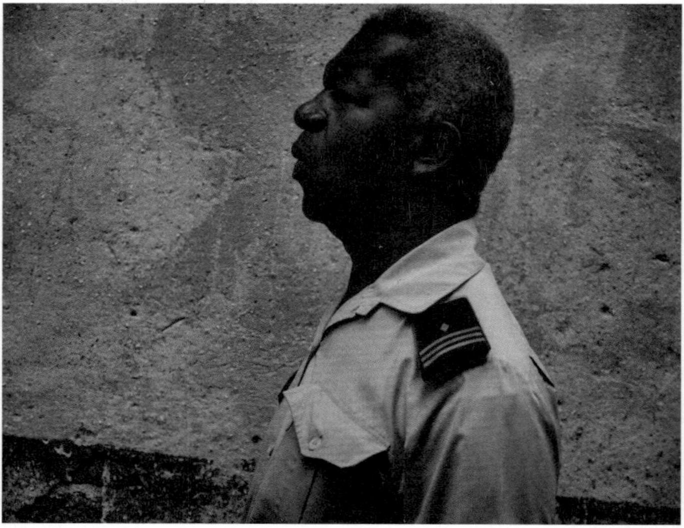

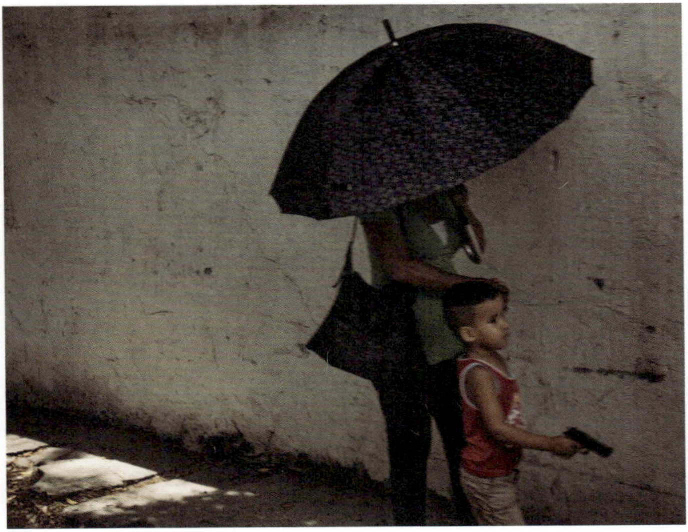

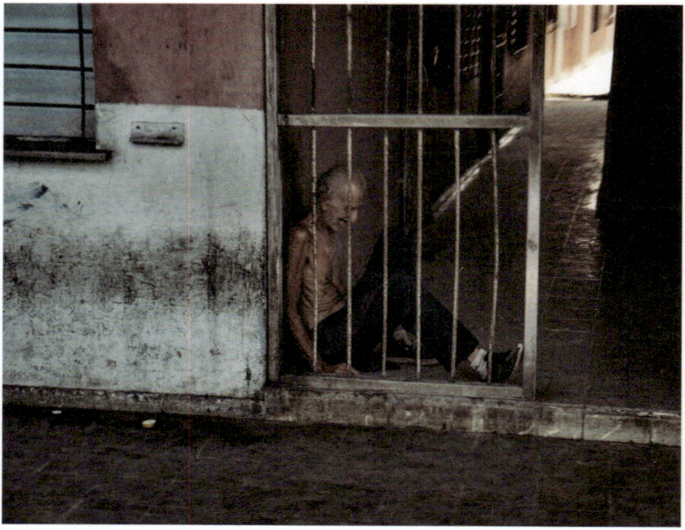

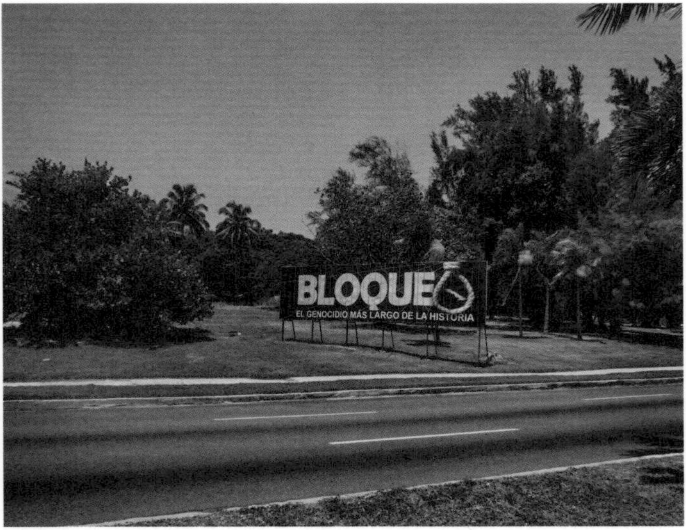
BLOQUEO
EL GENOCIDIO MÁS LARGO DE LA HISTORIA

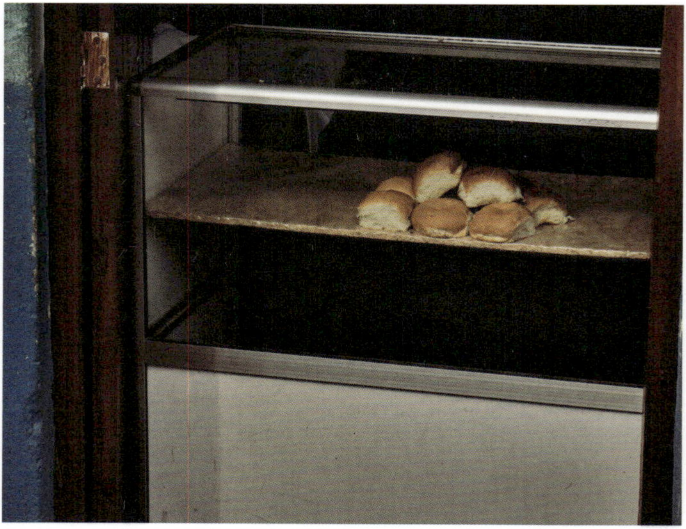

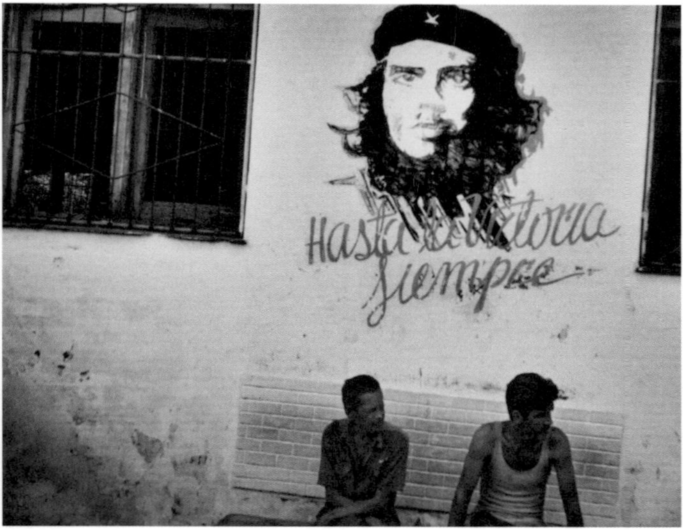
Hasta
Siempre

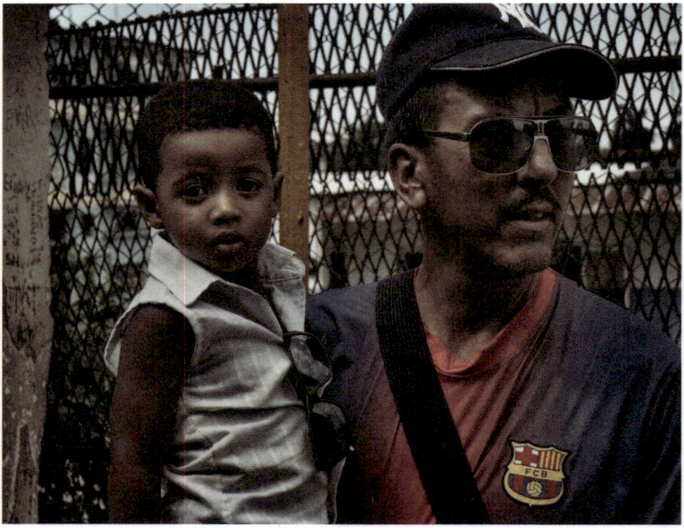
FCB

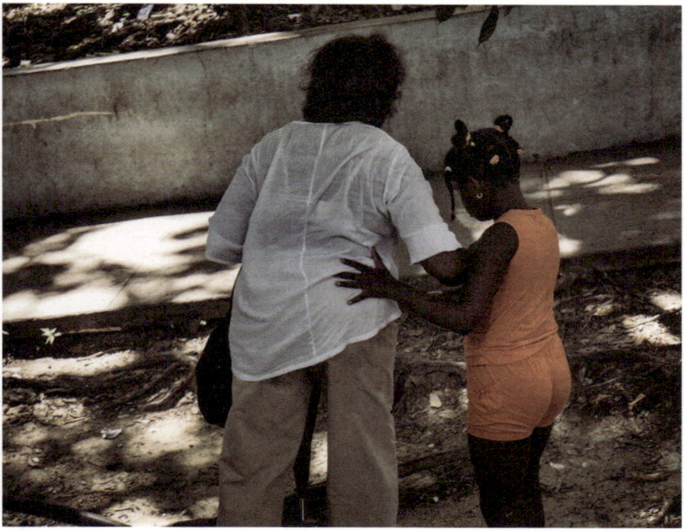

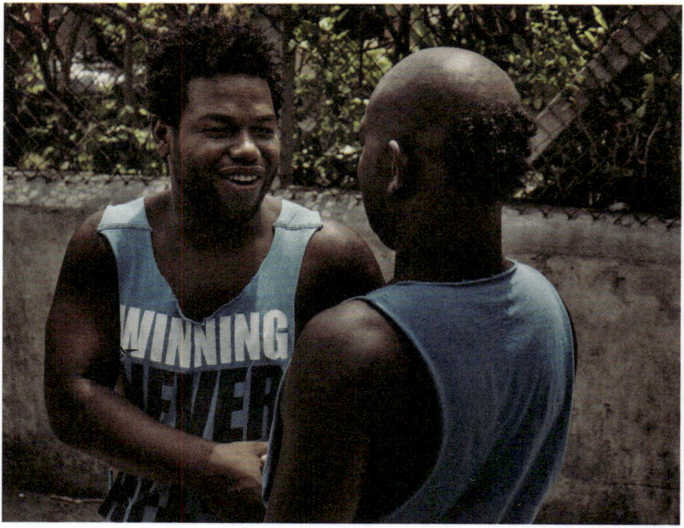
WINNING

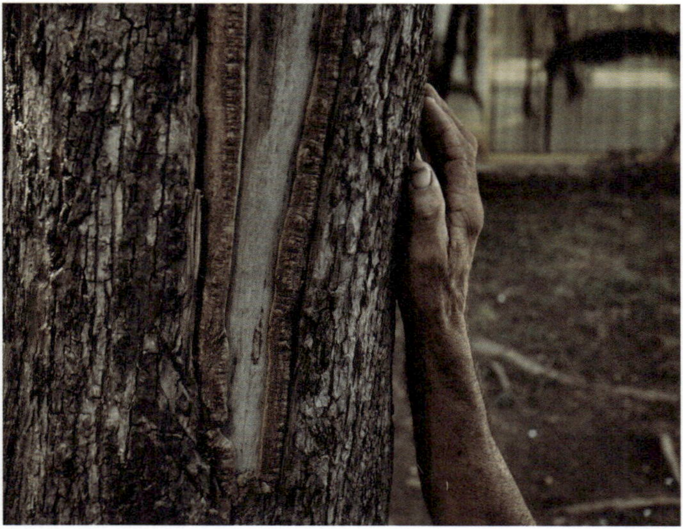

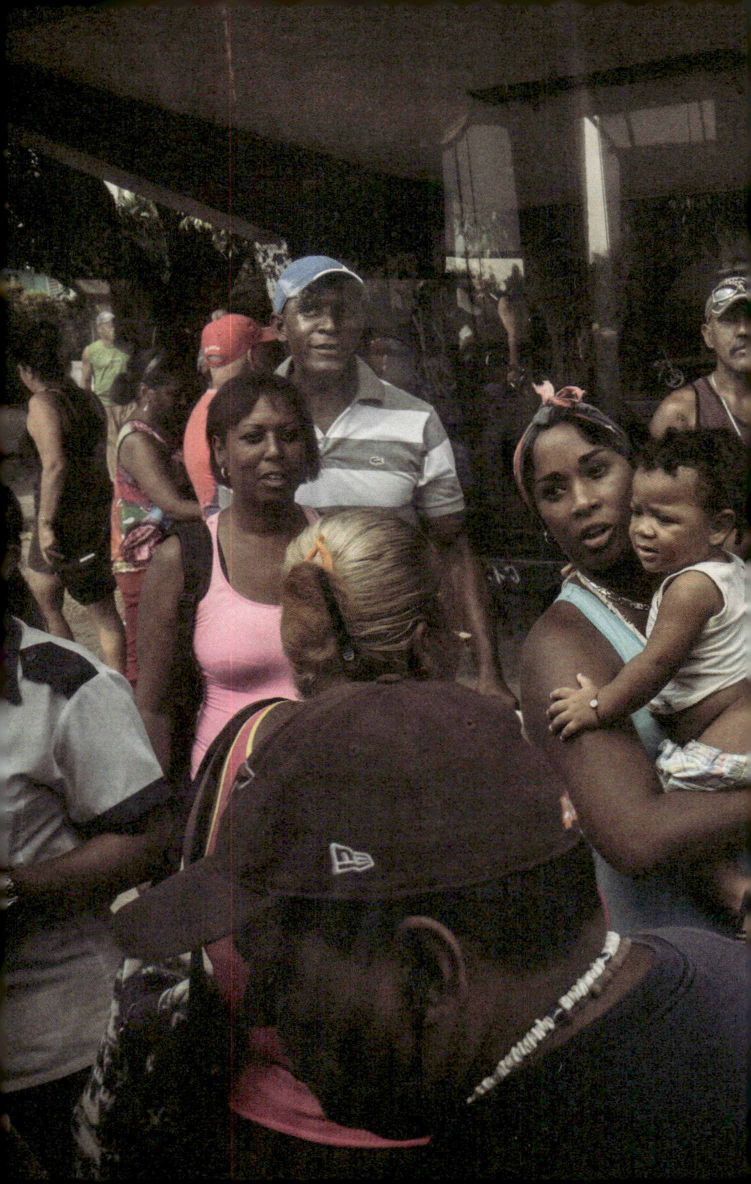

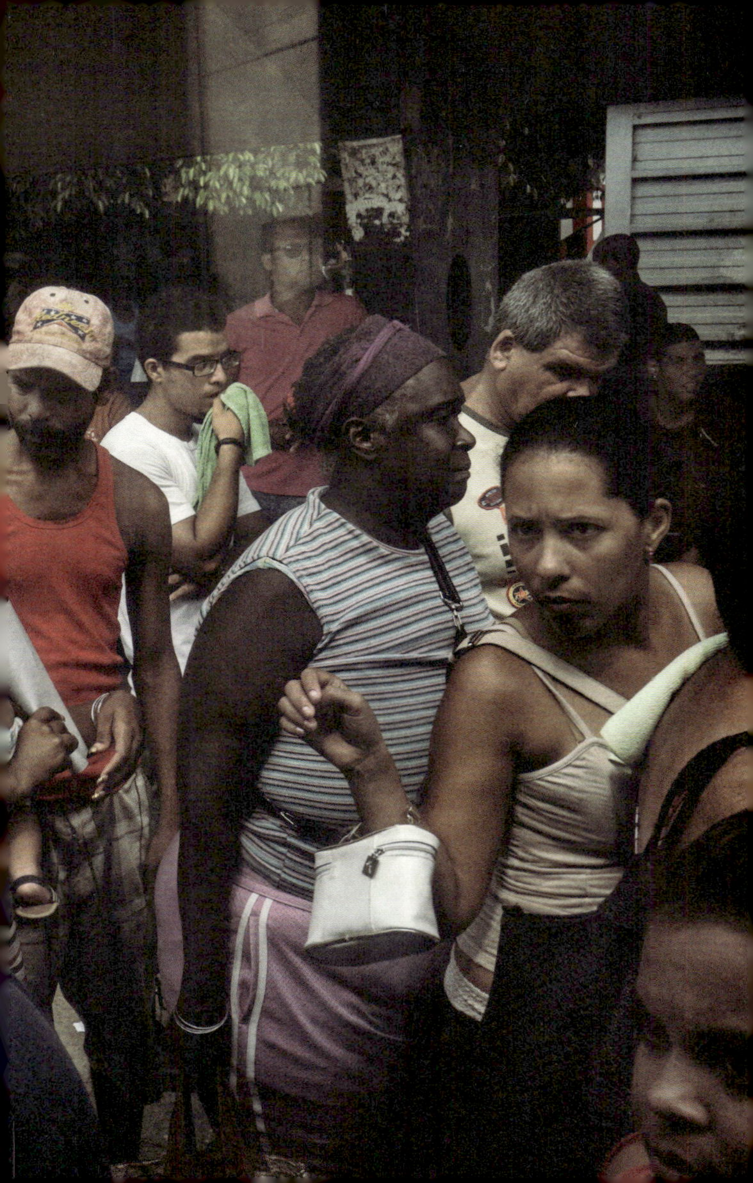

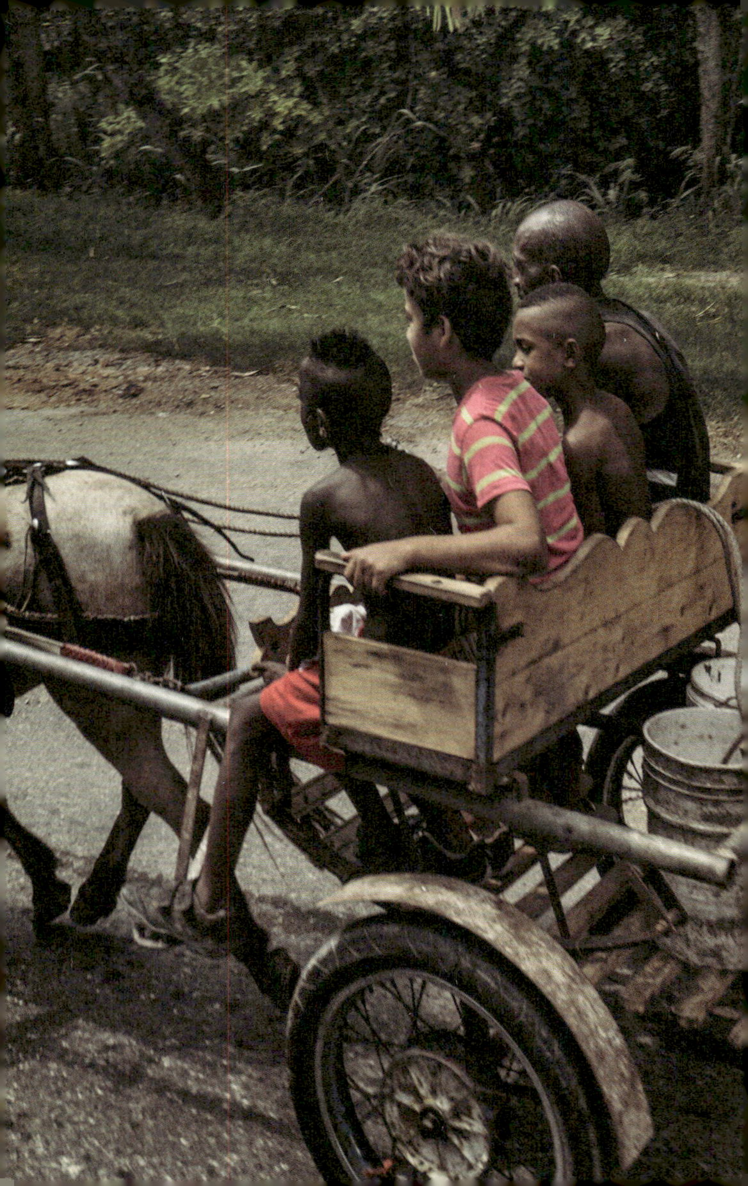

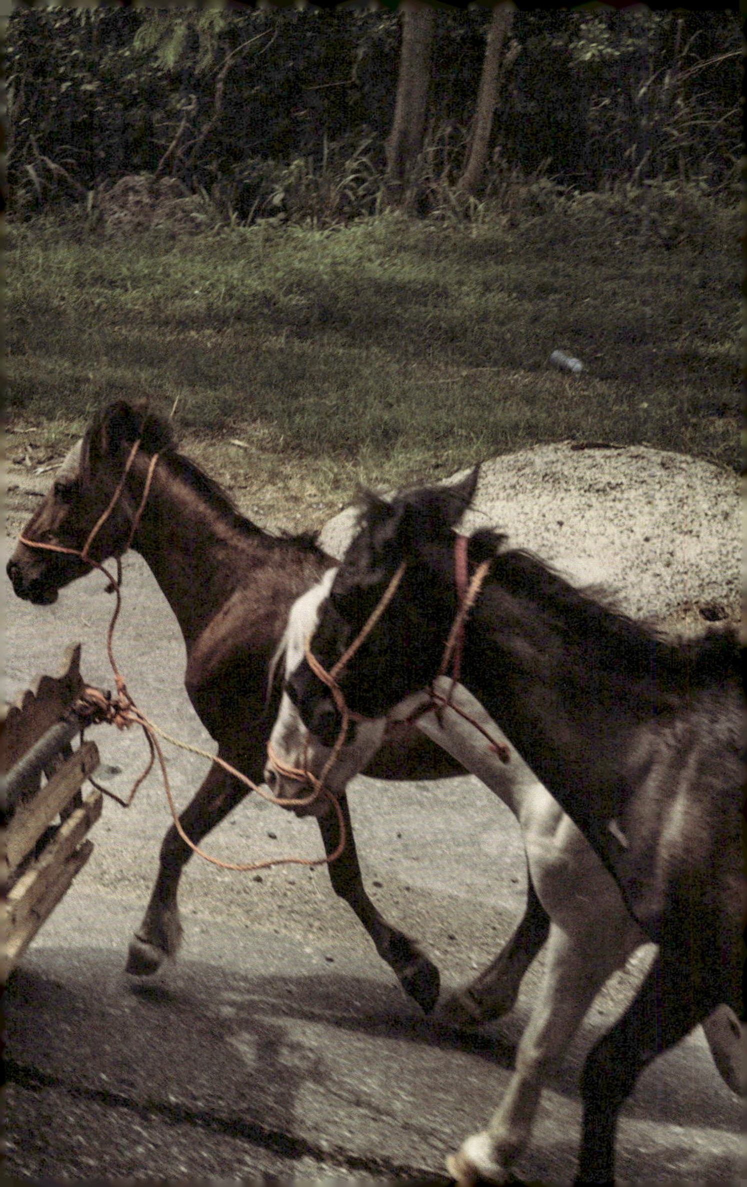

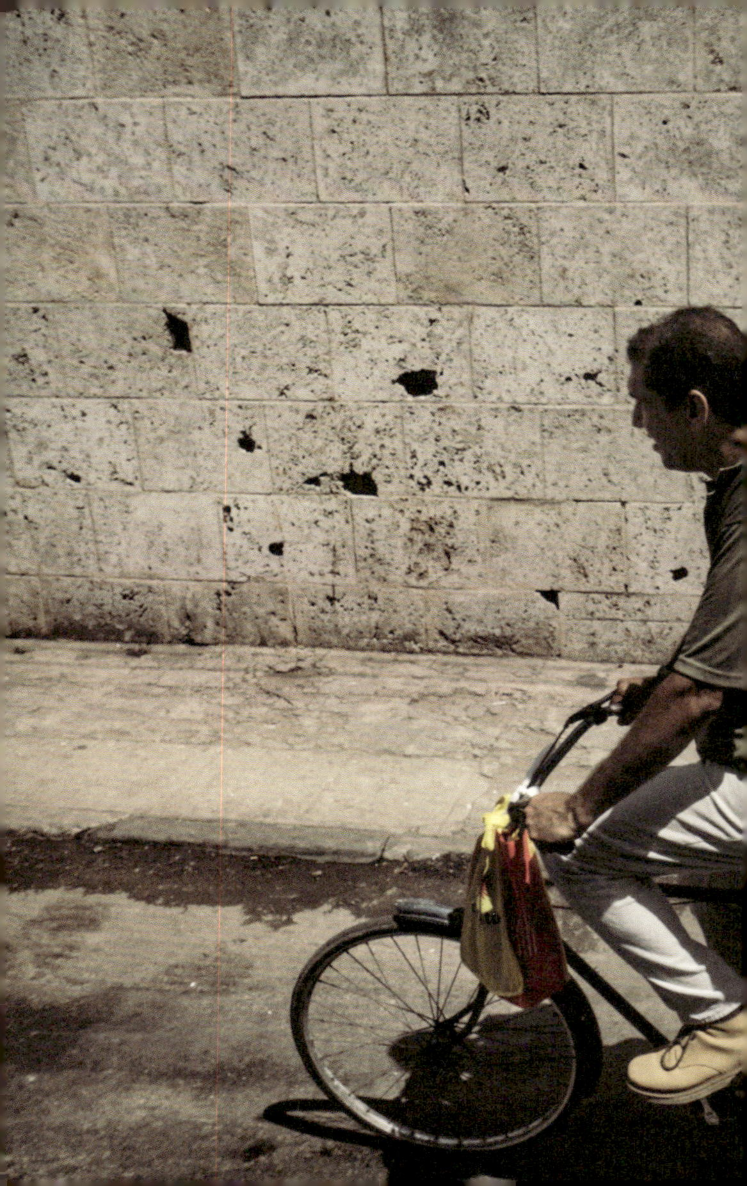

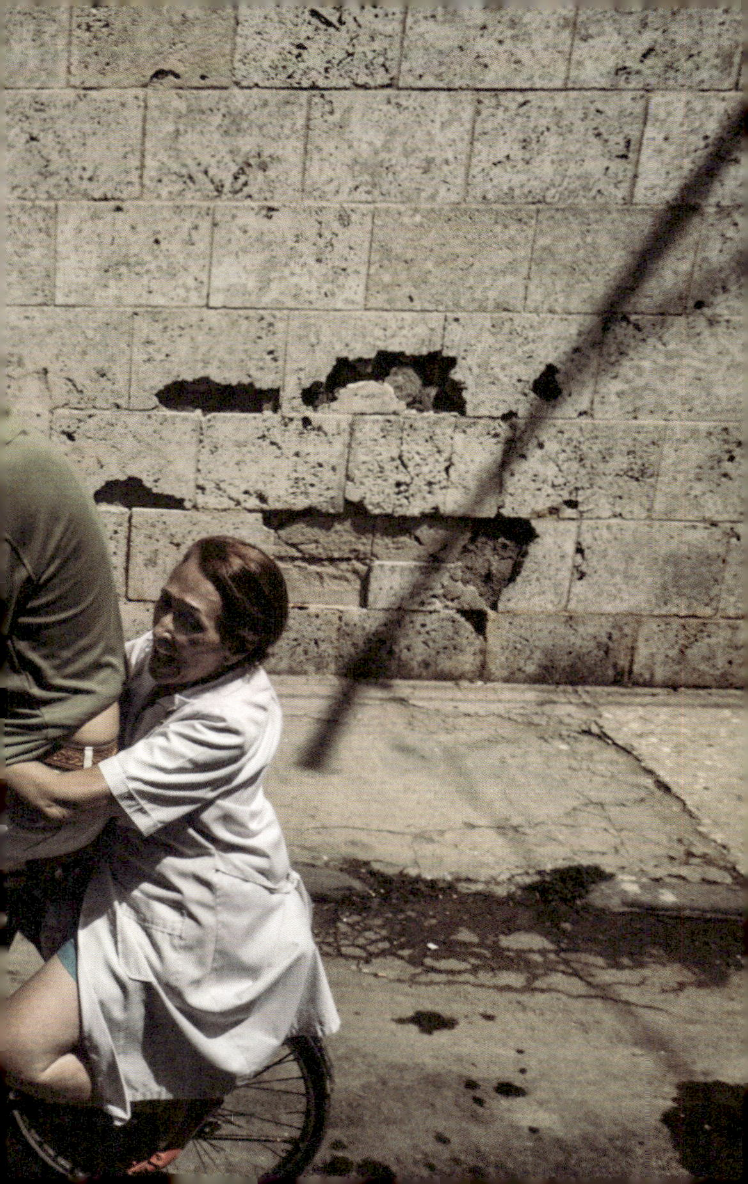

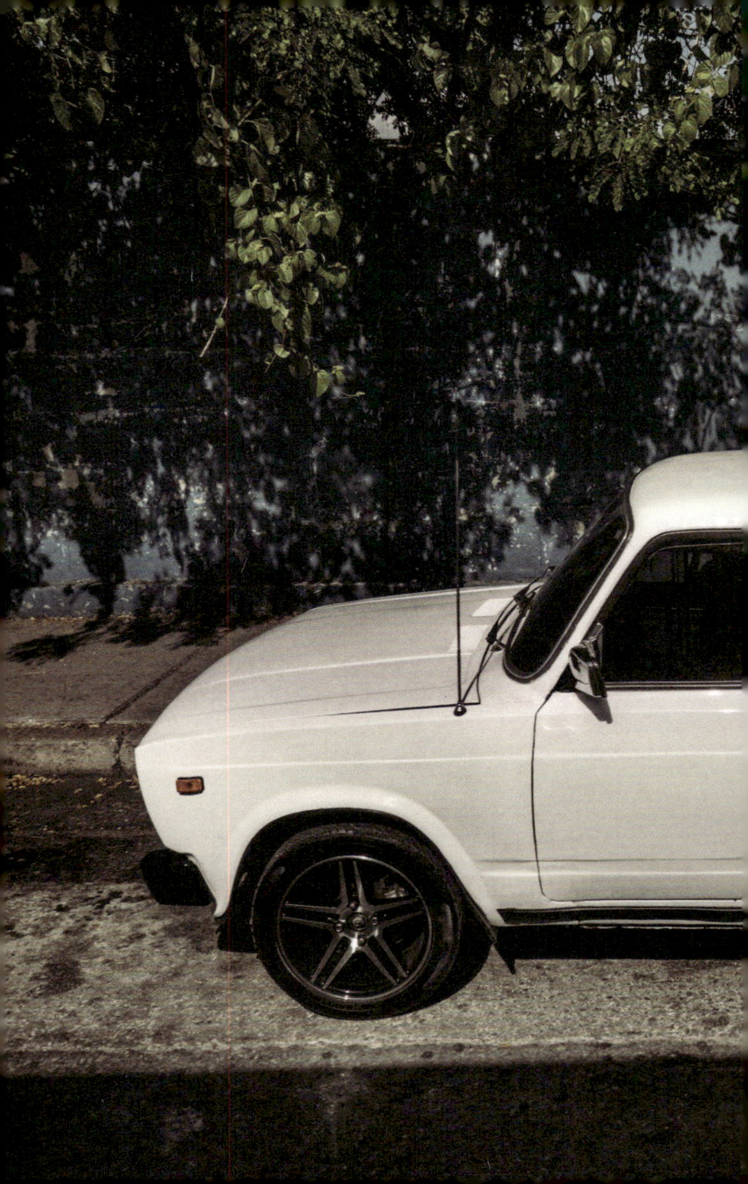

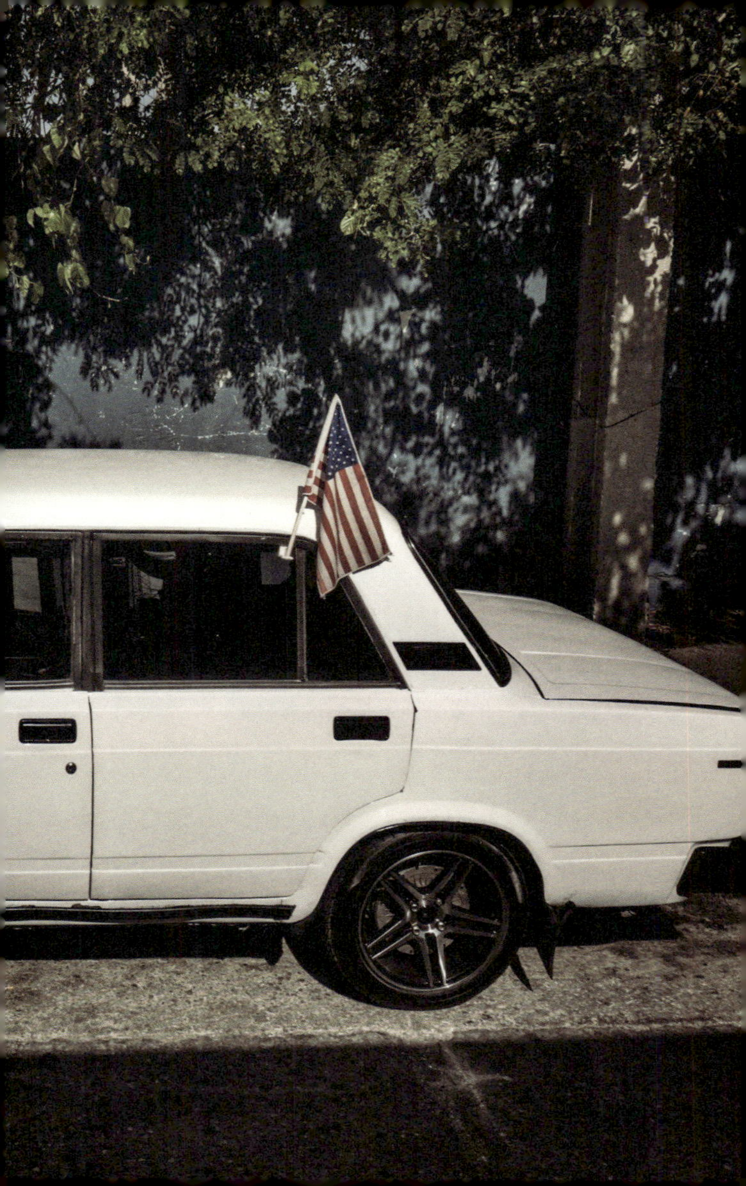

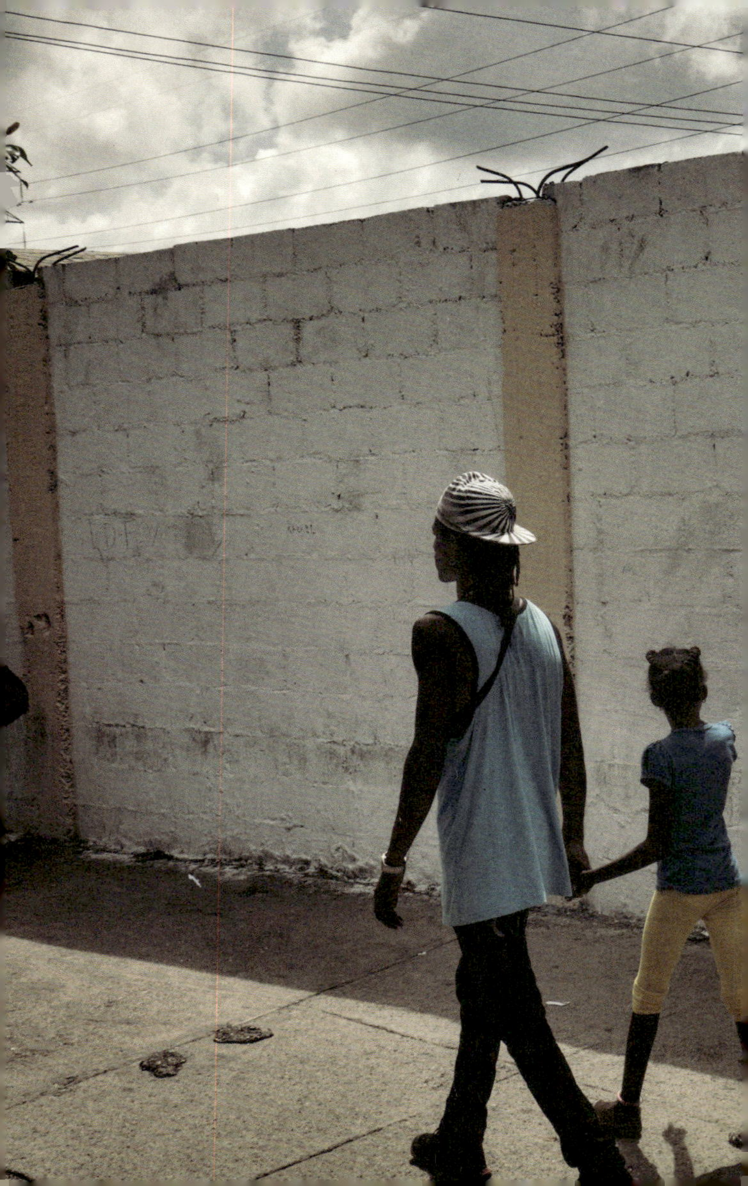

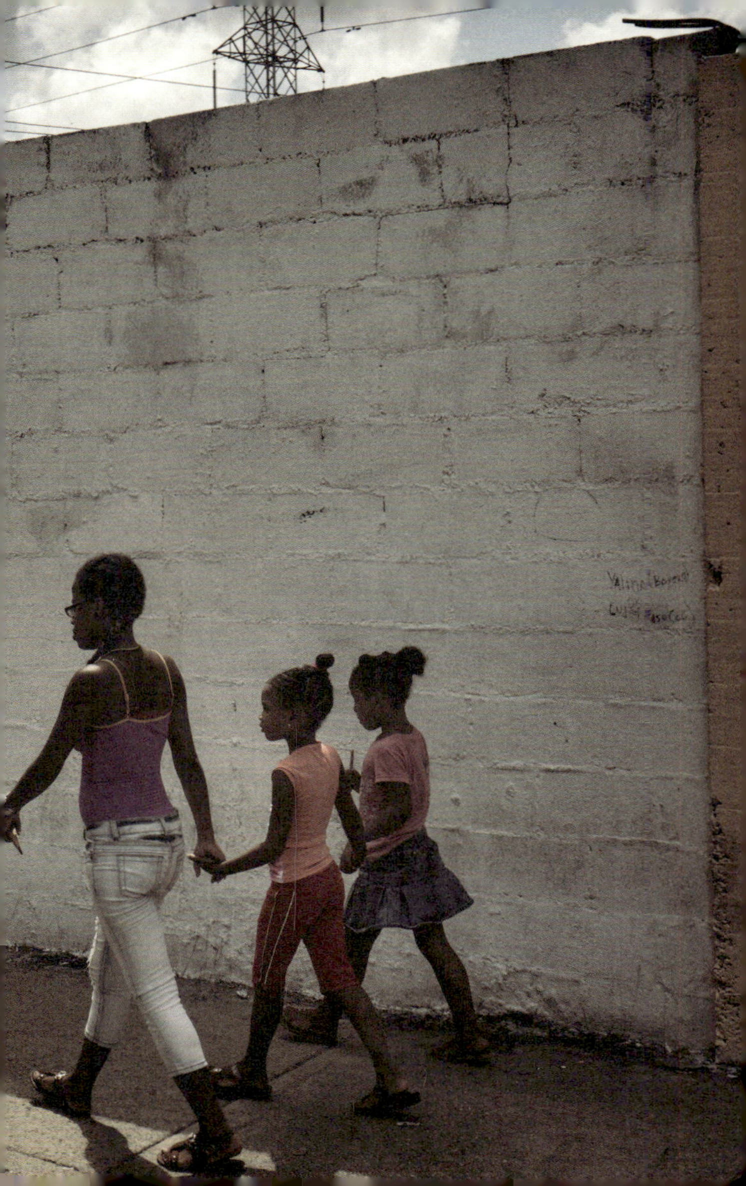

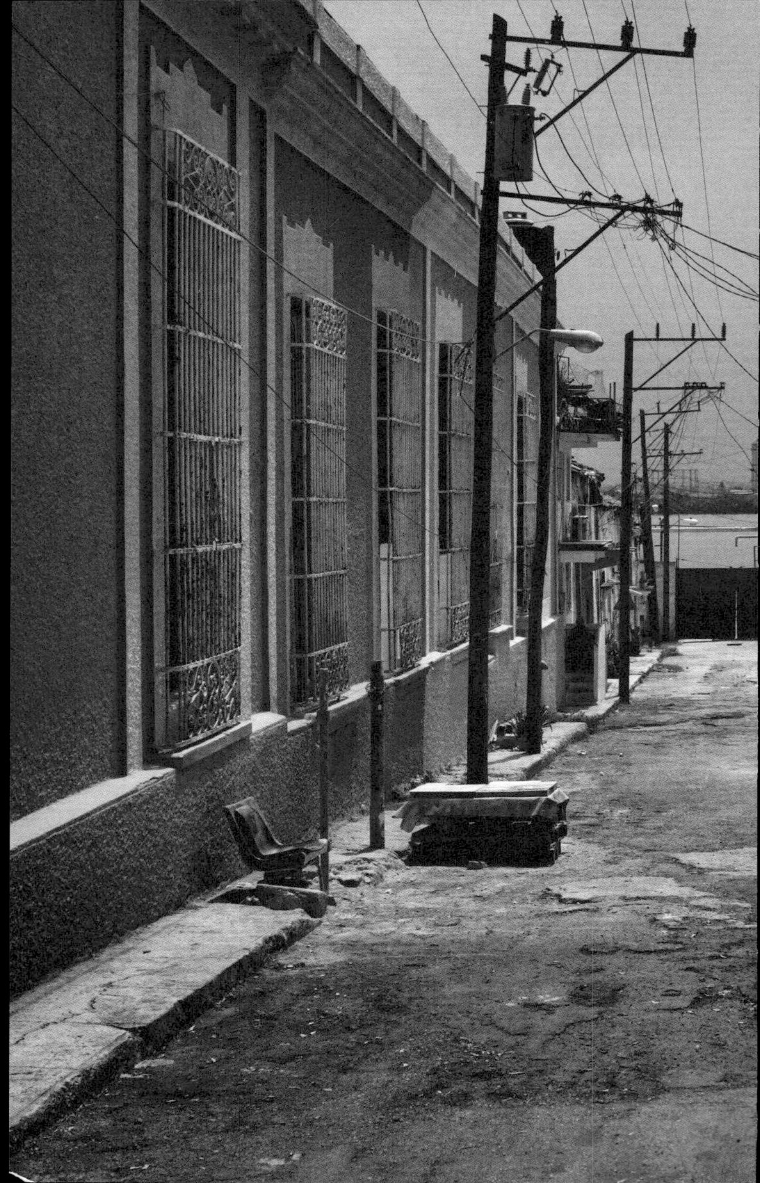

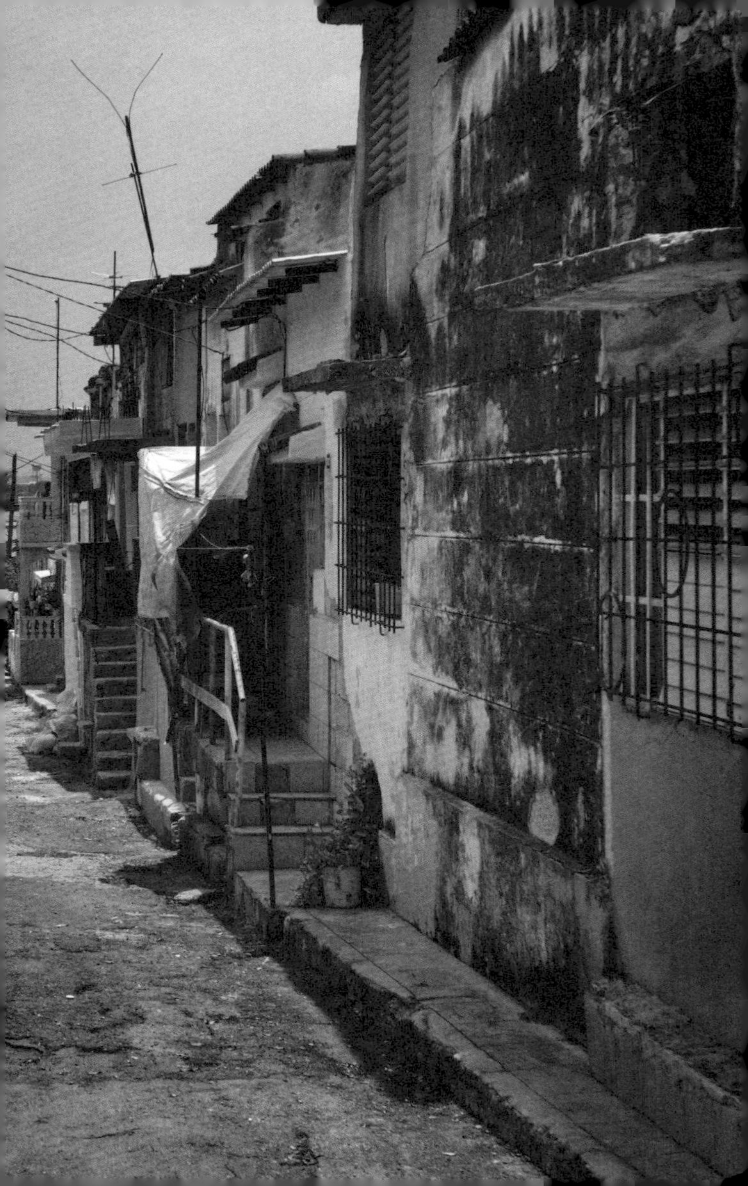

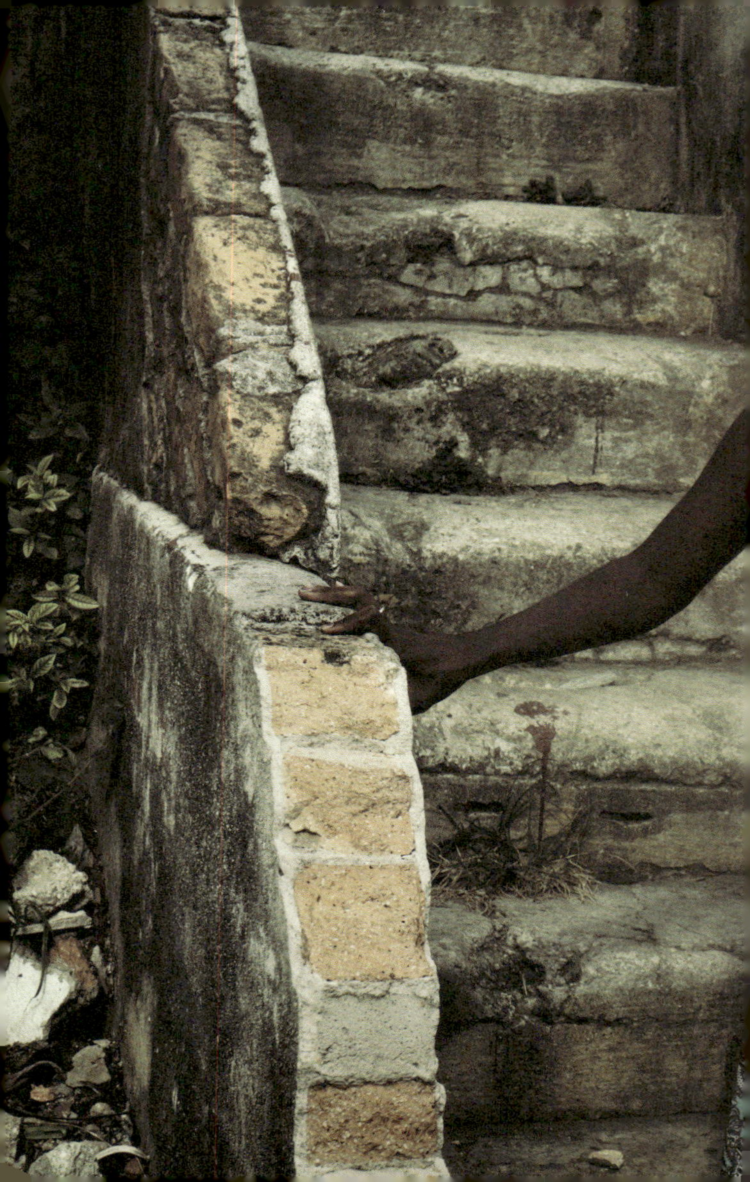

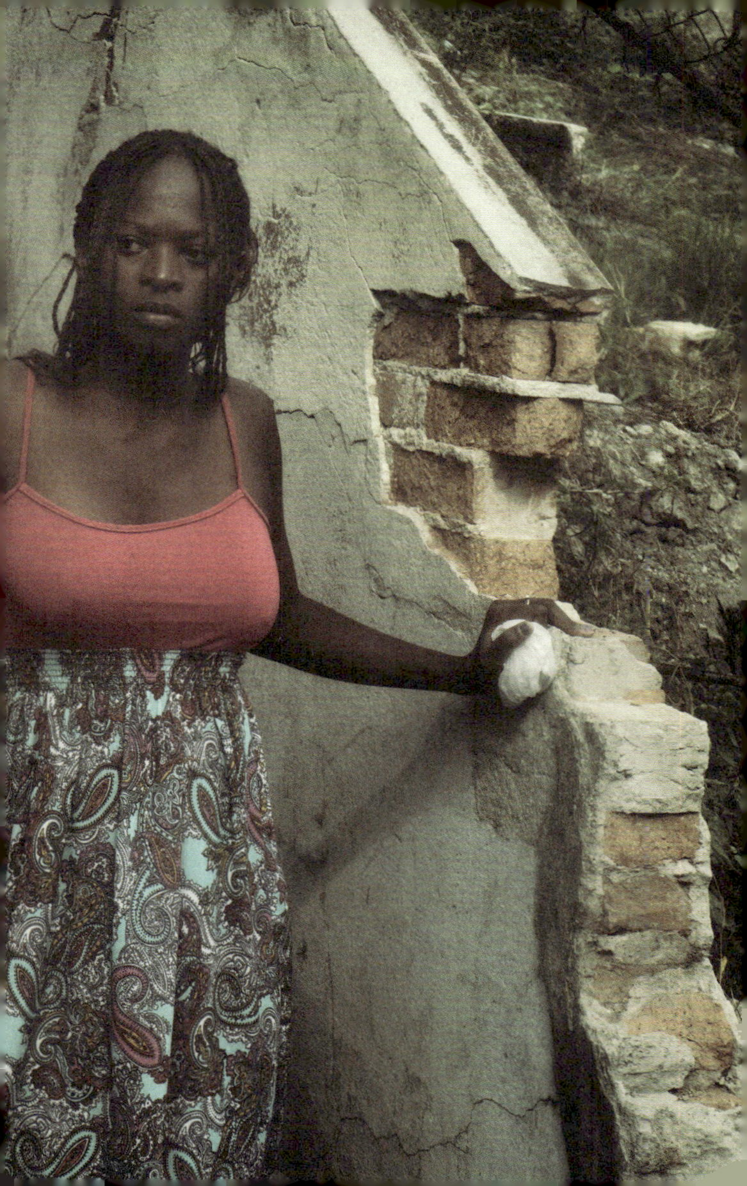

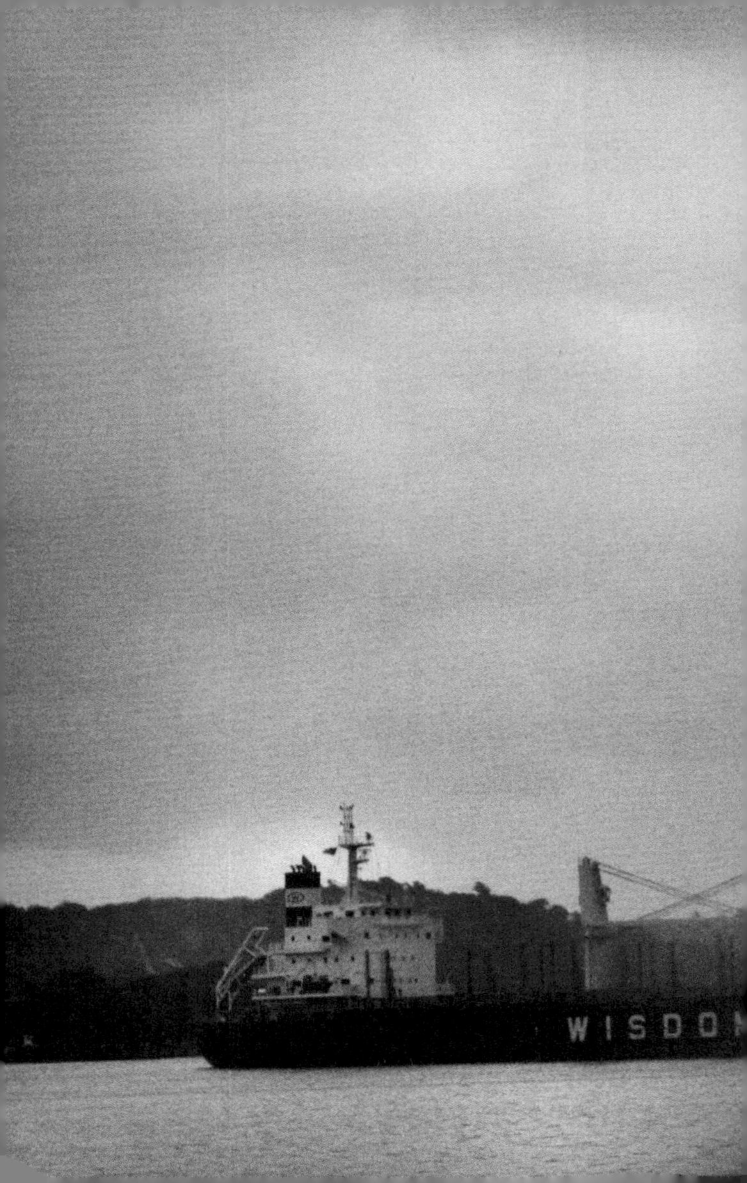
WISDO

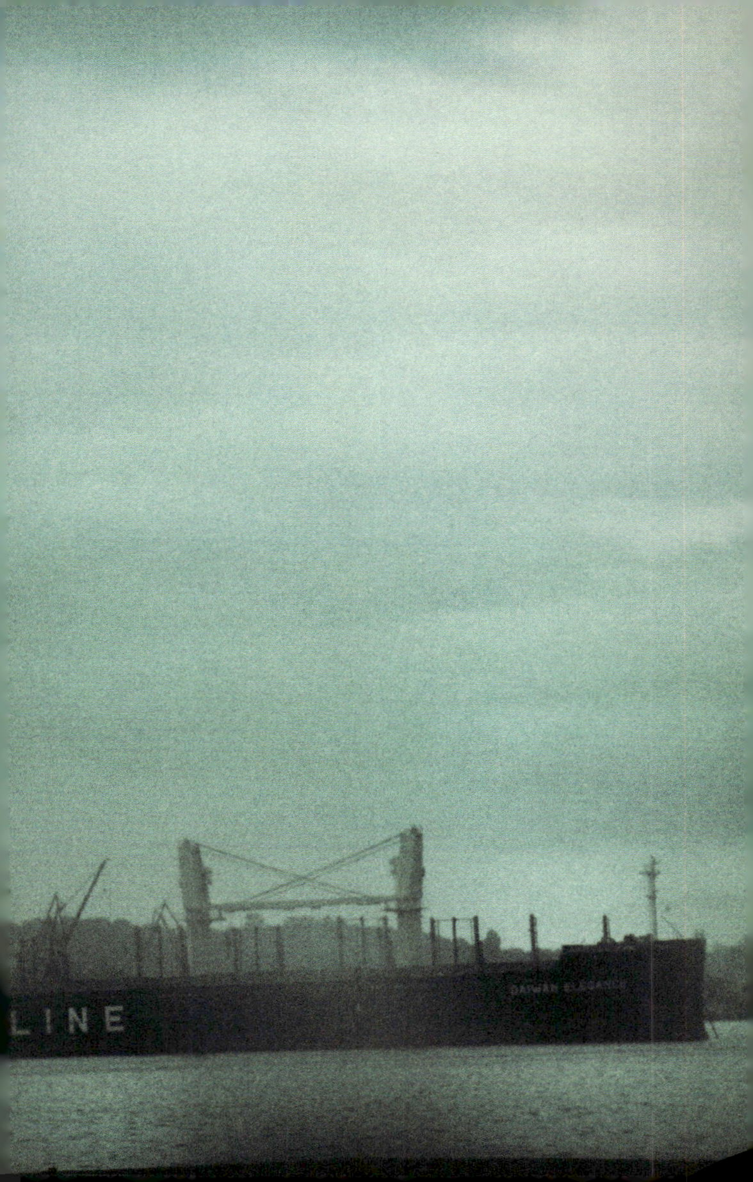
LINE

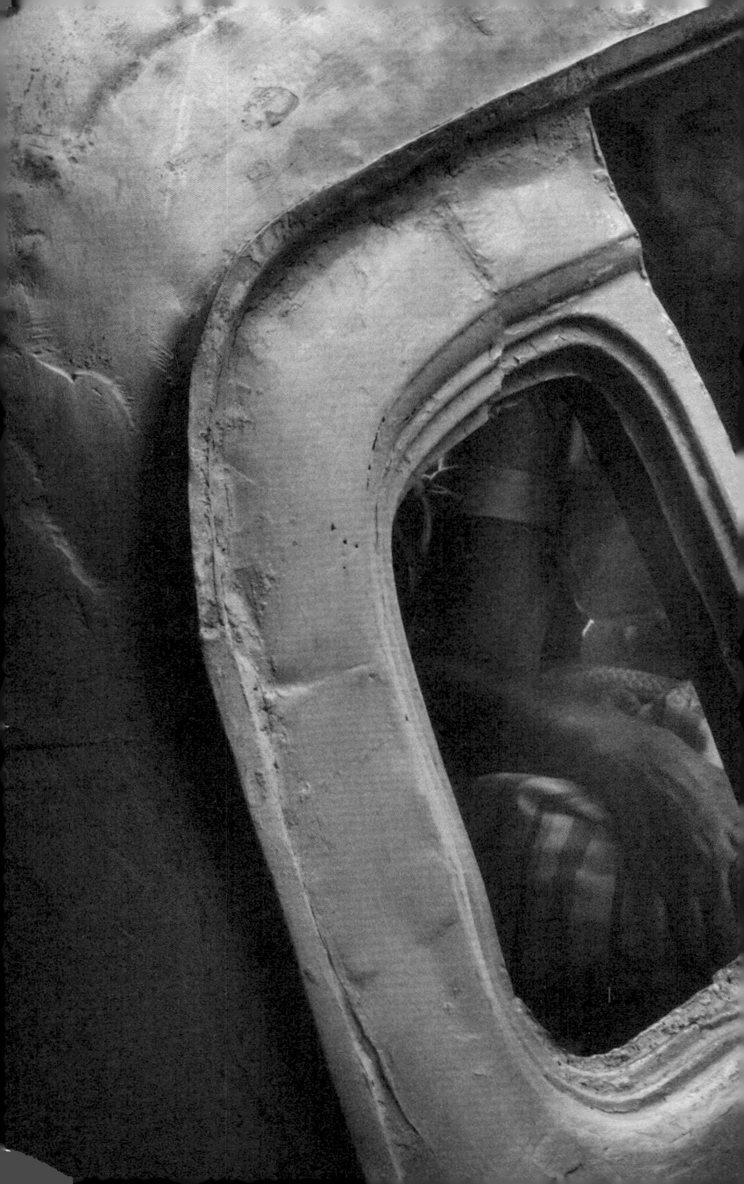

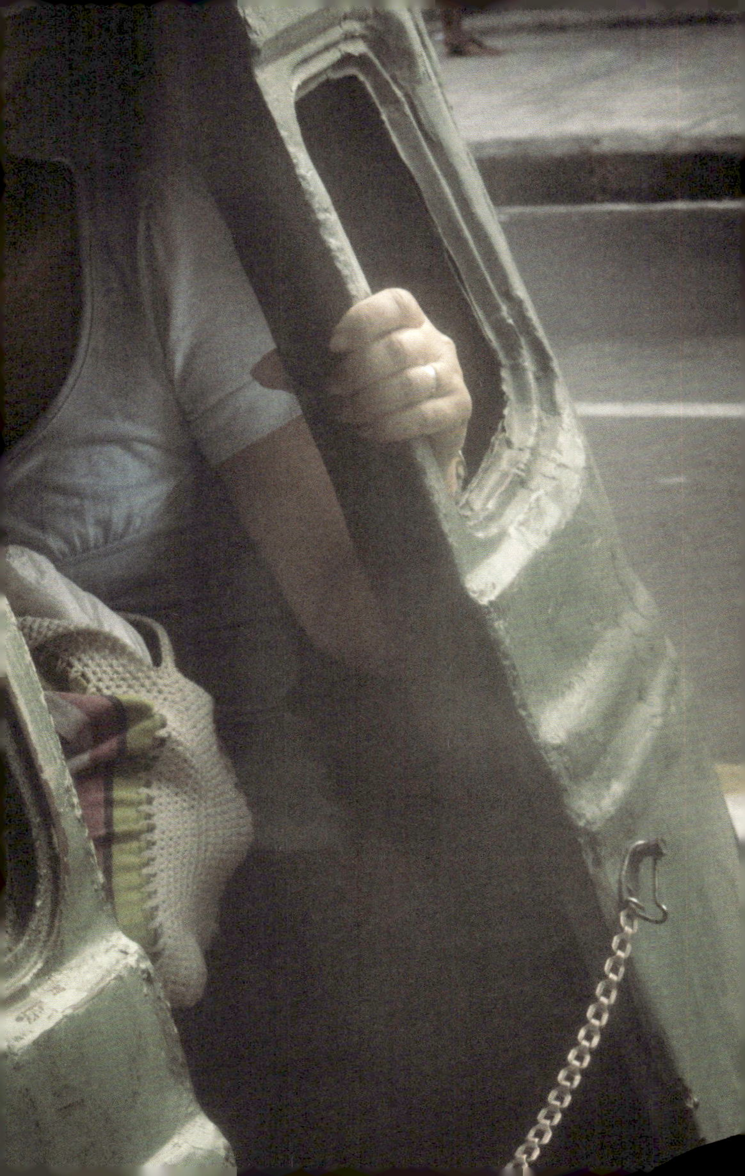

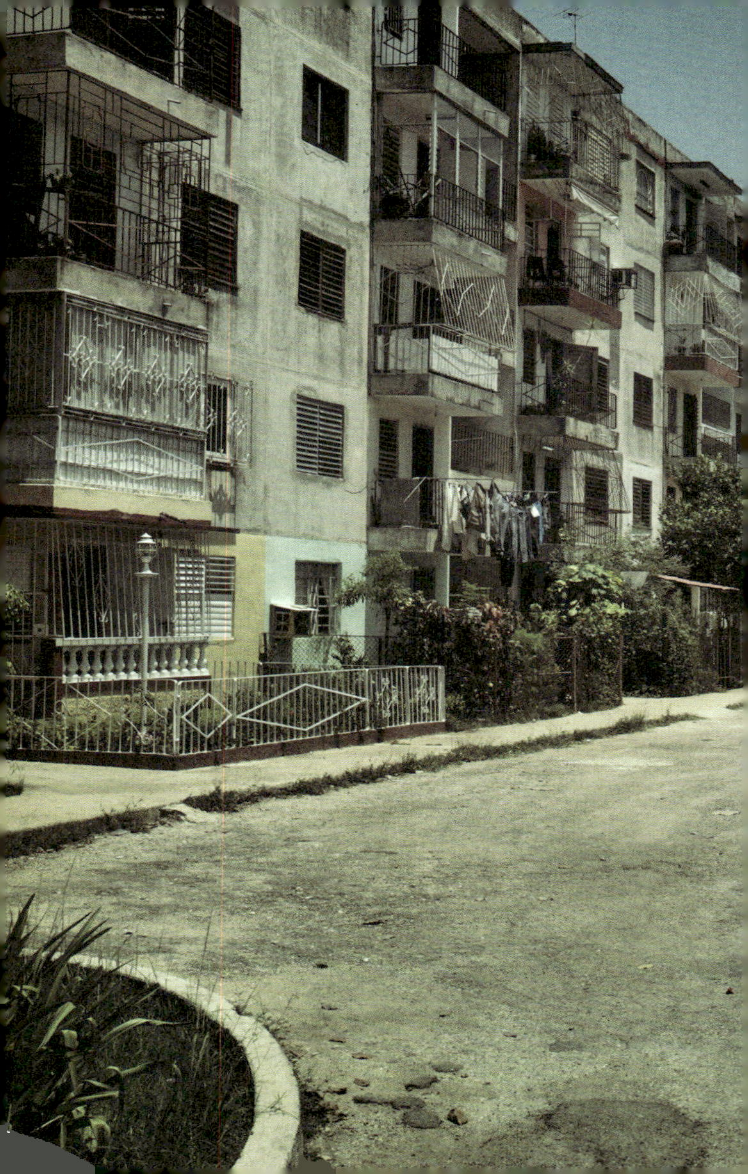

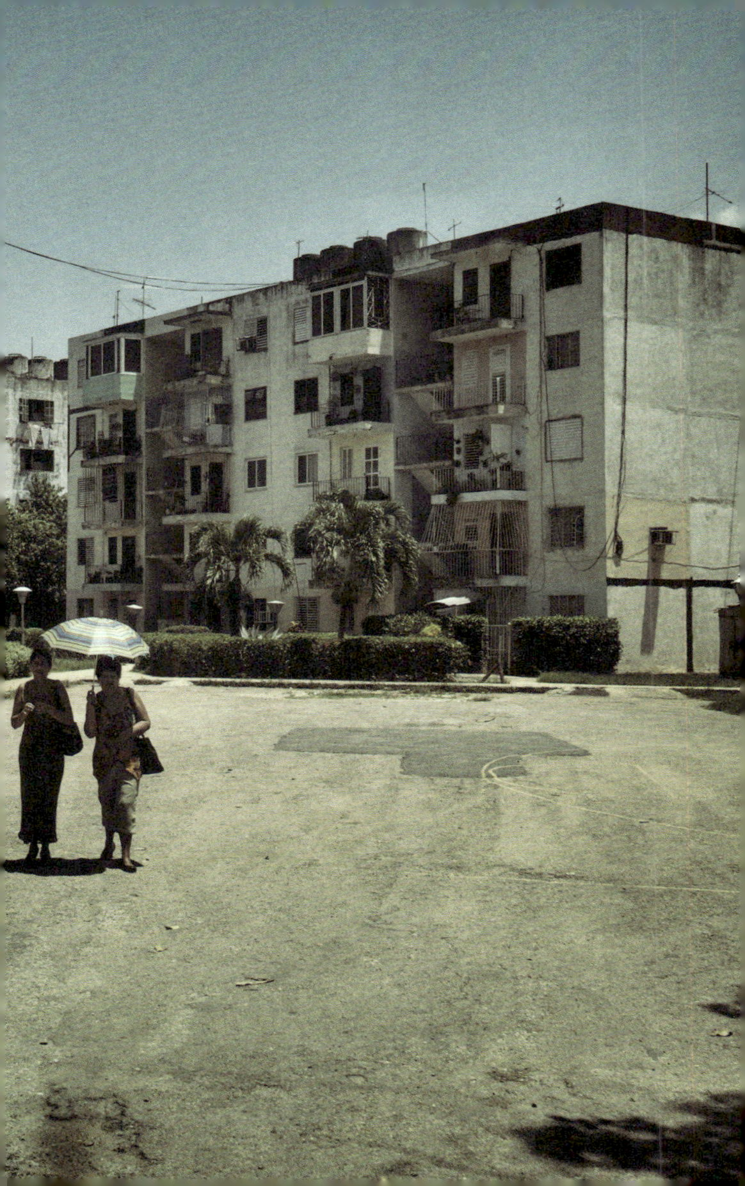

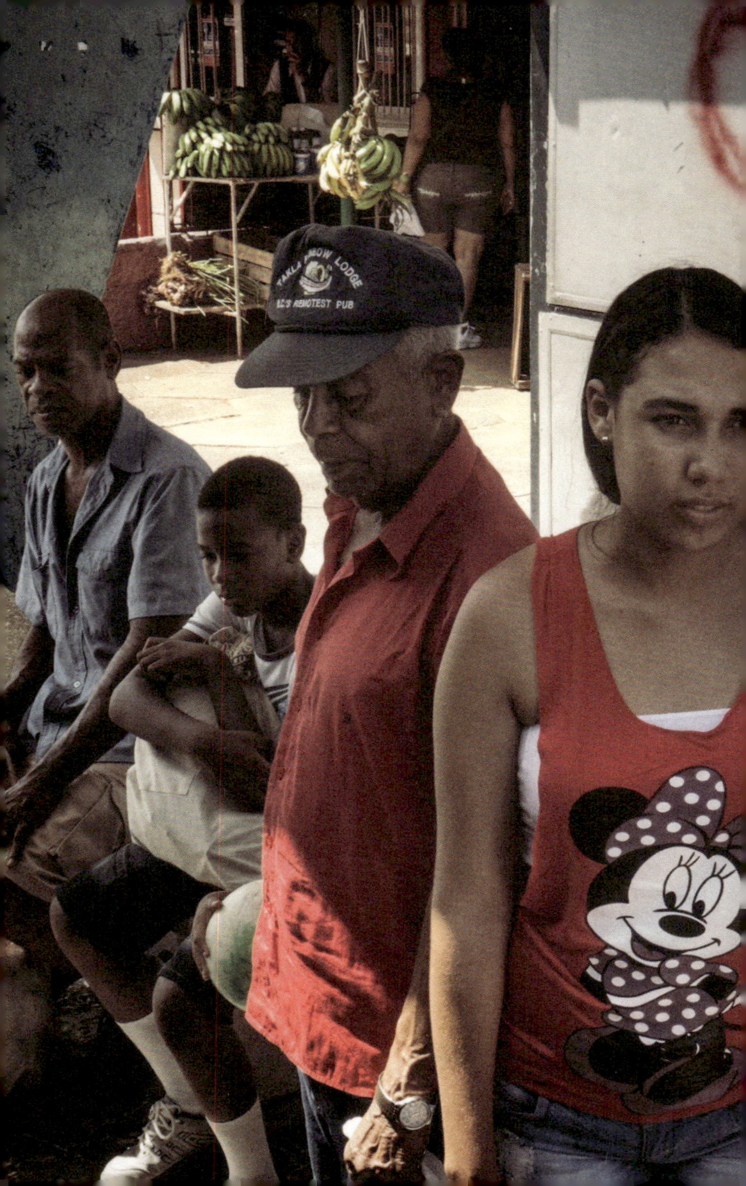
LODGE
REMOTEST PUB

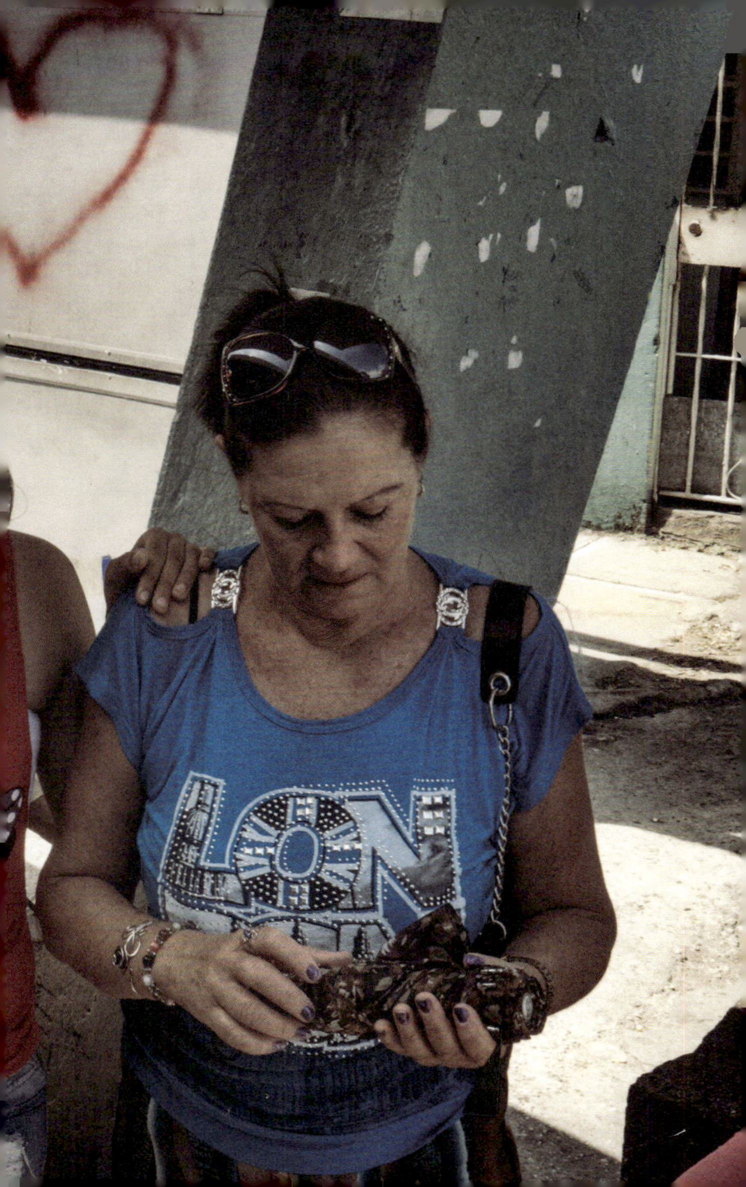
LON

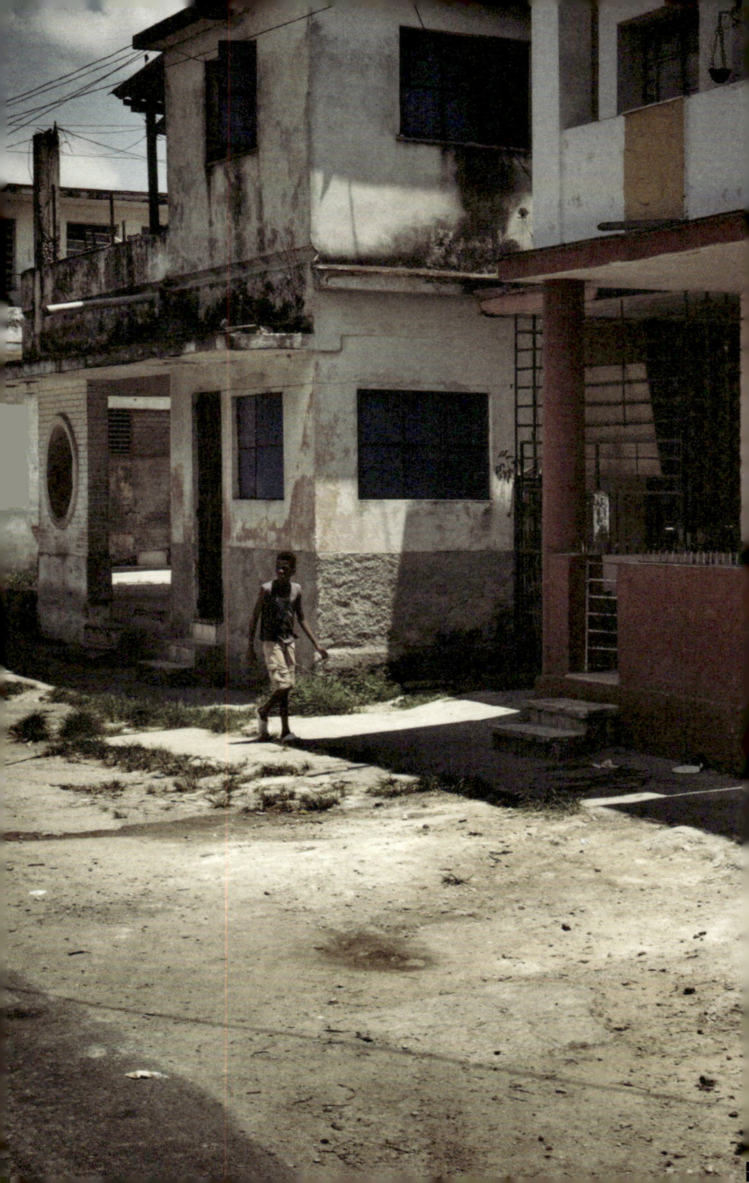

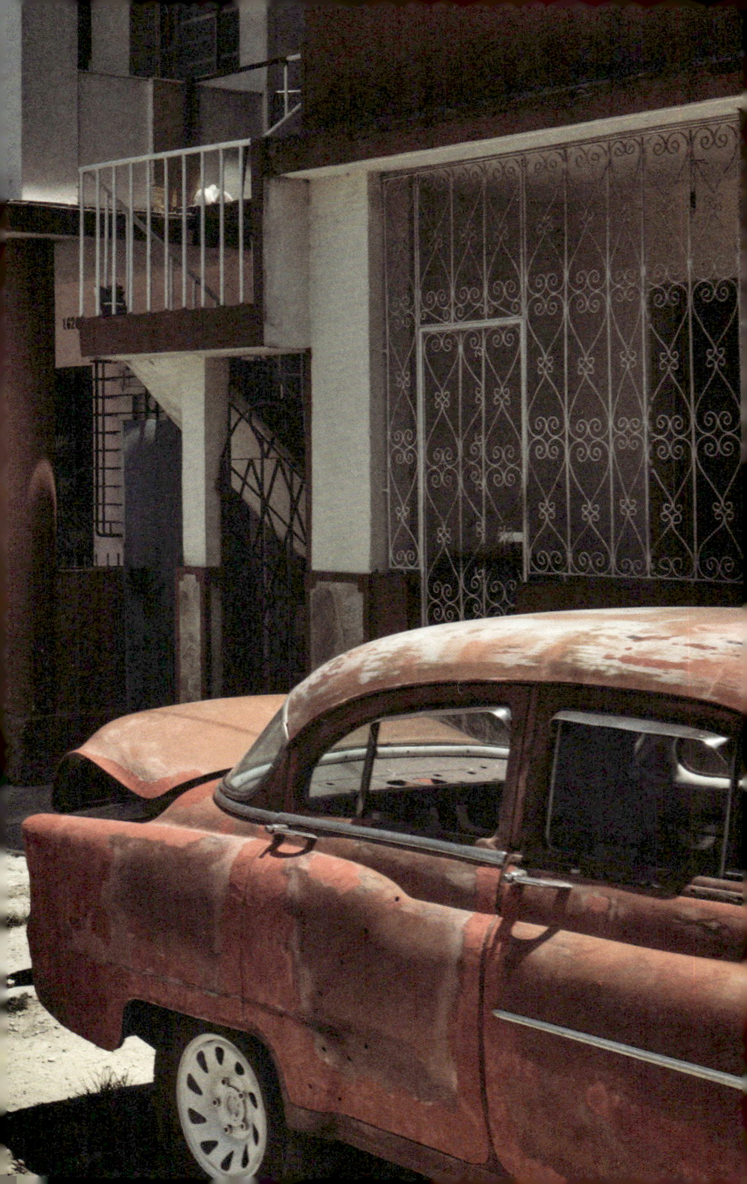

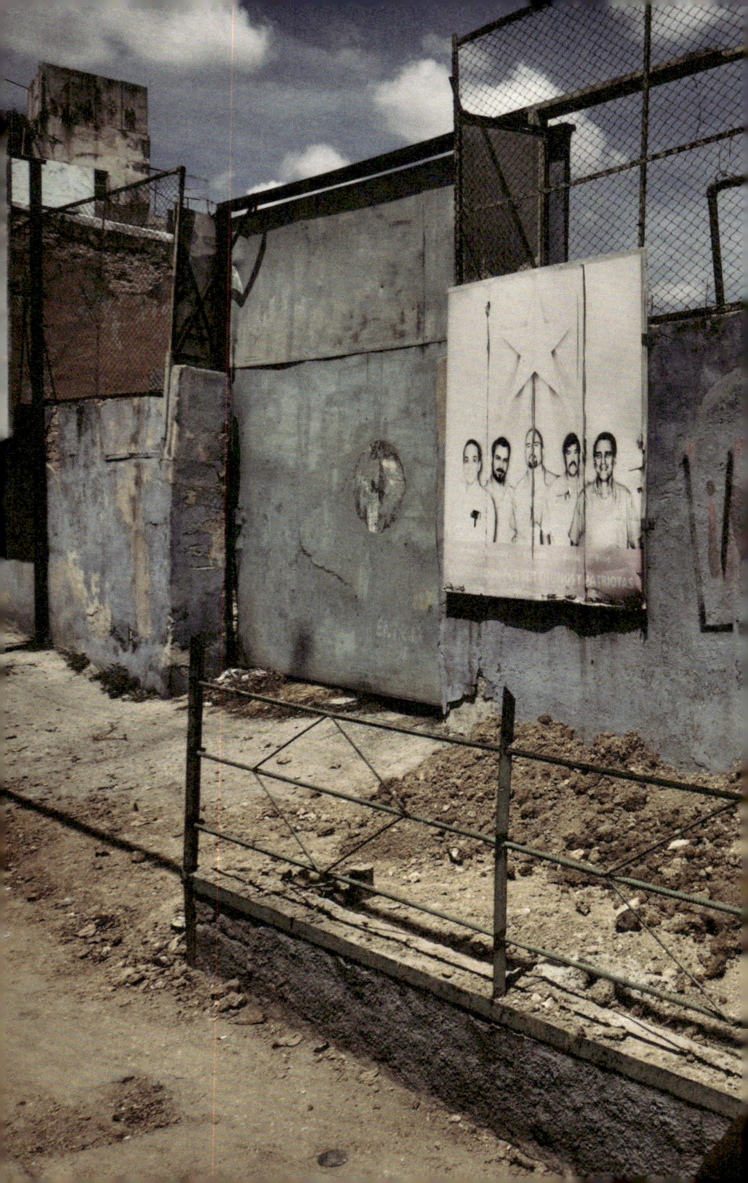

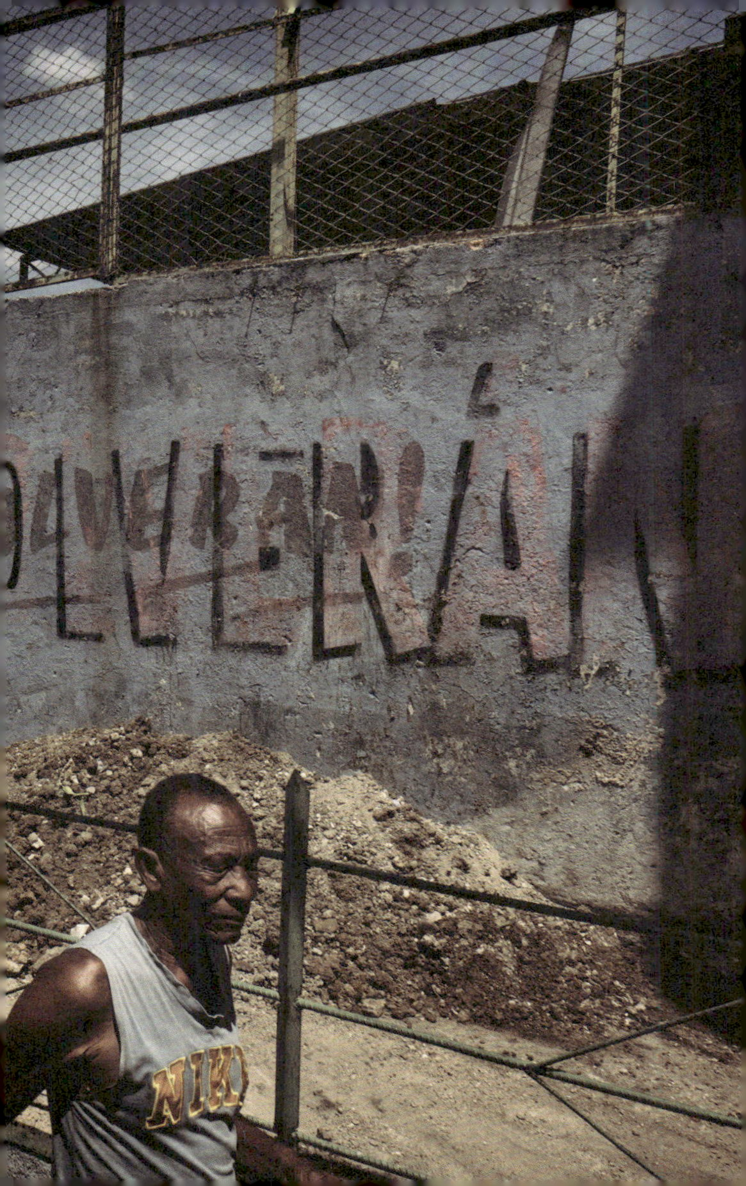

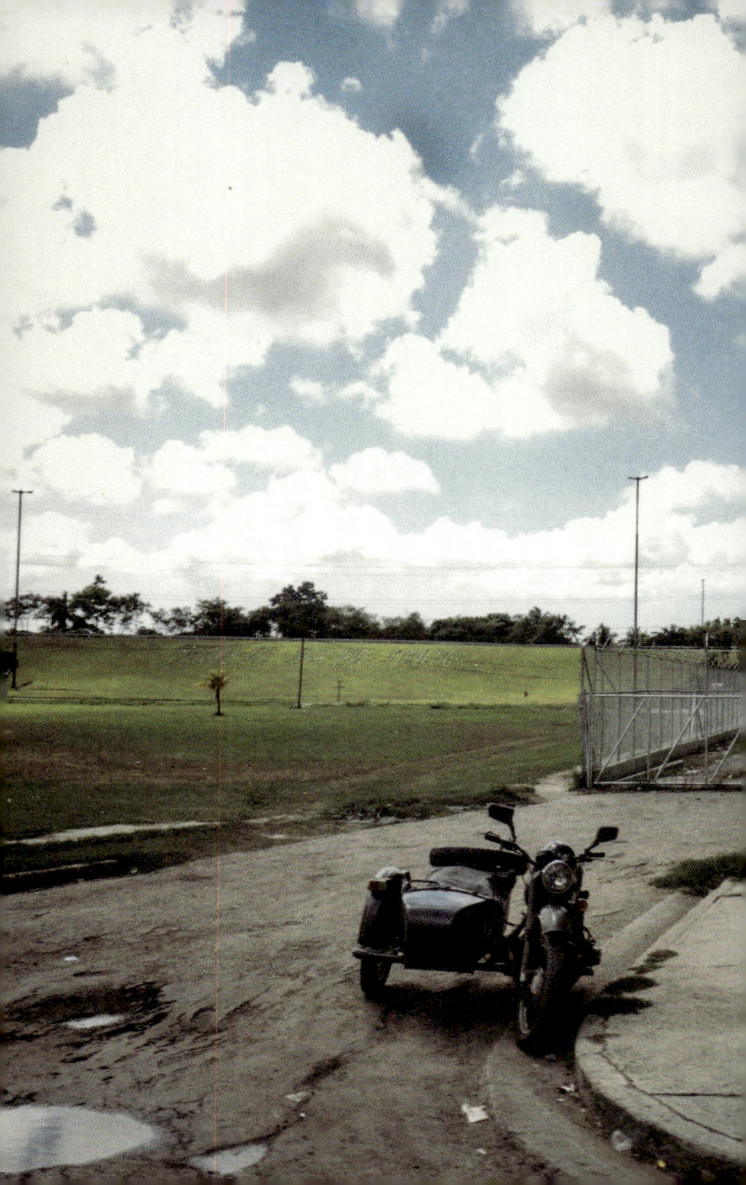

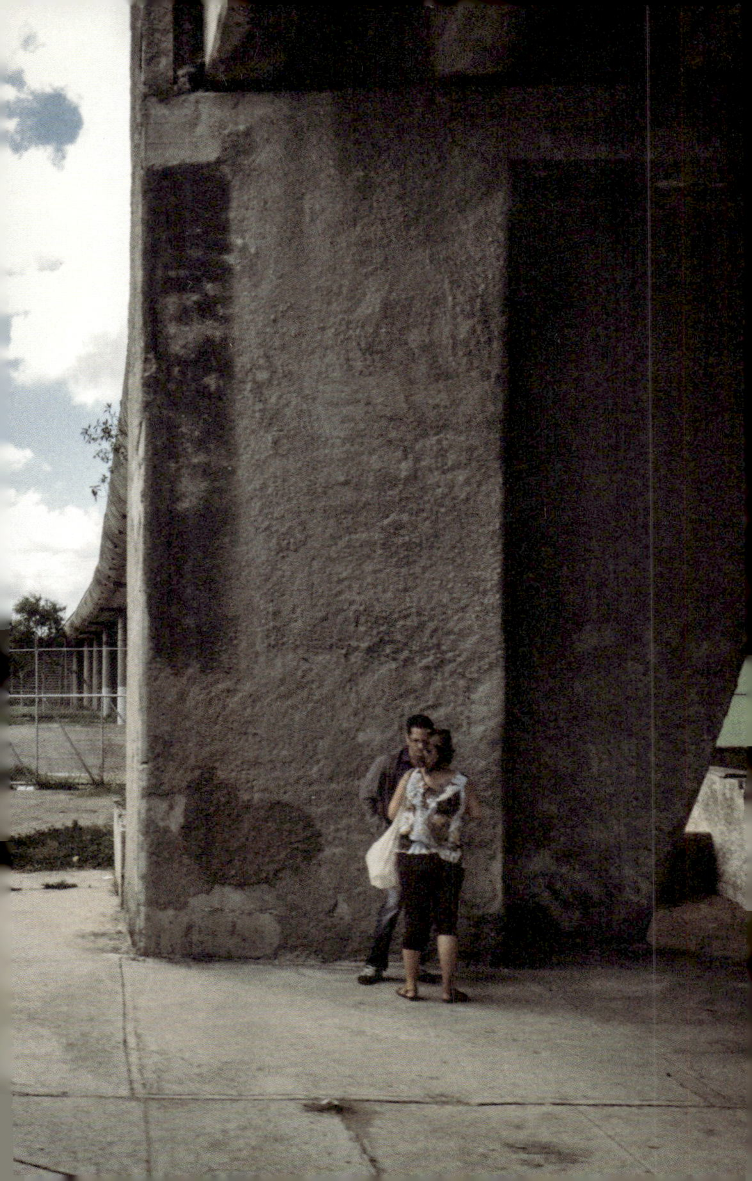

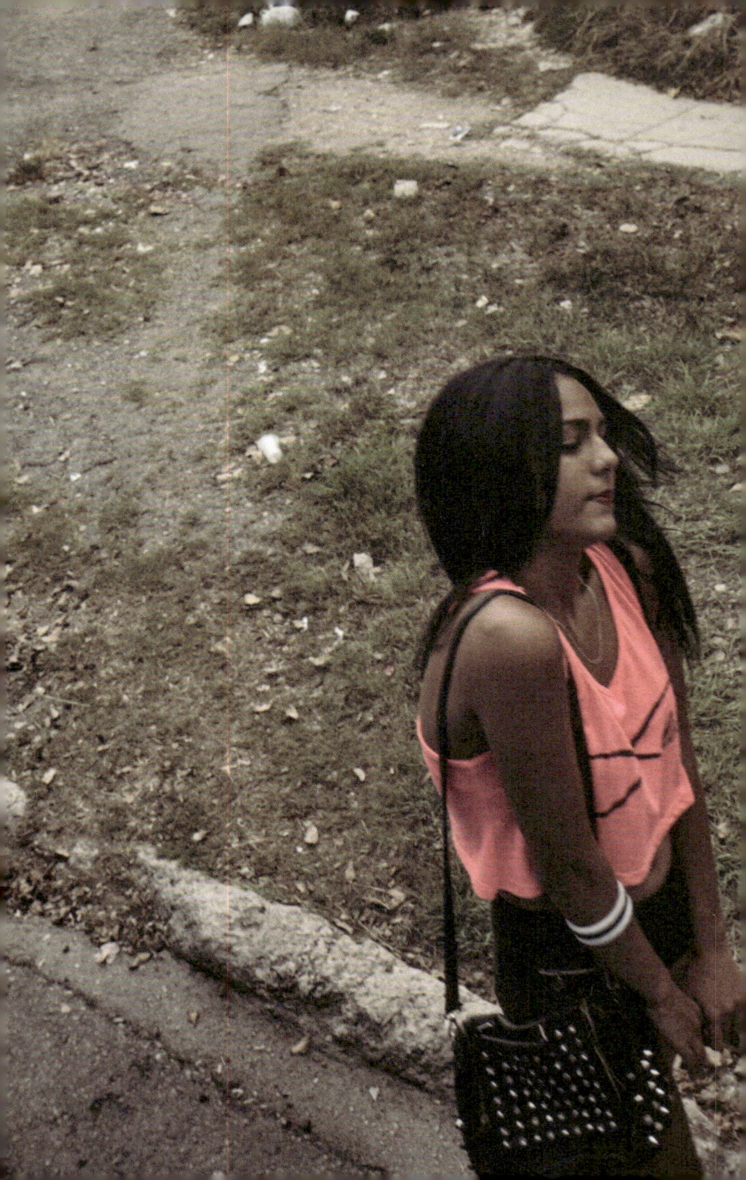

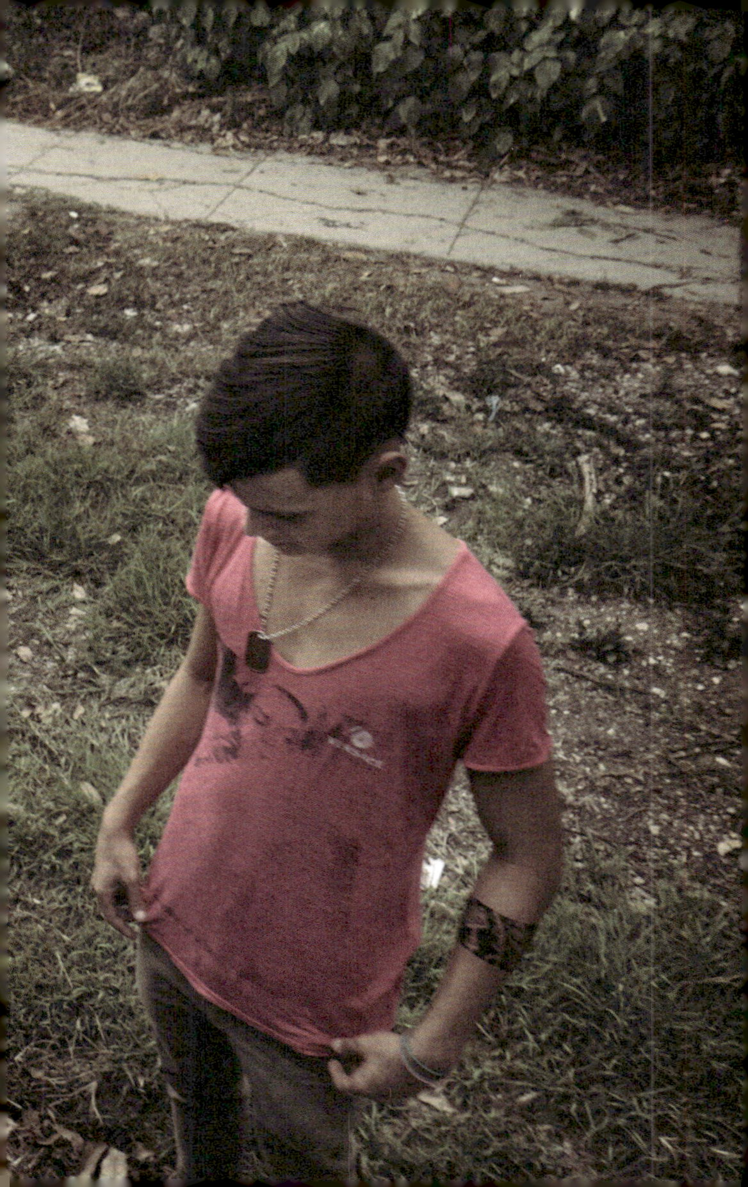

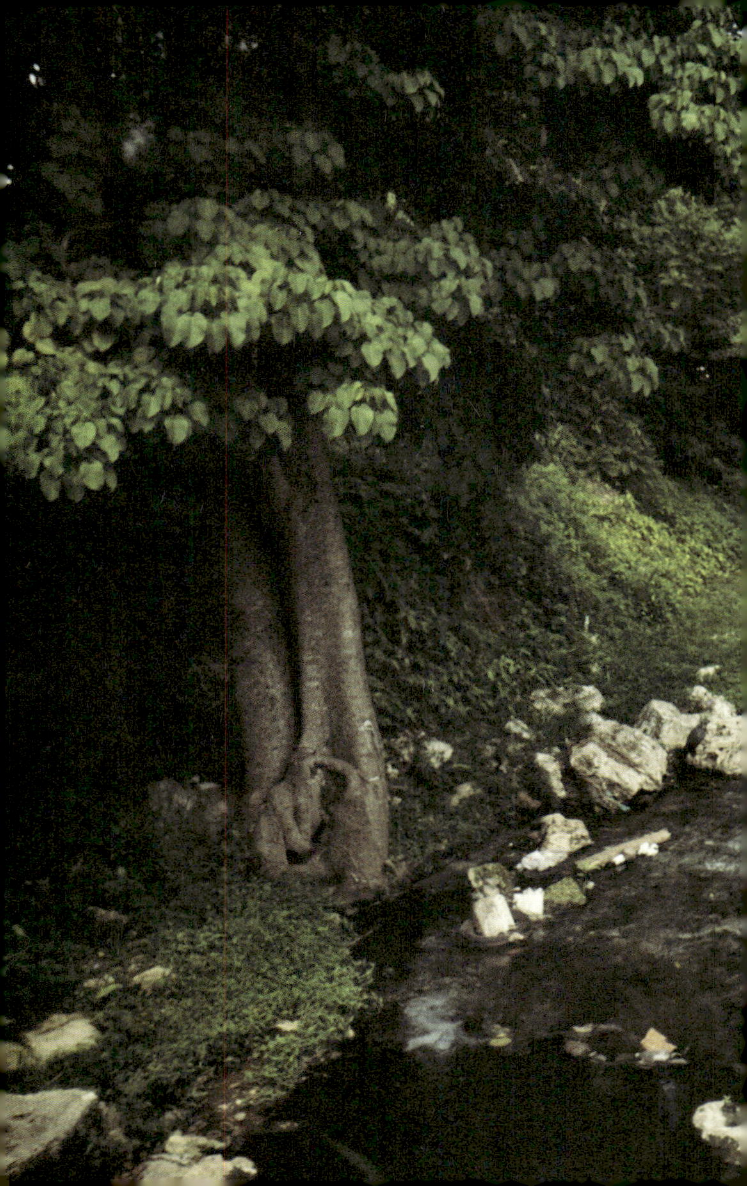

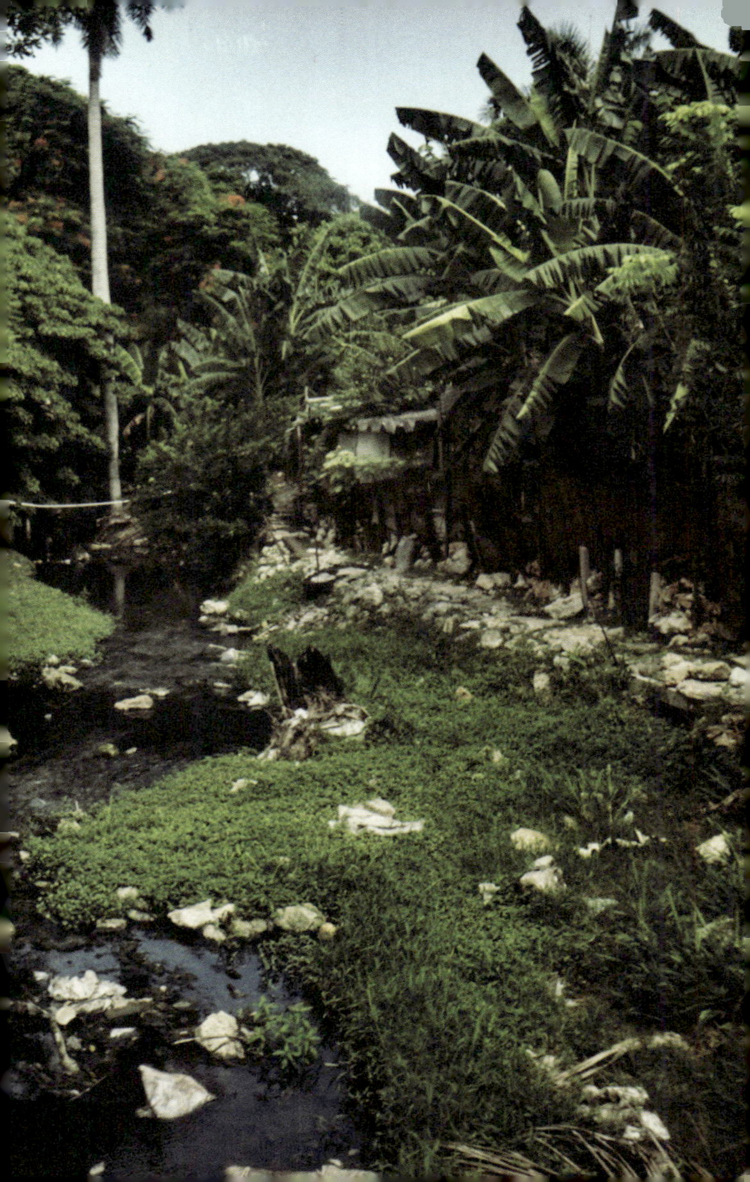

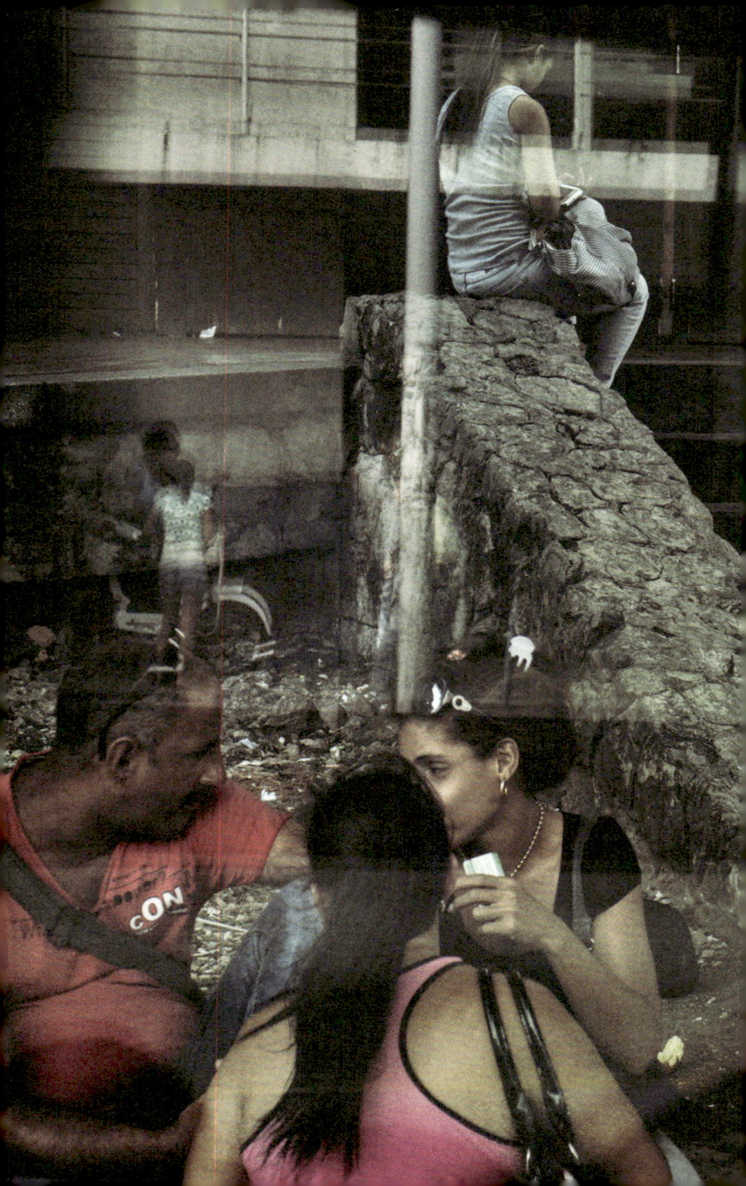
CON

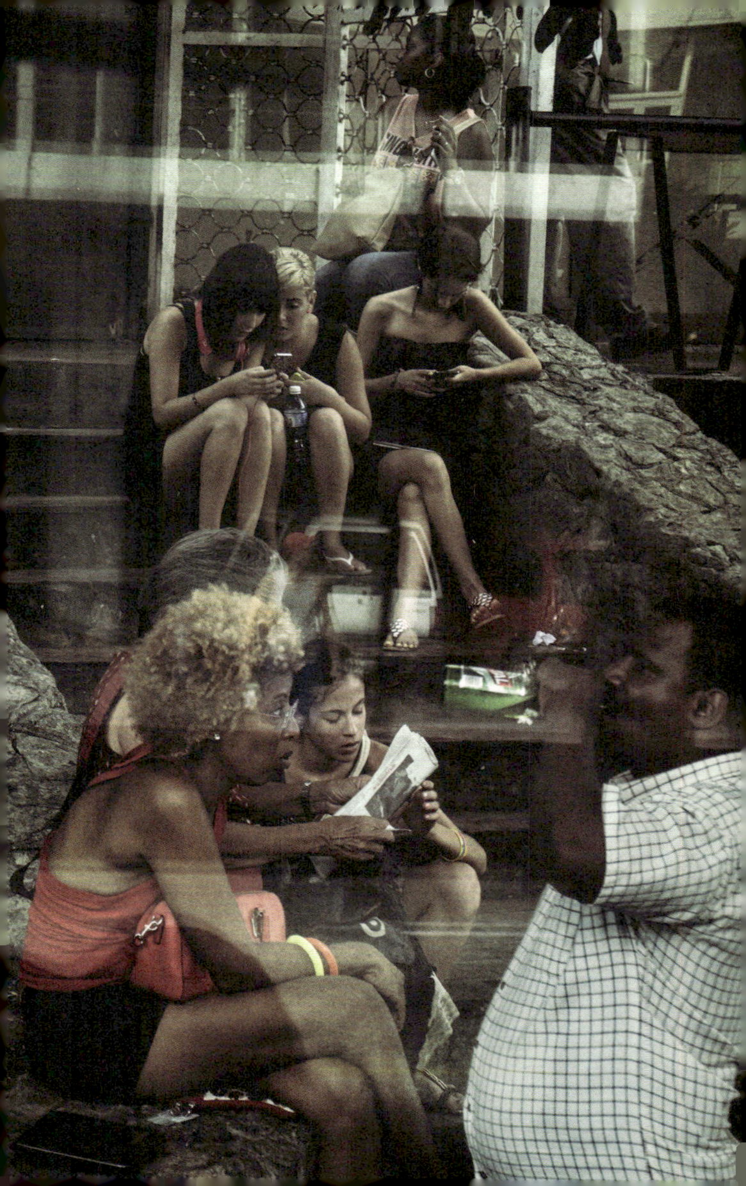

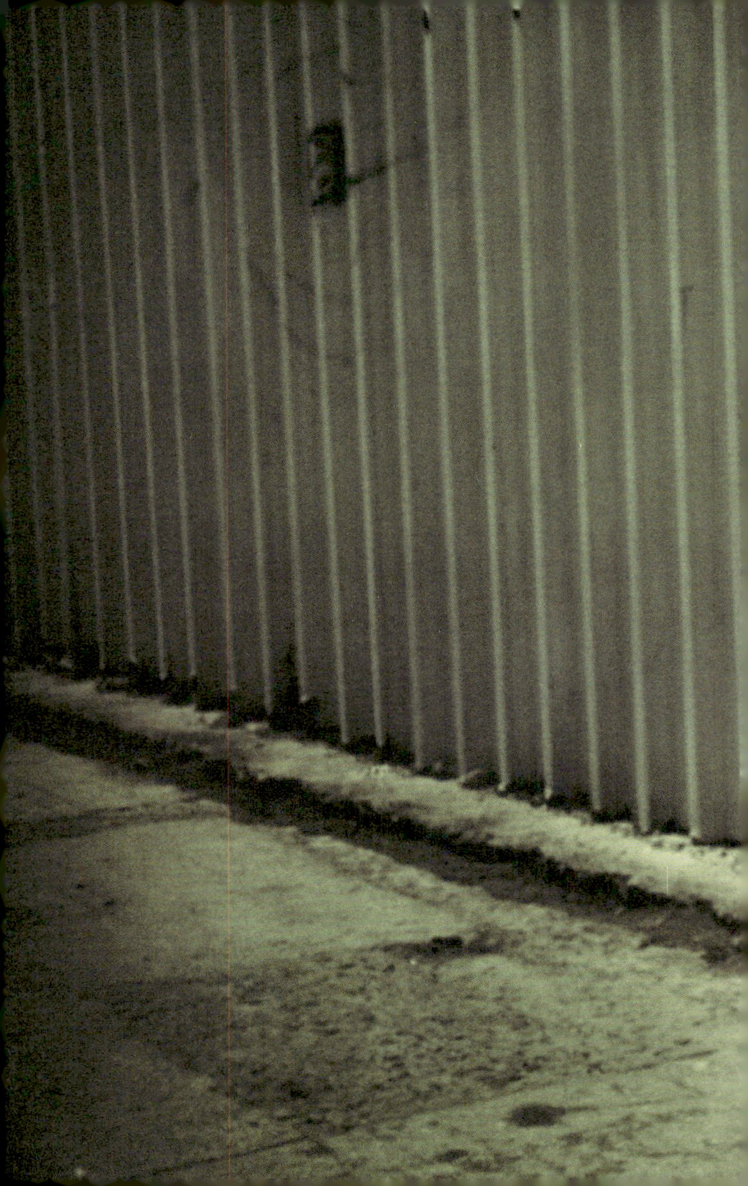

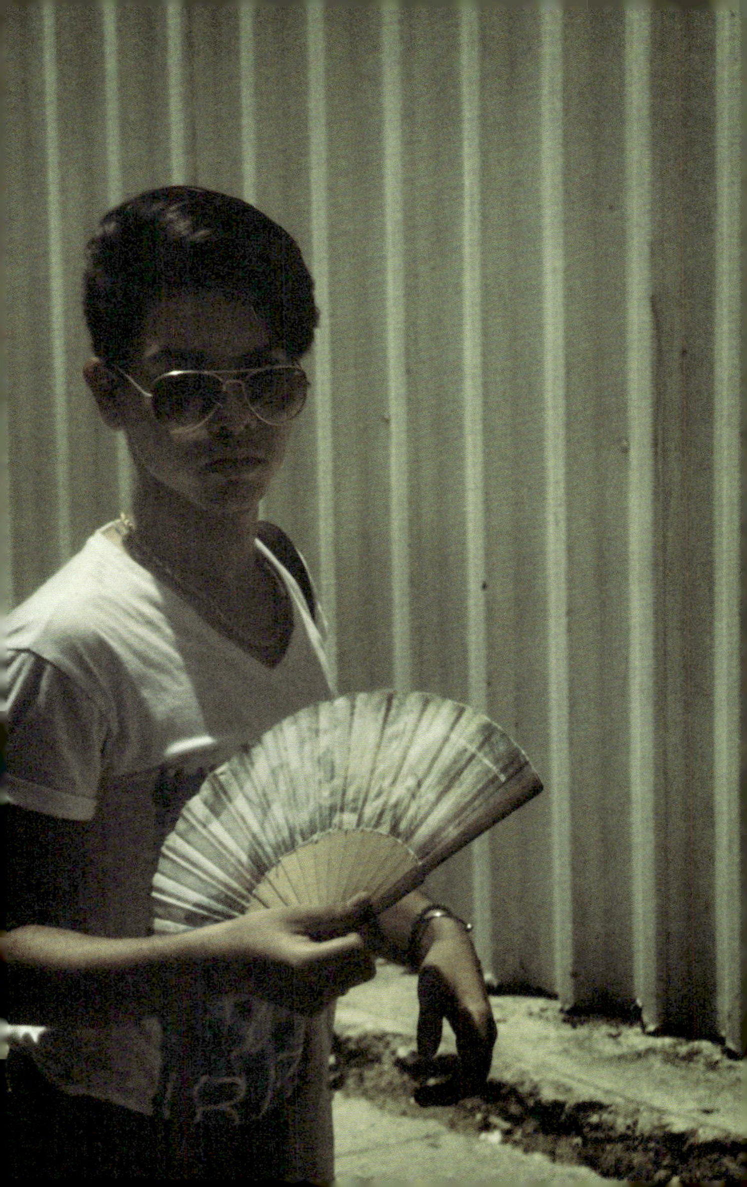

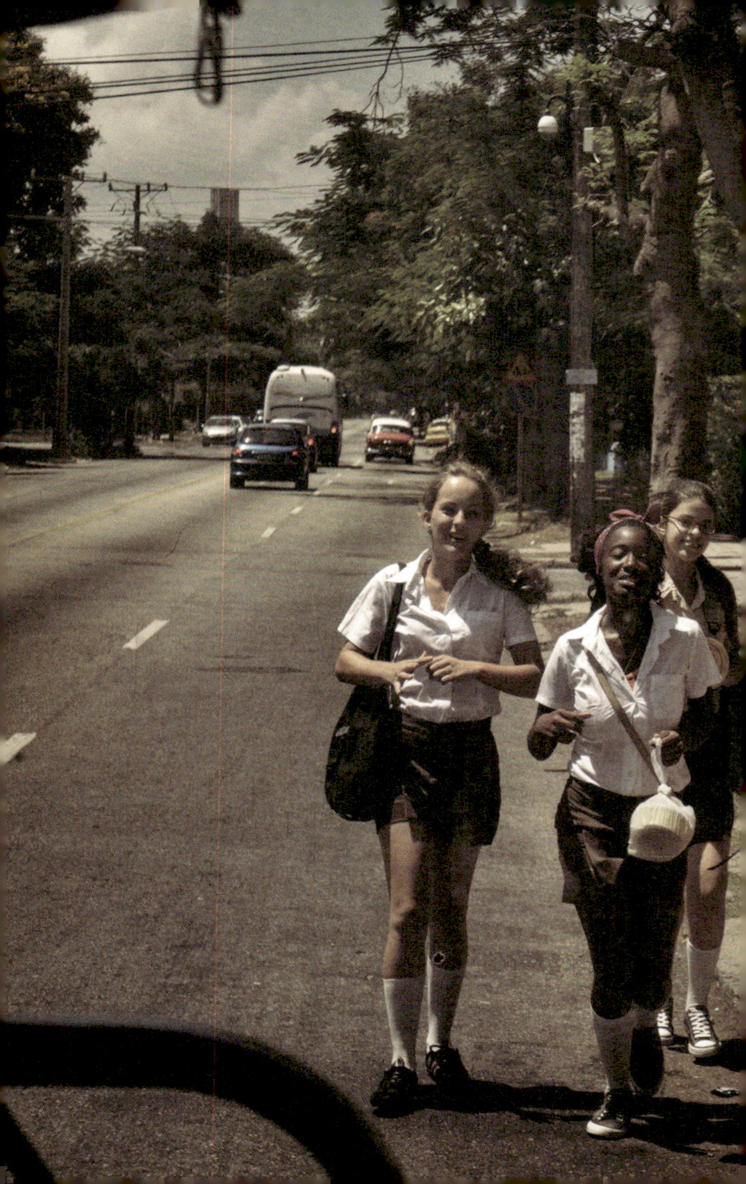

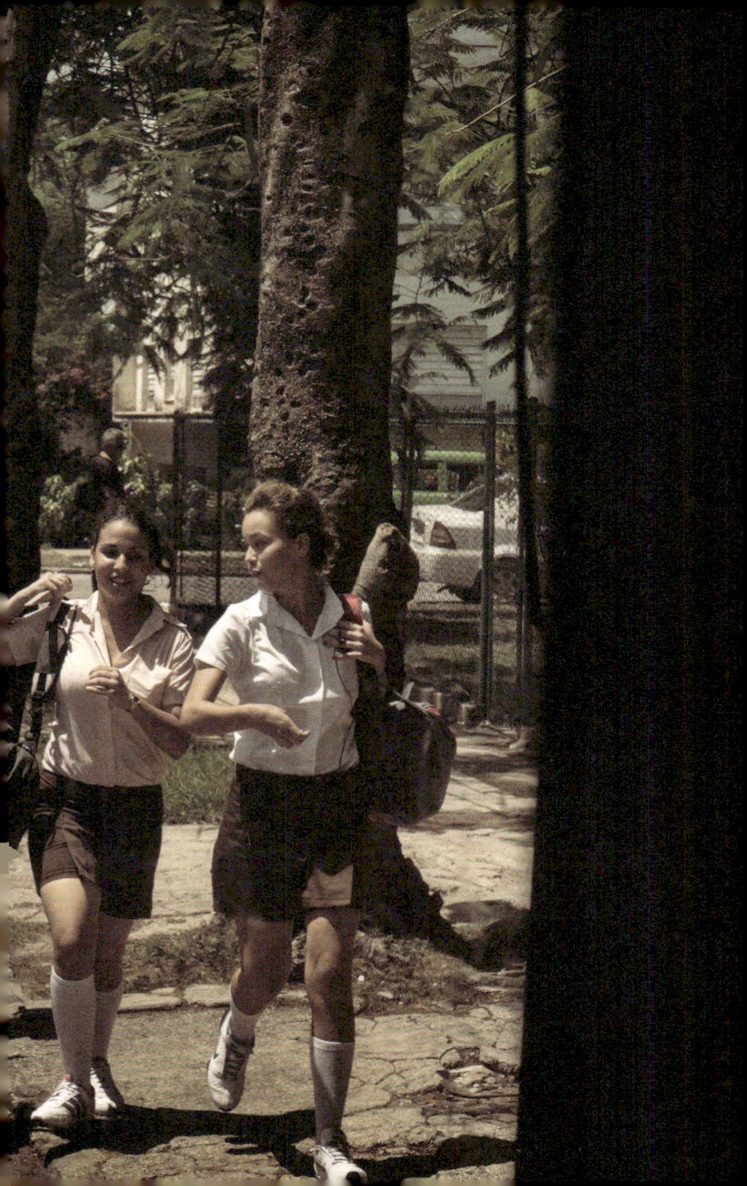

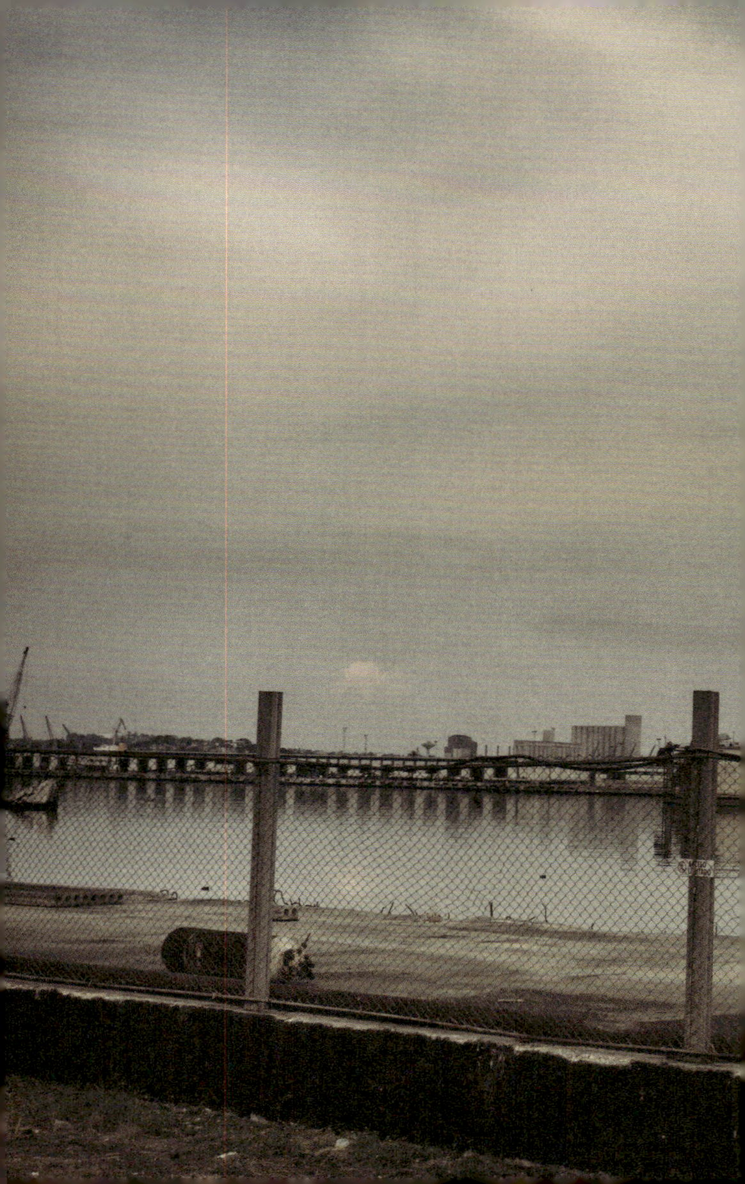

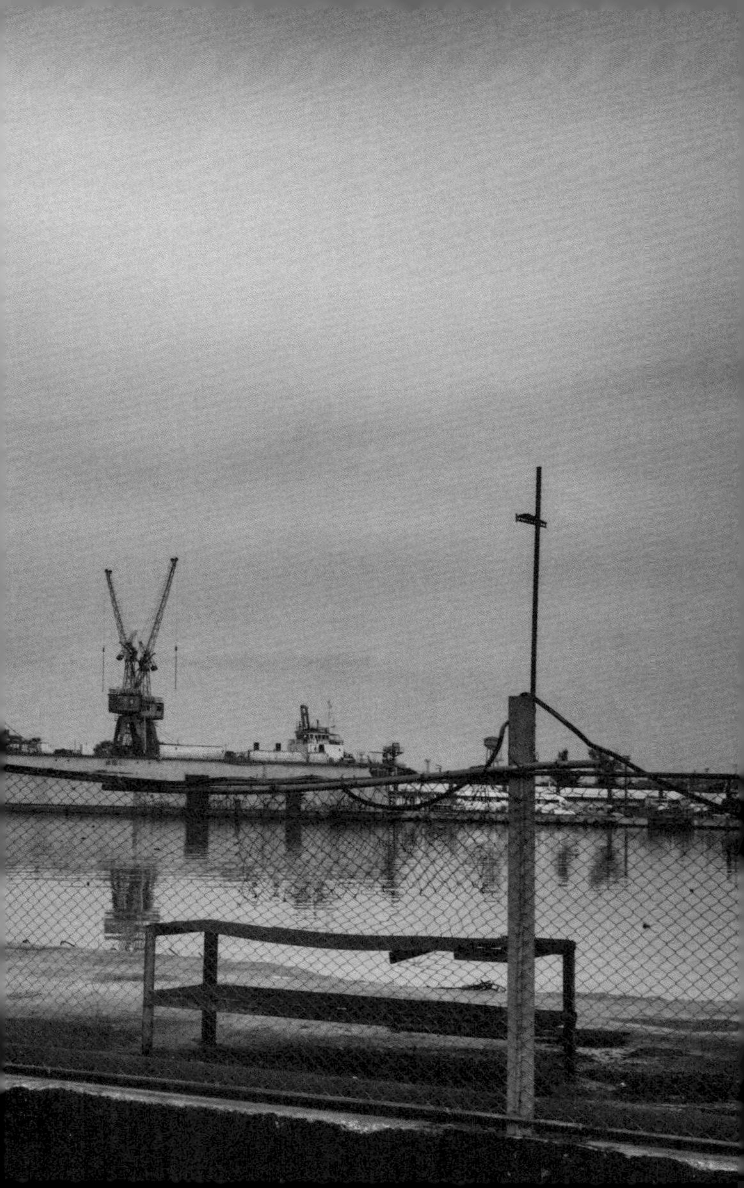

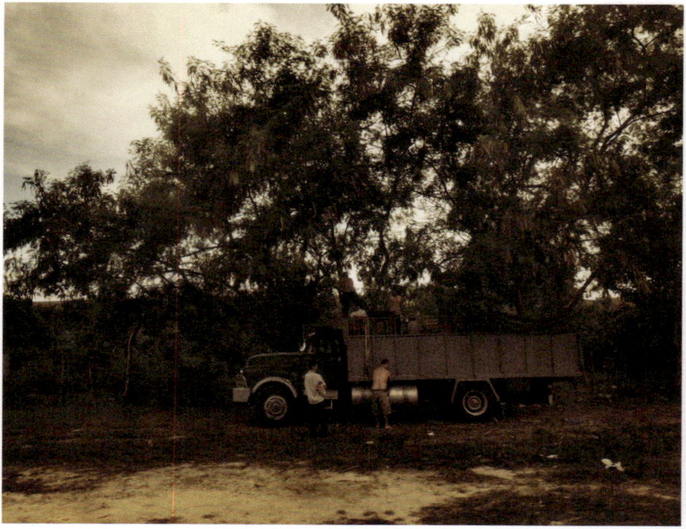

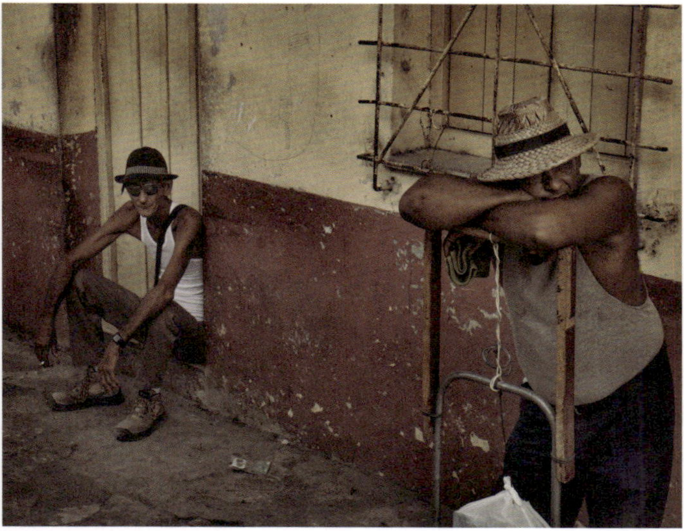

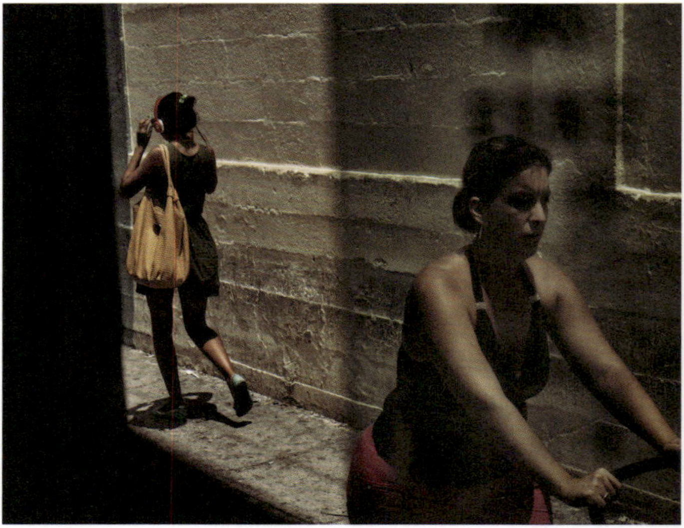

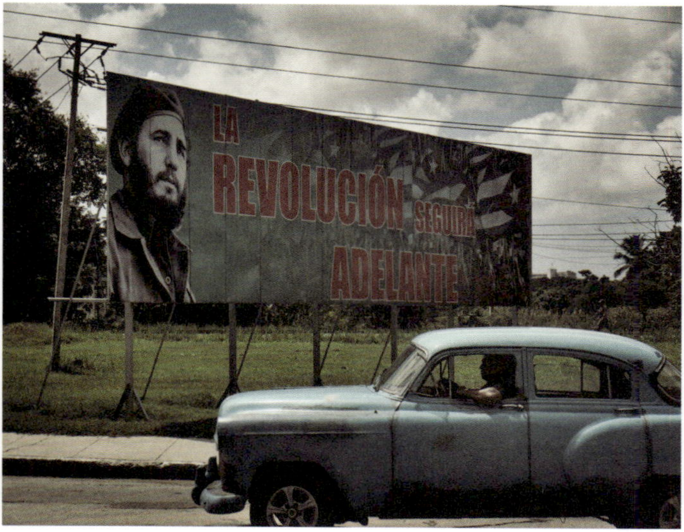
LA
REVOLUCIÓN
SEGUIRÁ
ADELANTE

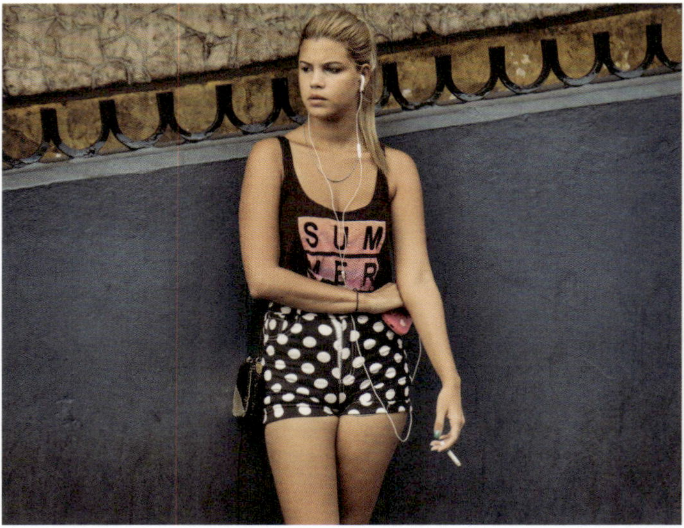
SUM
MER

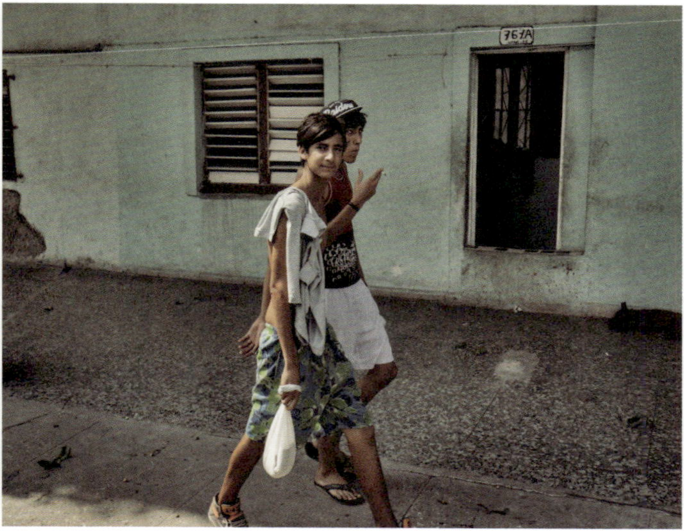

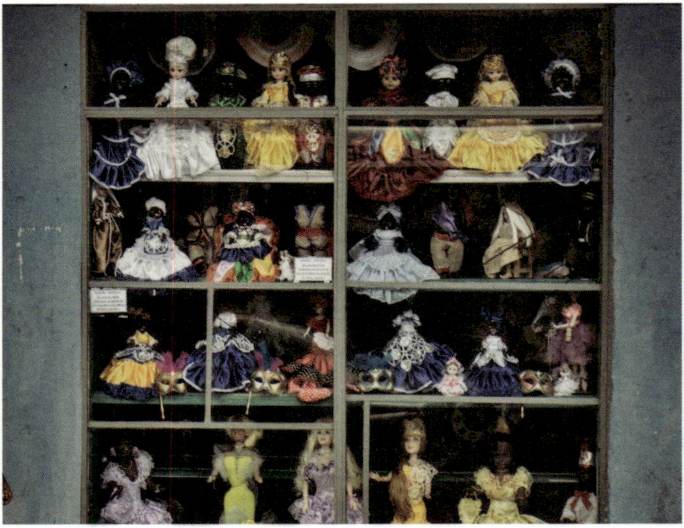

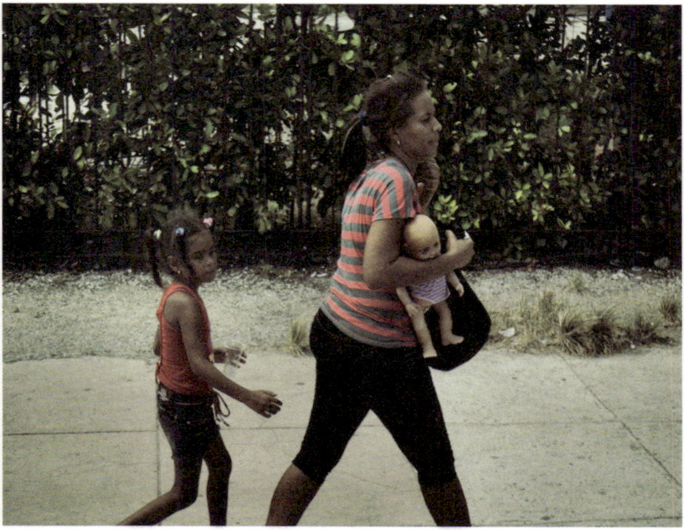

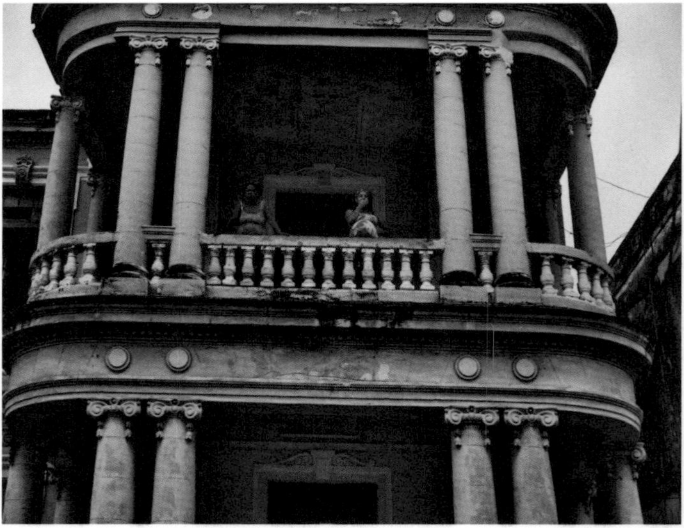

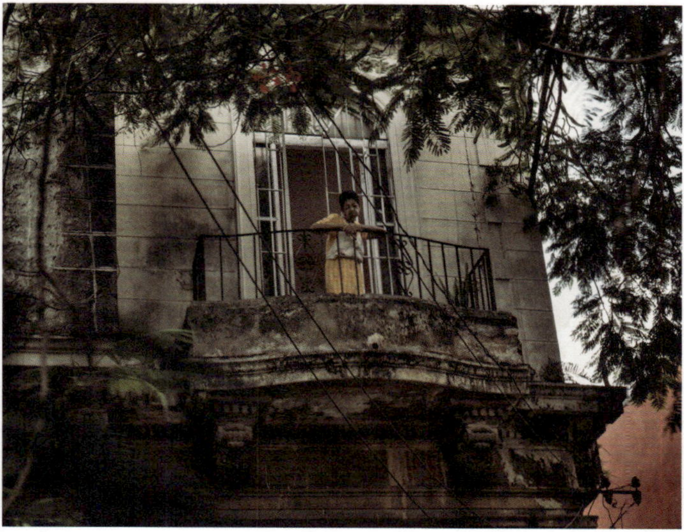

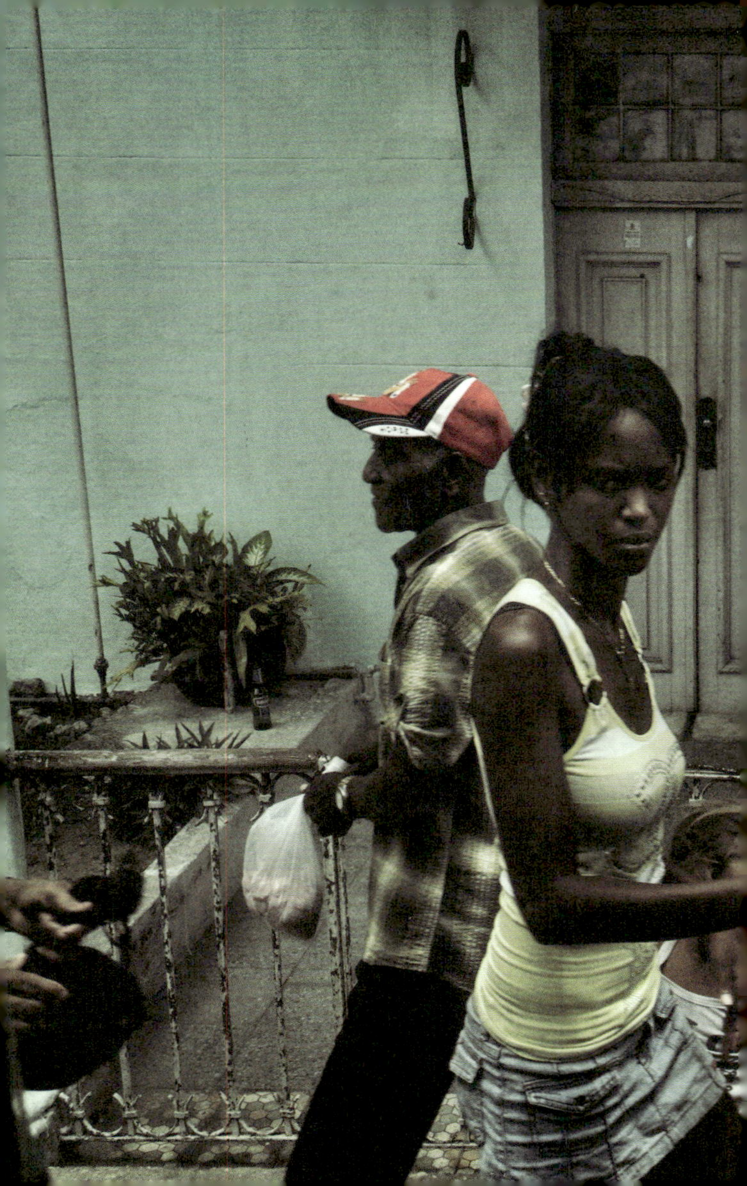

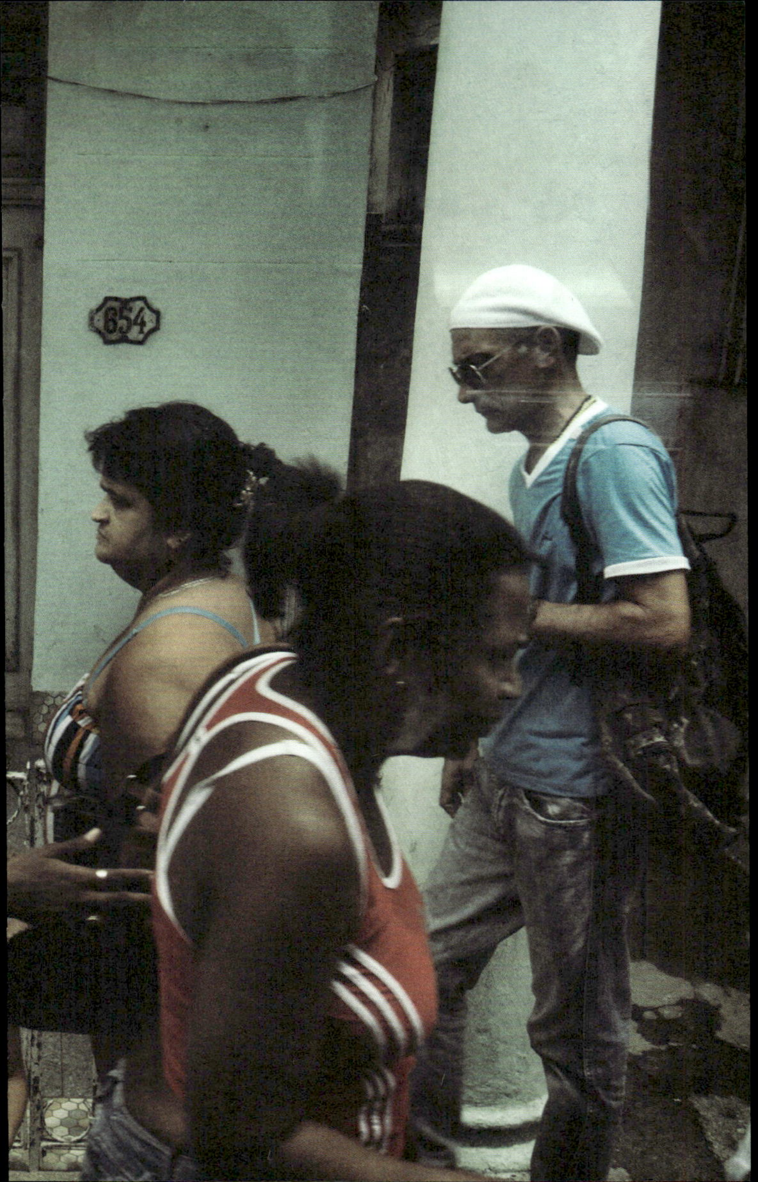
654

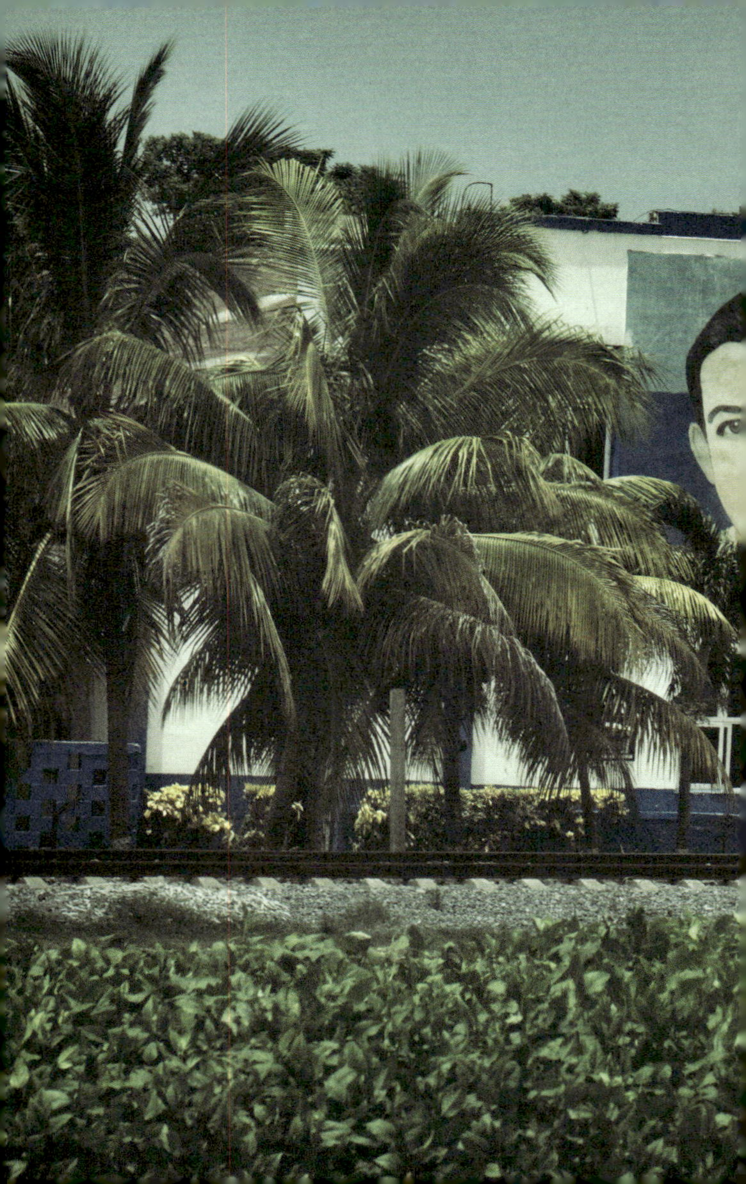

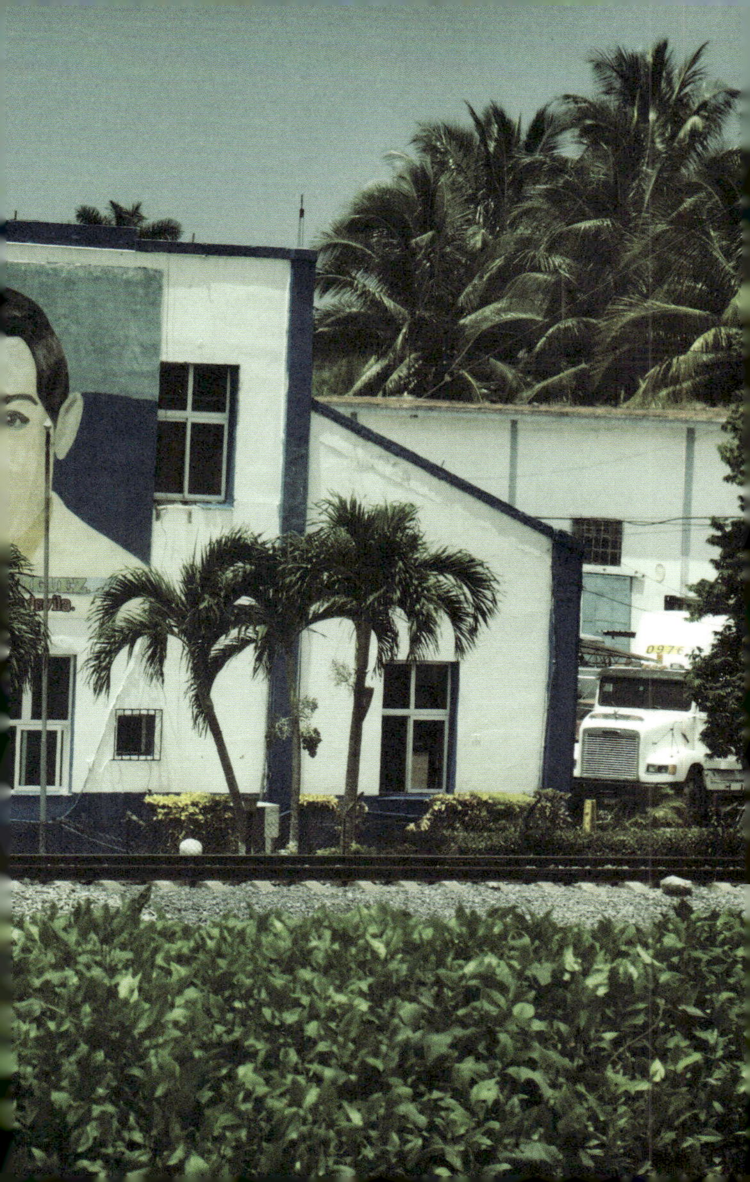

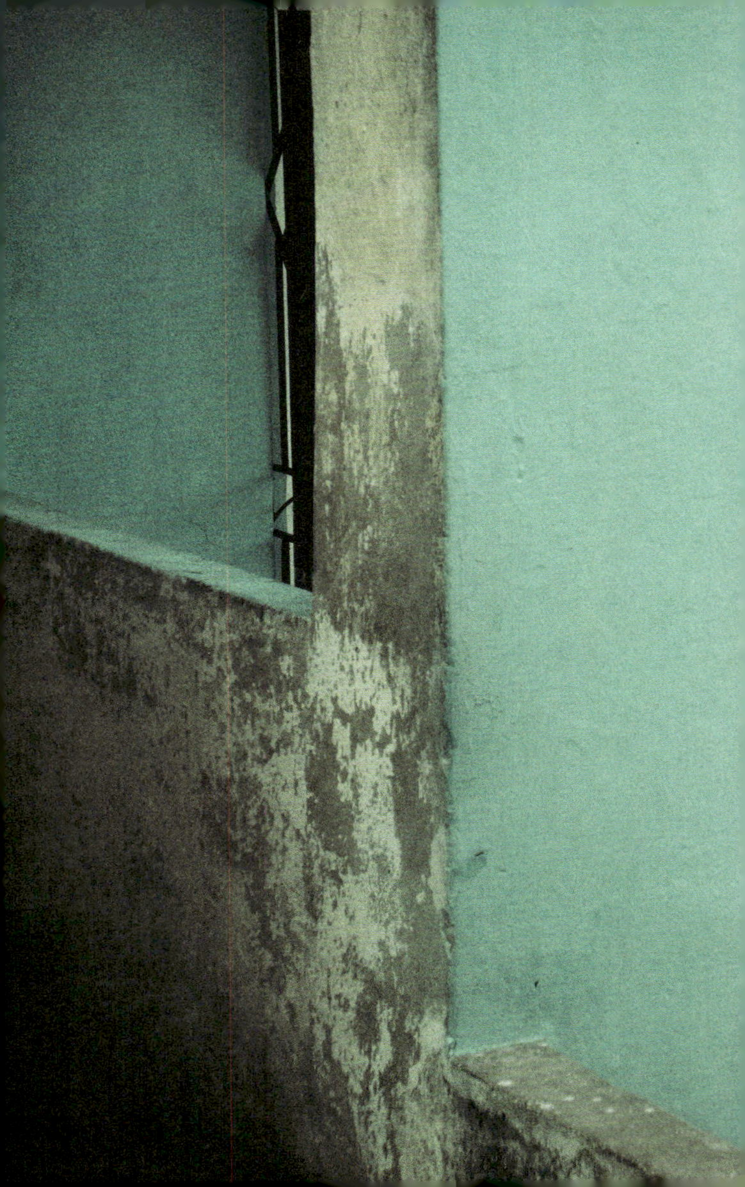

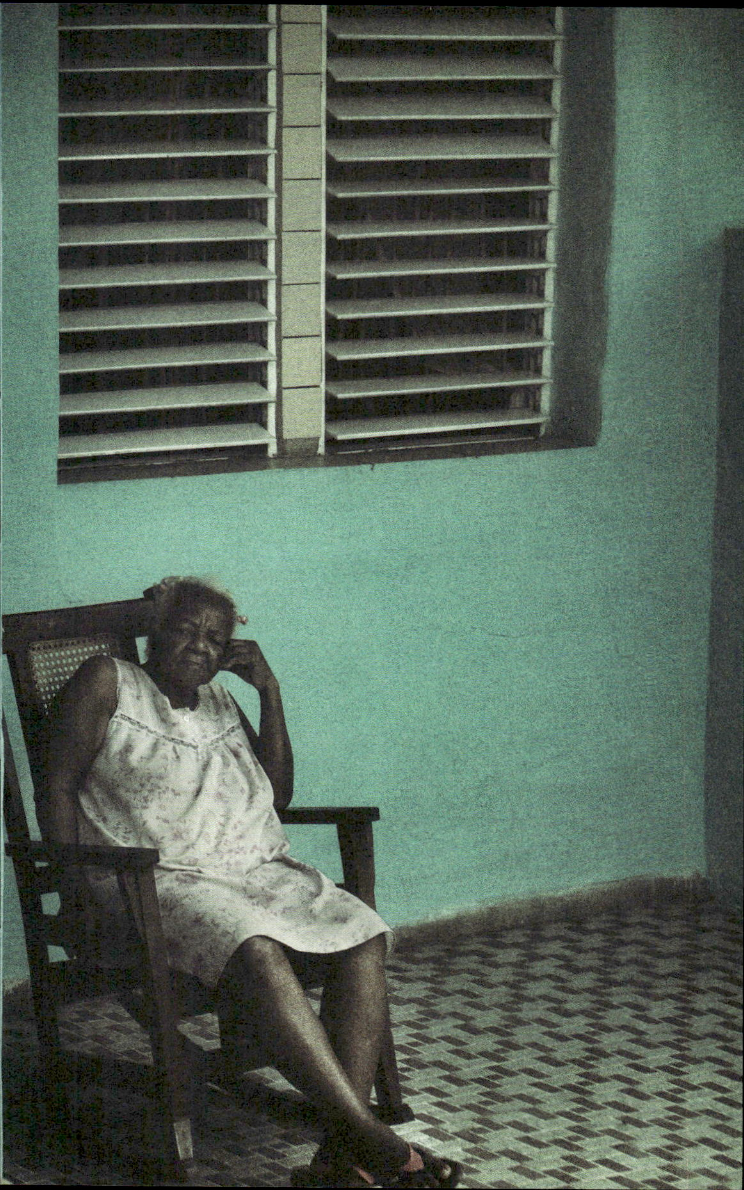

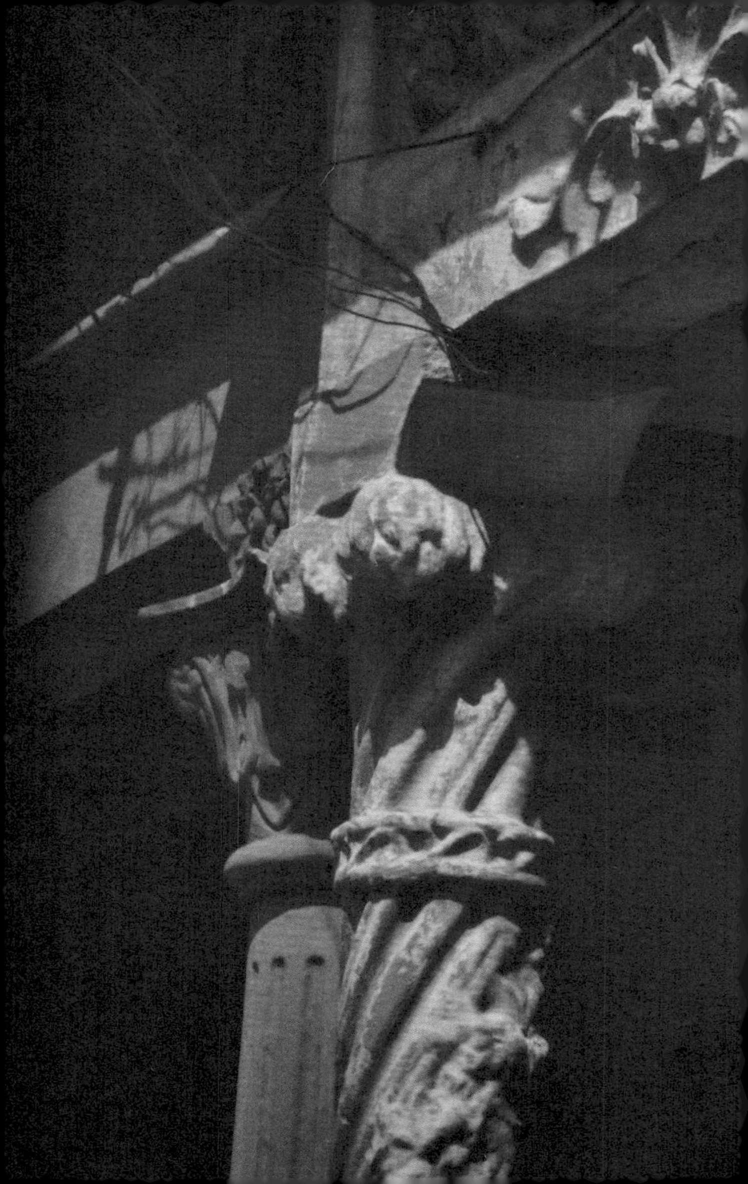

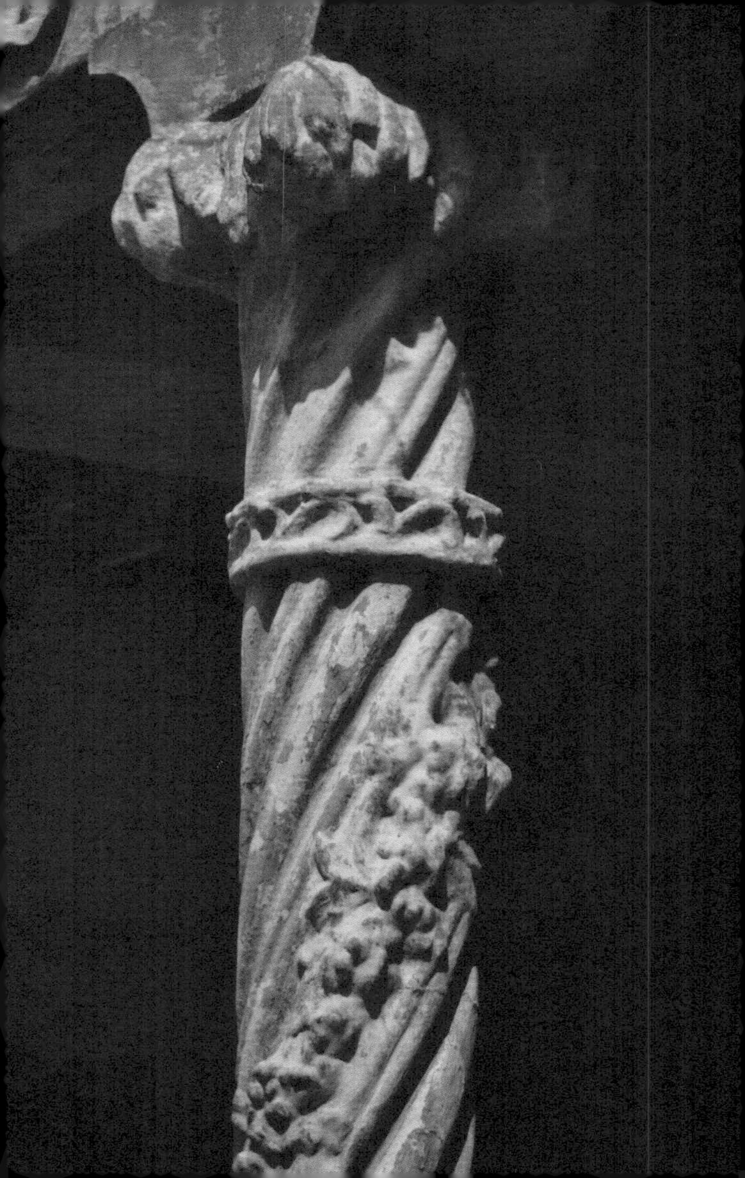

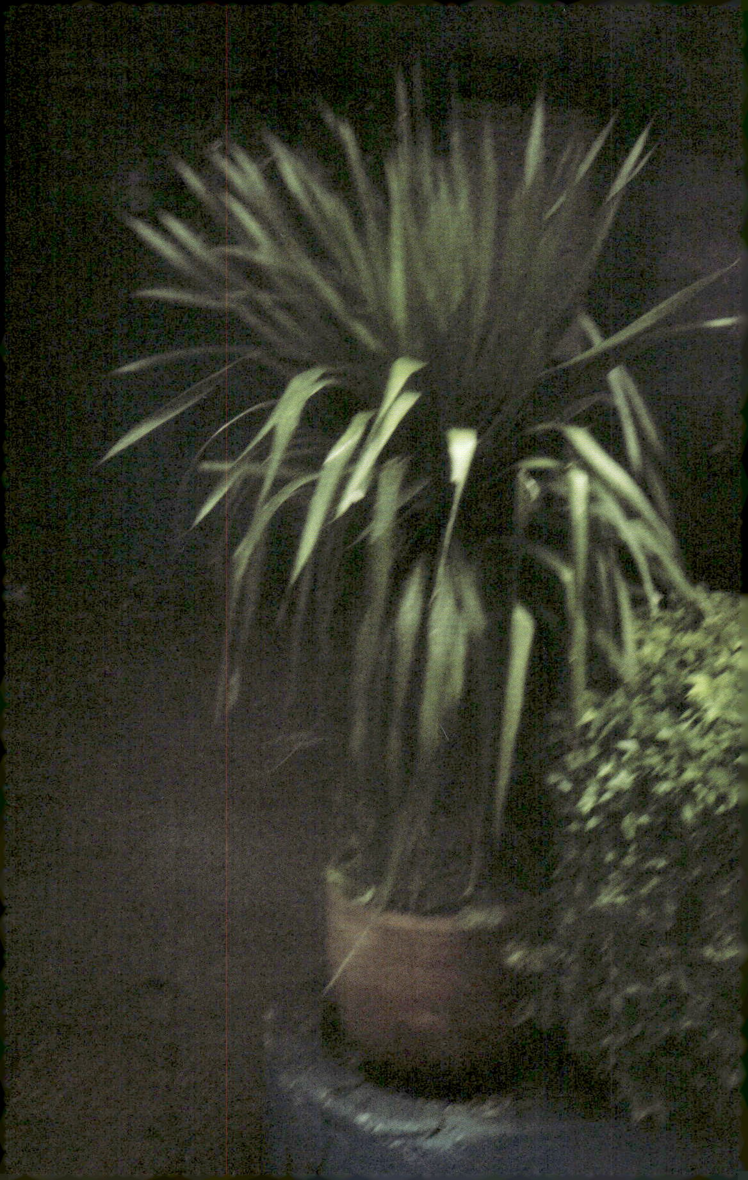

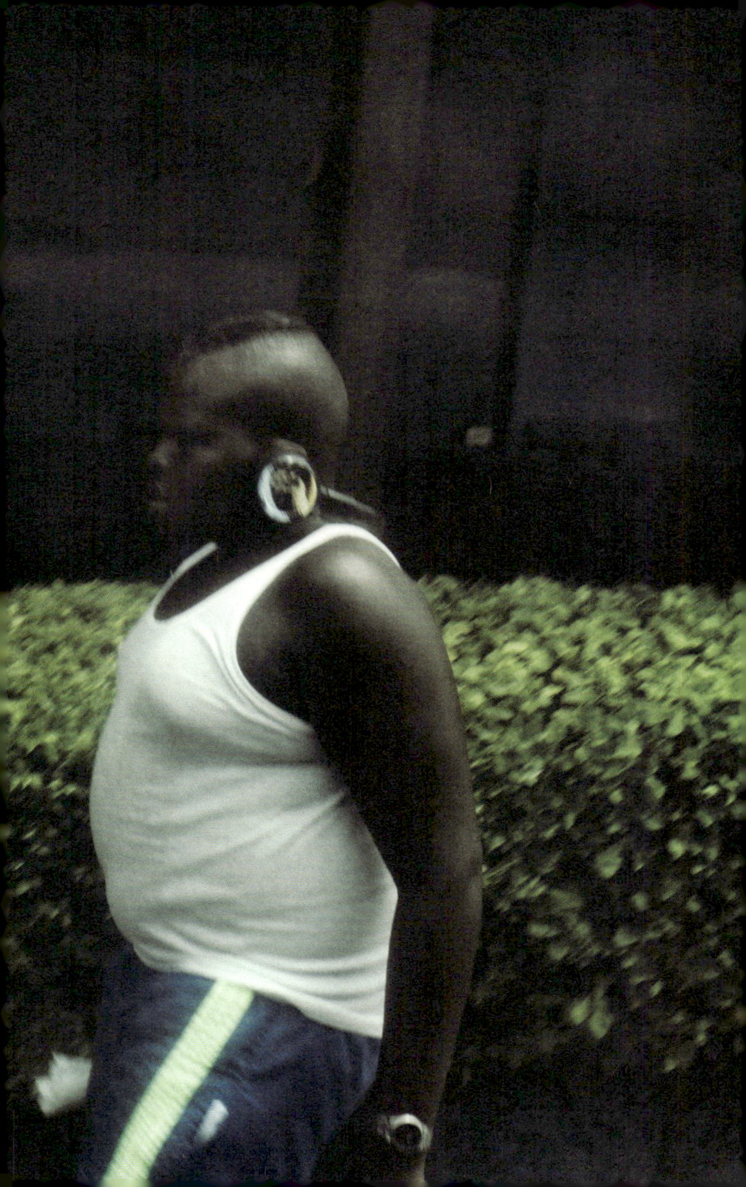

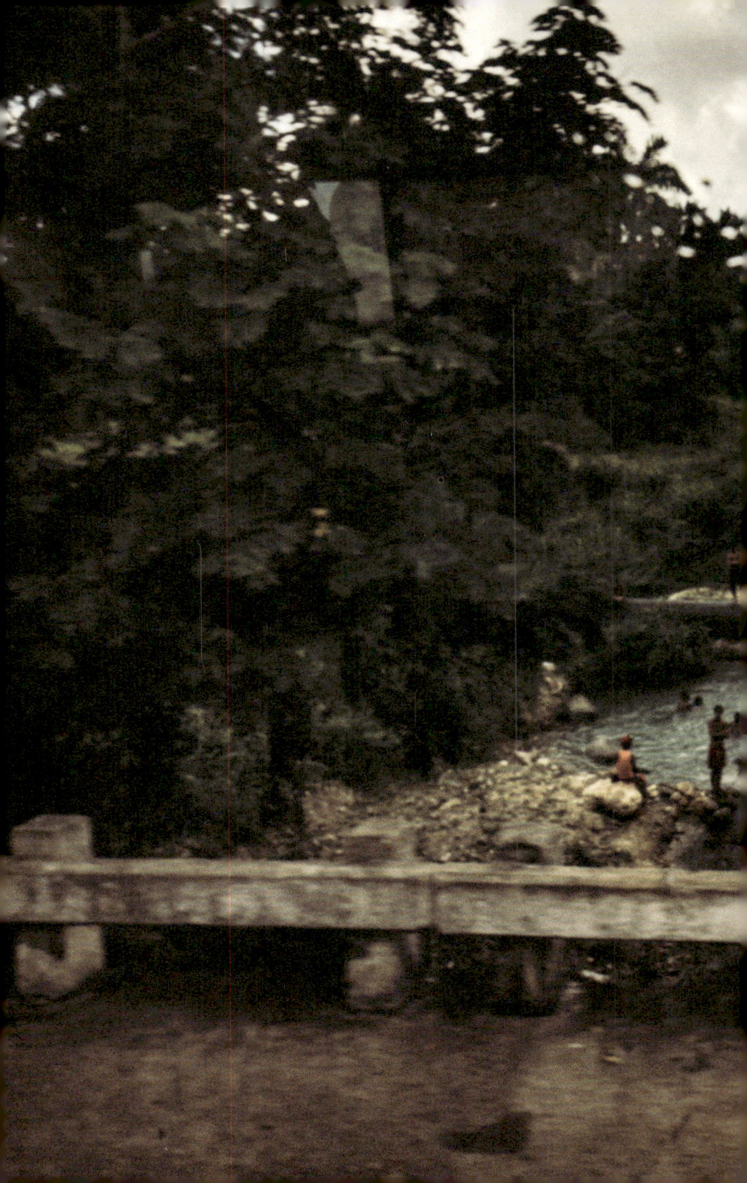

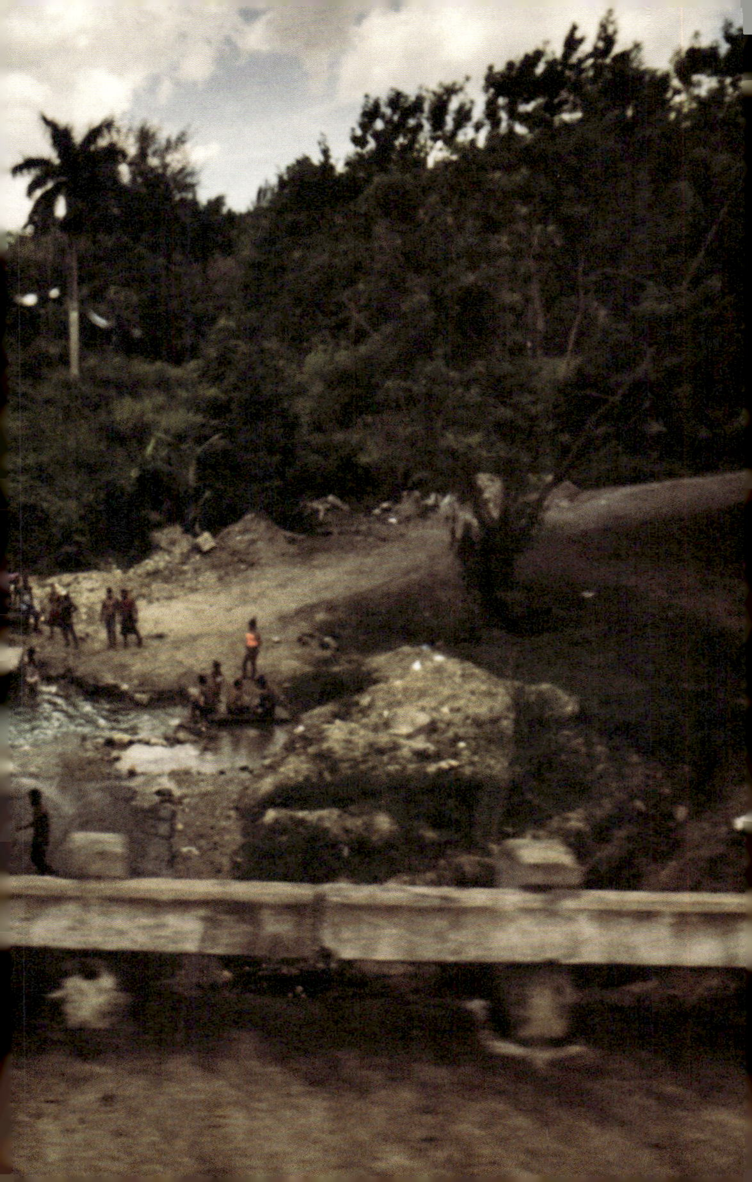

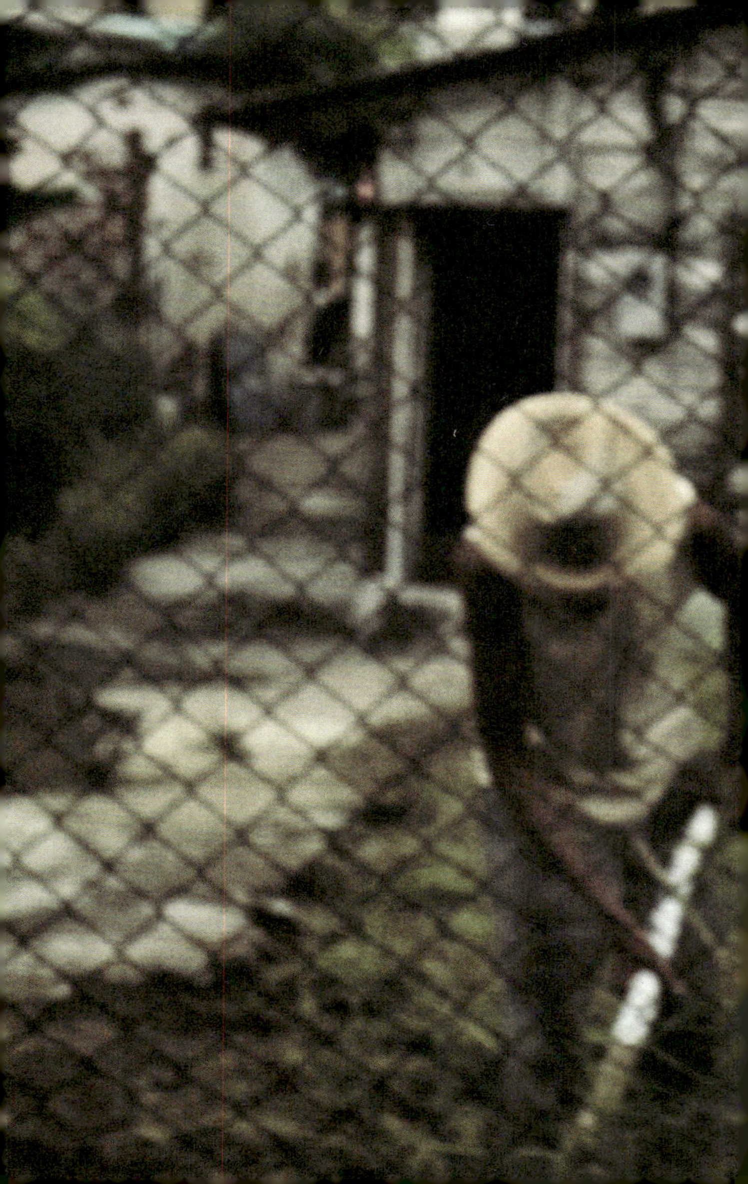

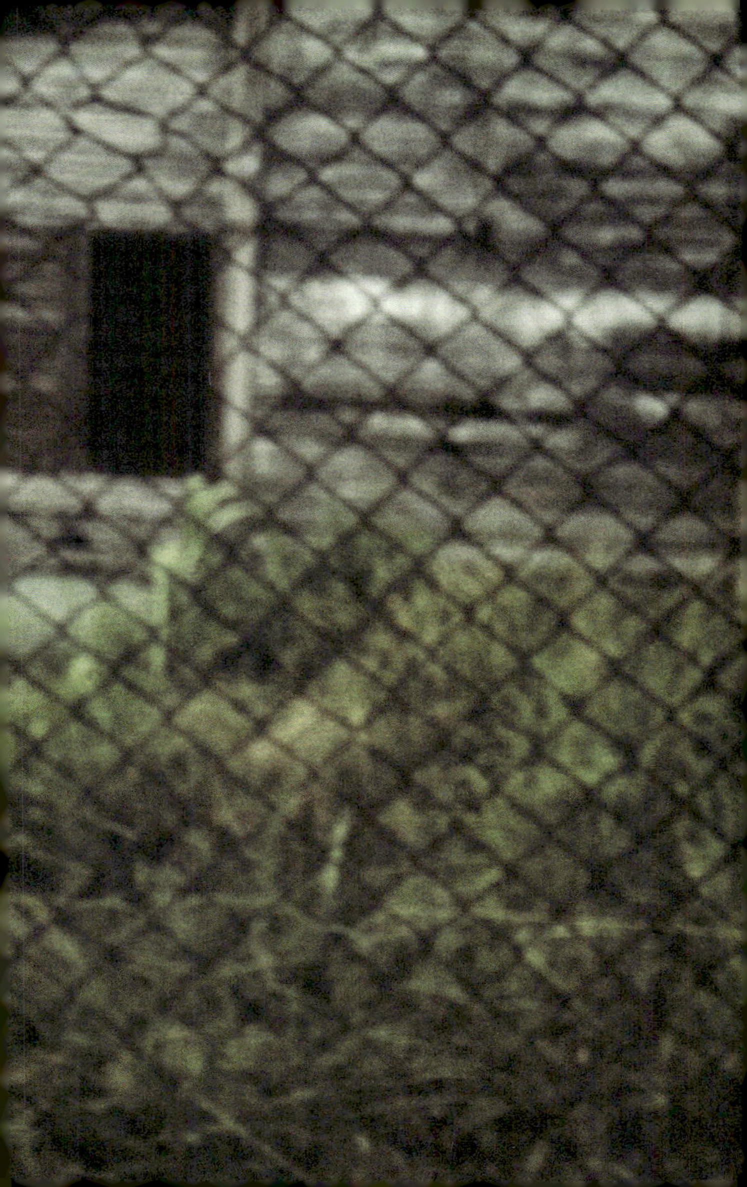

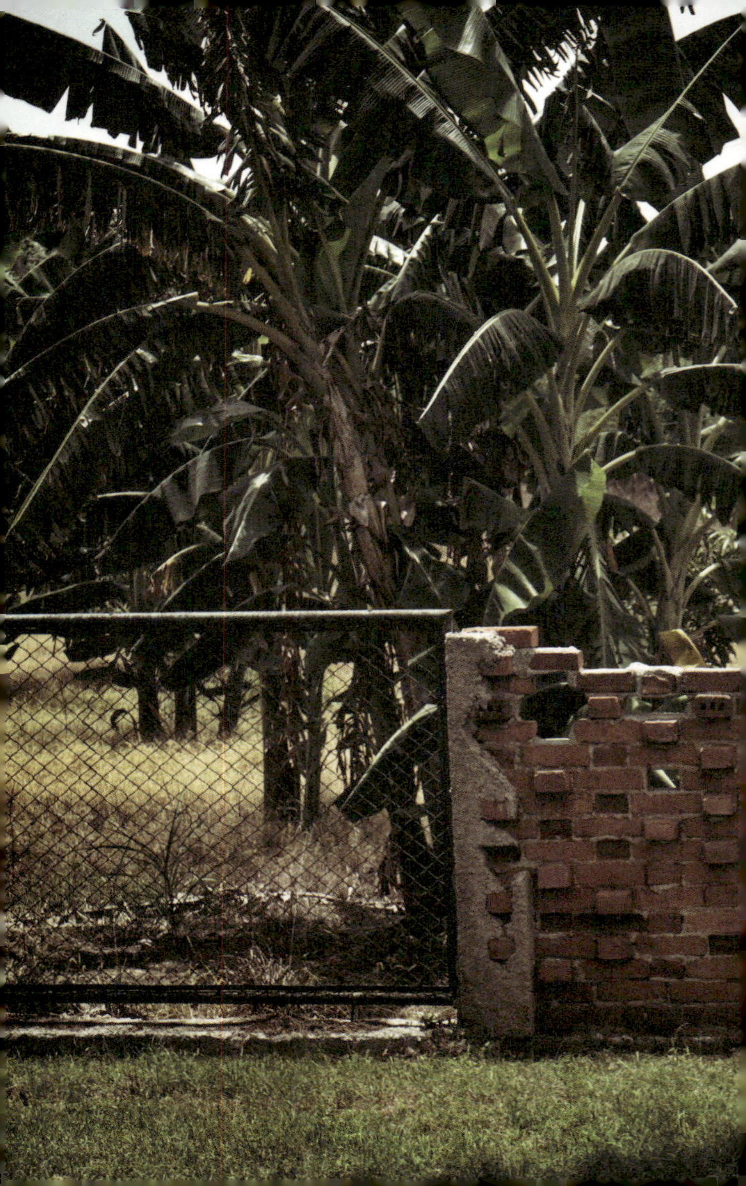

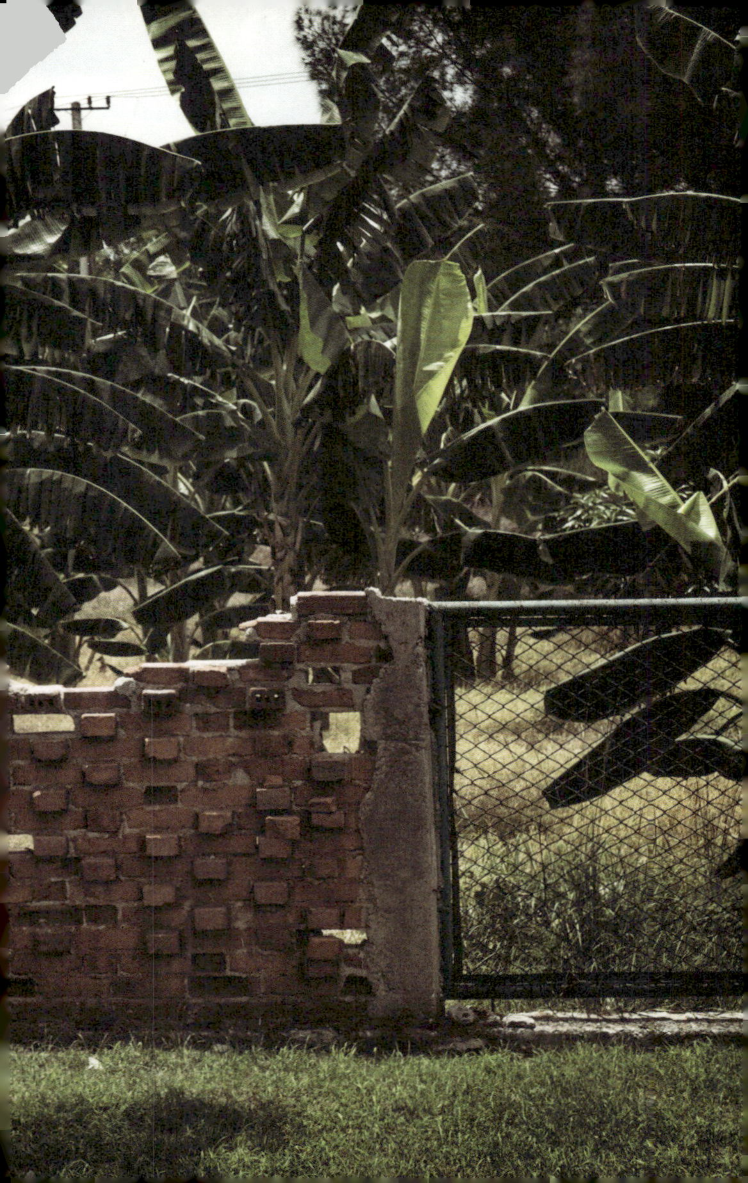

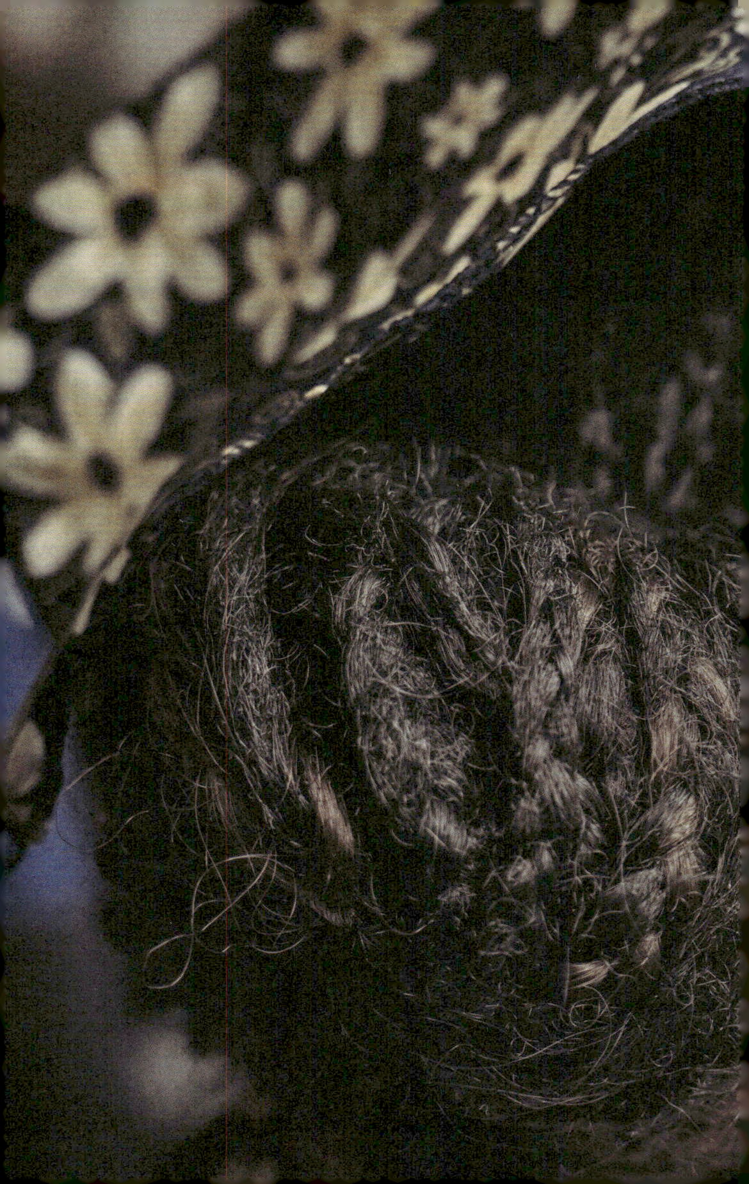

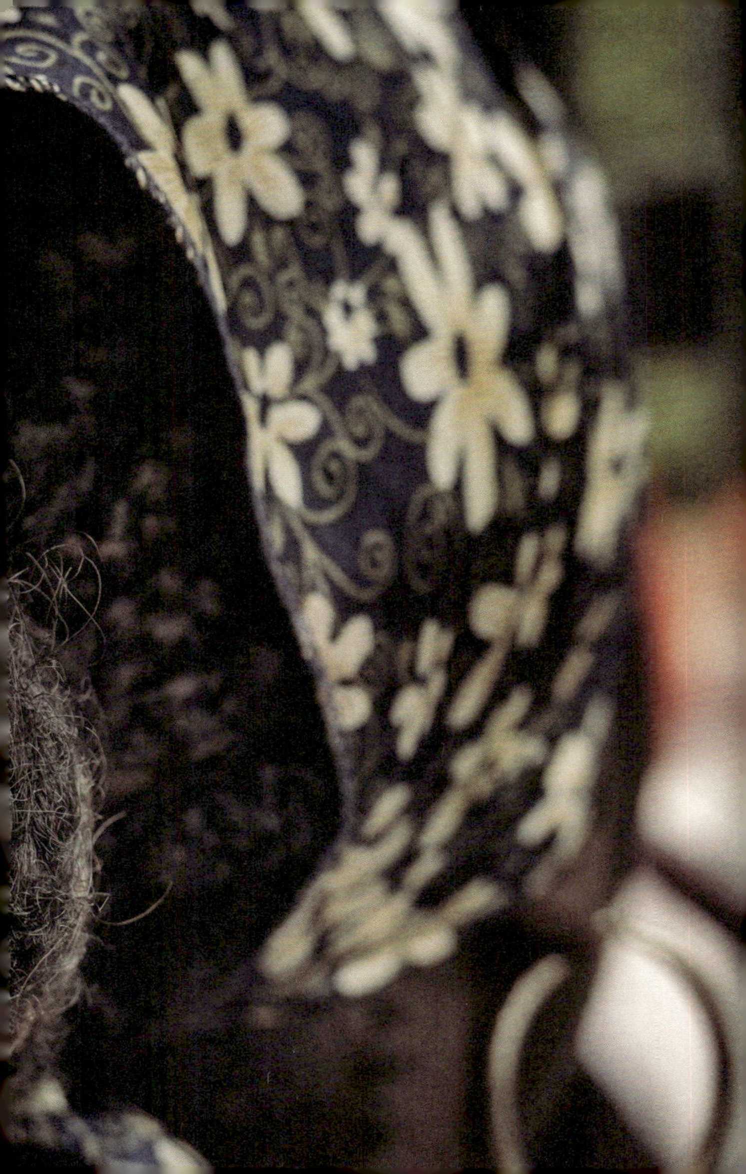

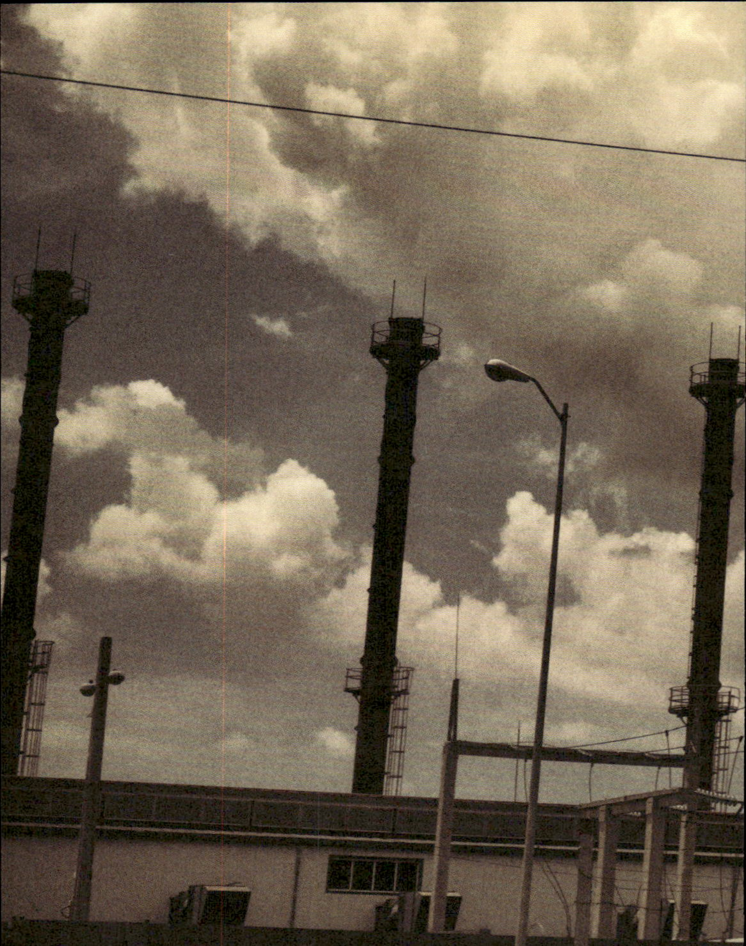

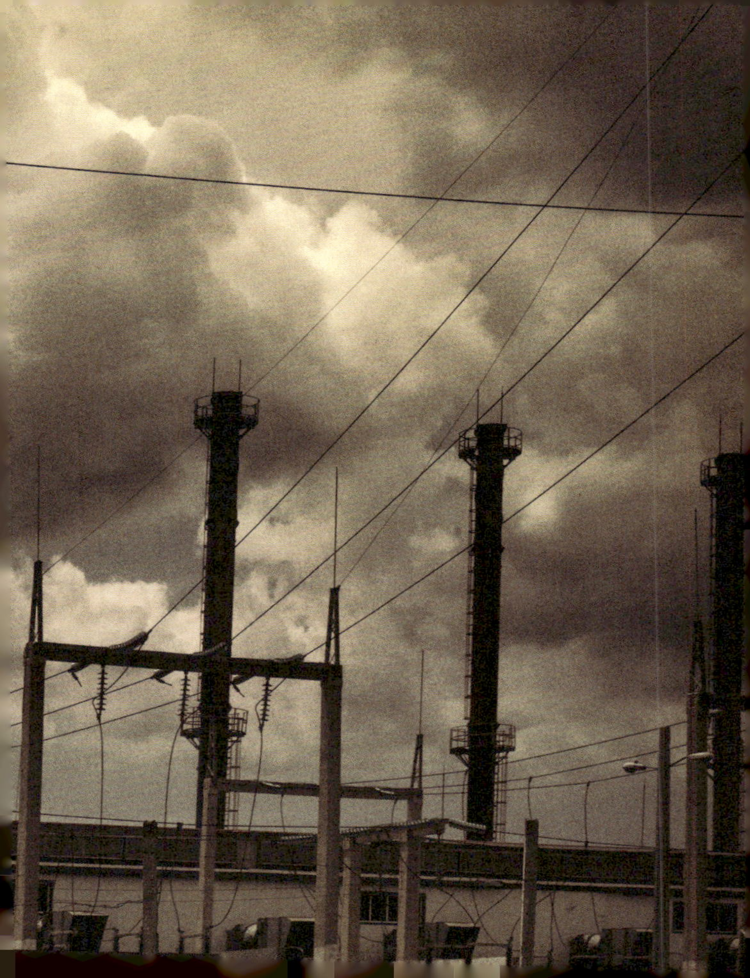

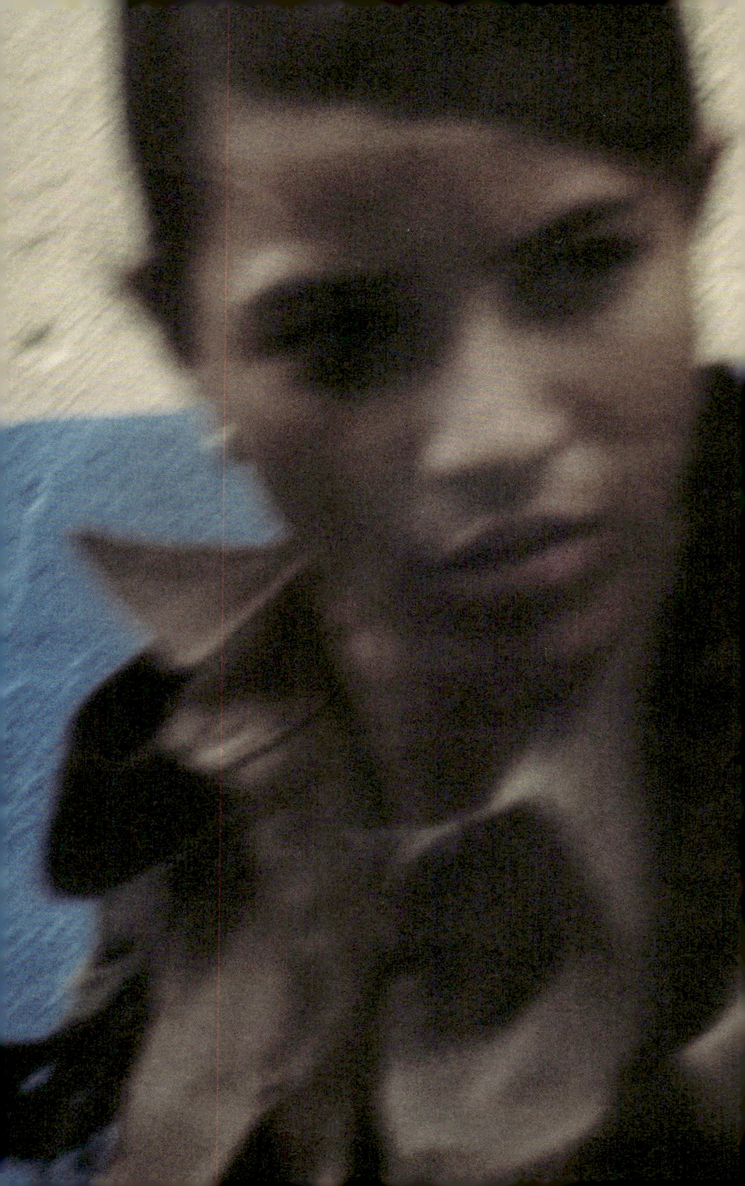

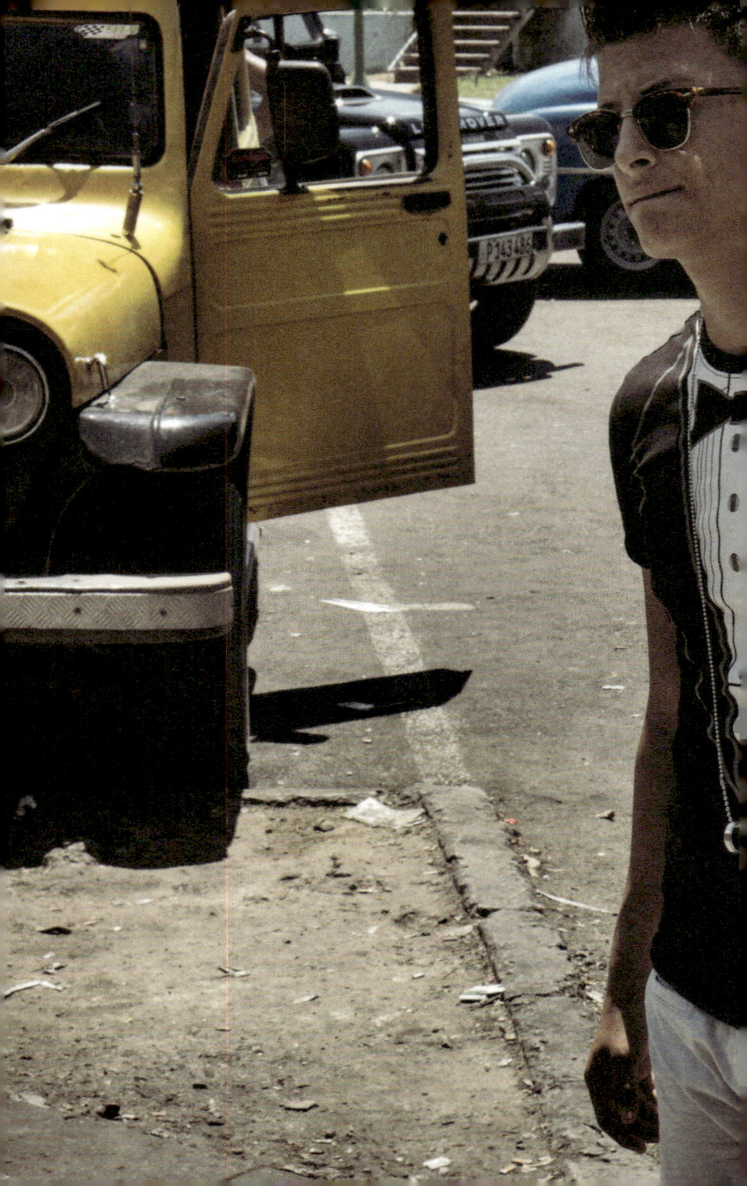
ROVER

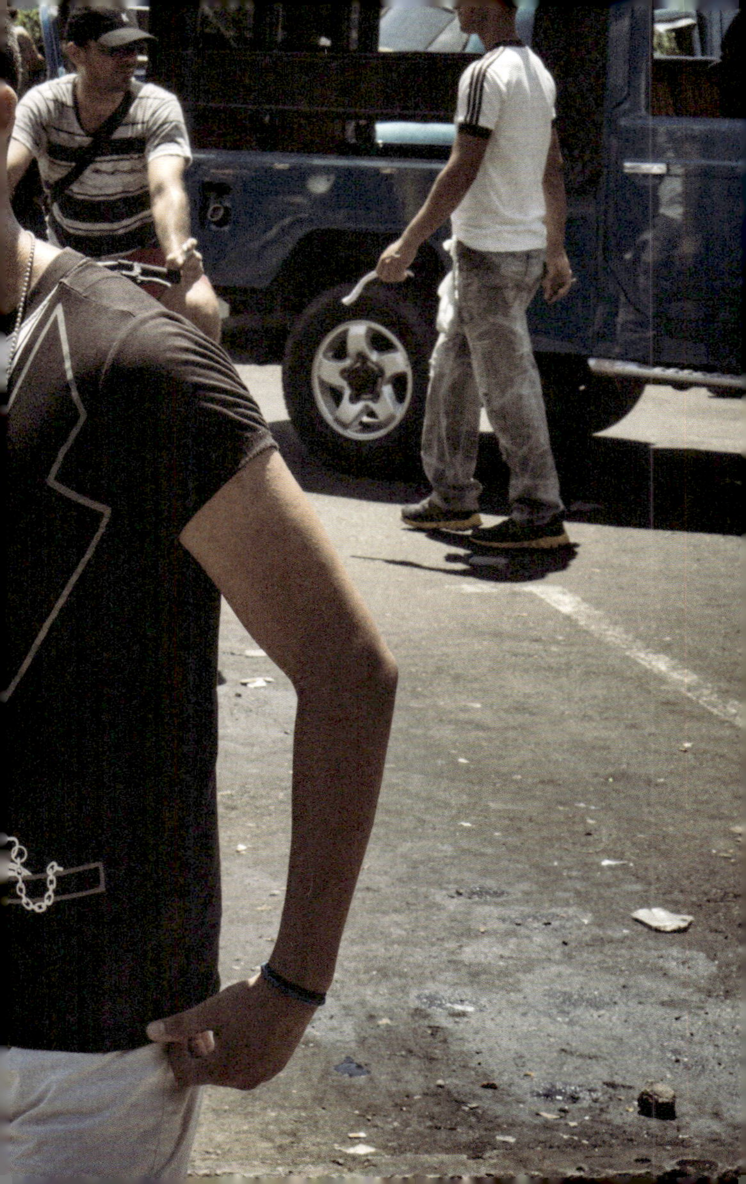

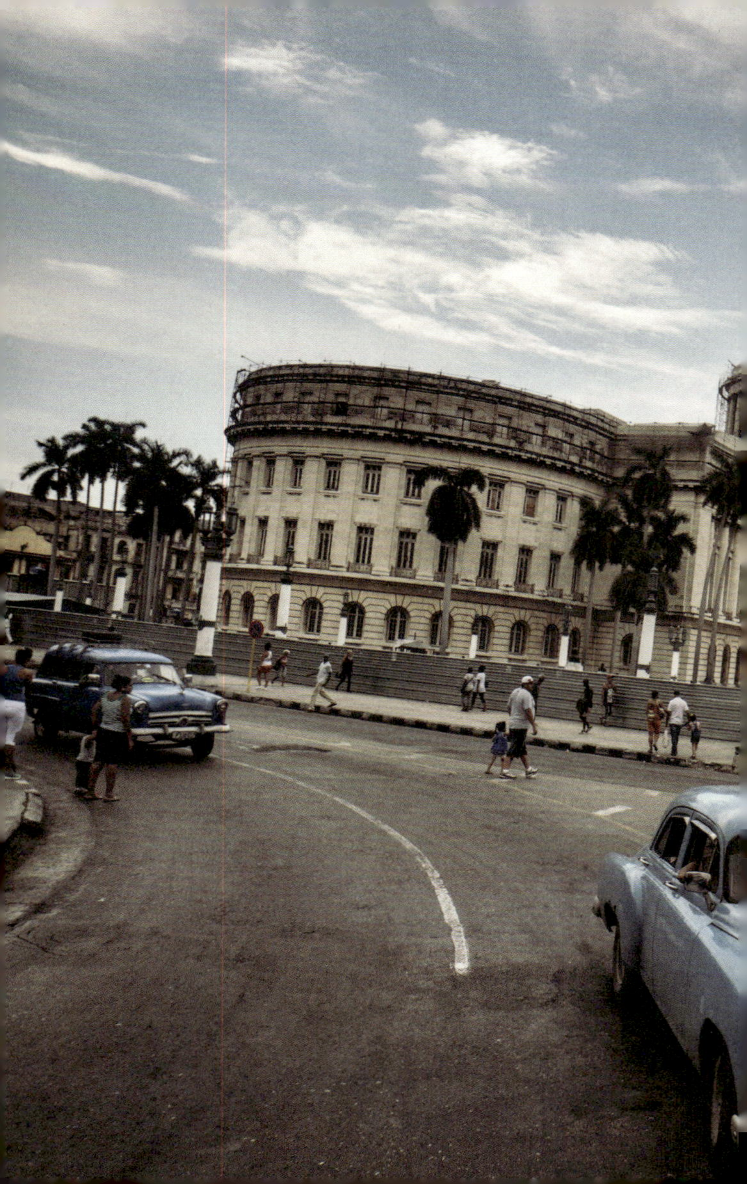

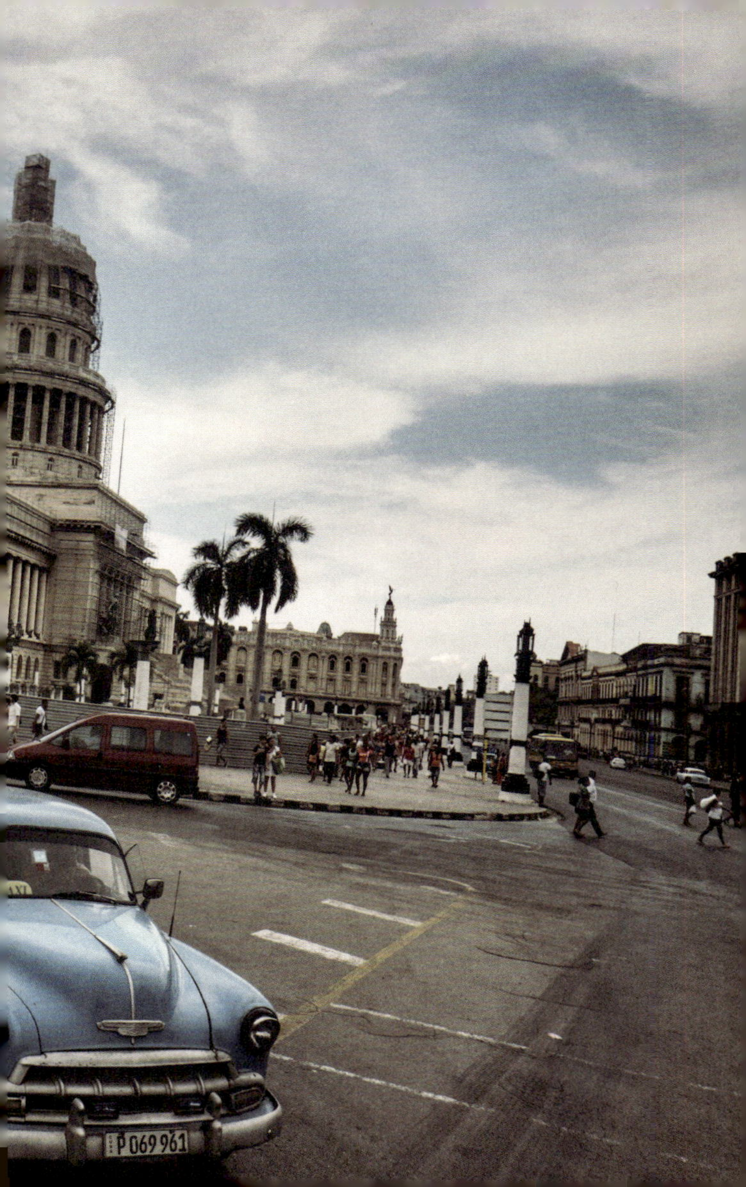
P069 961

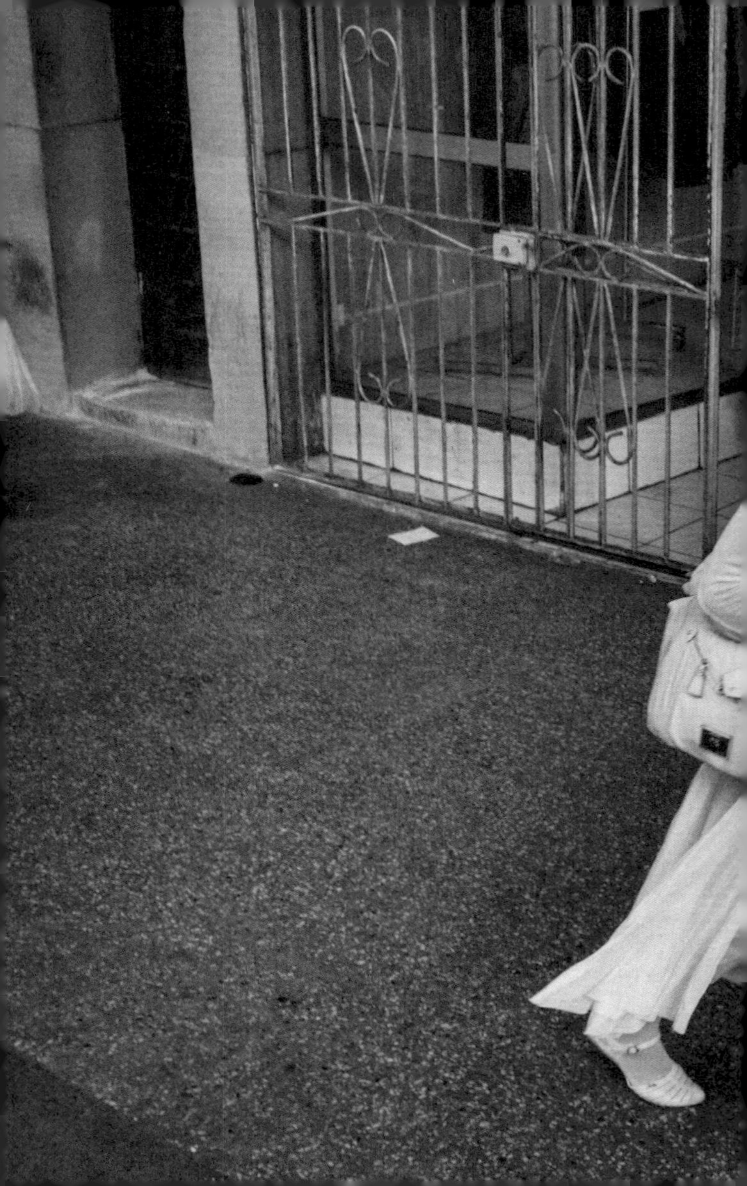

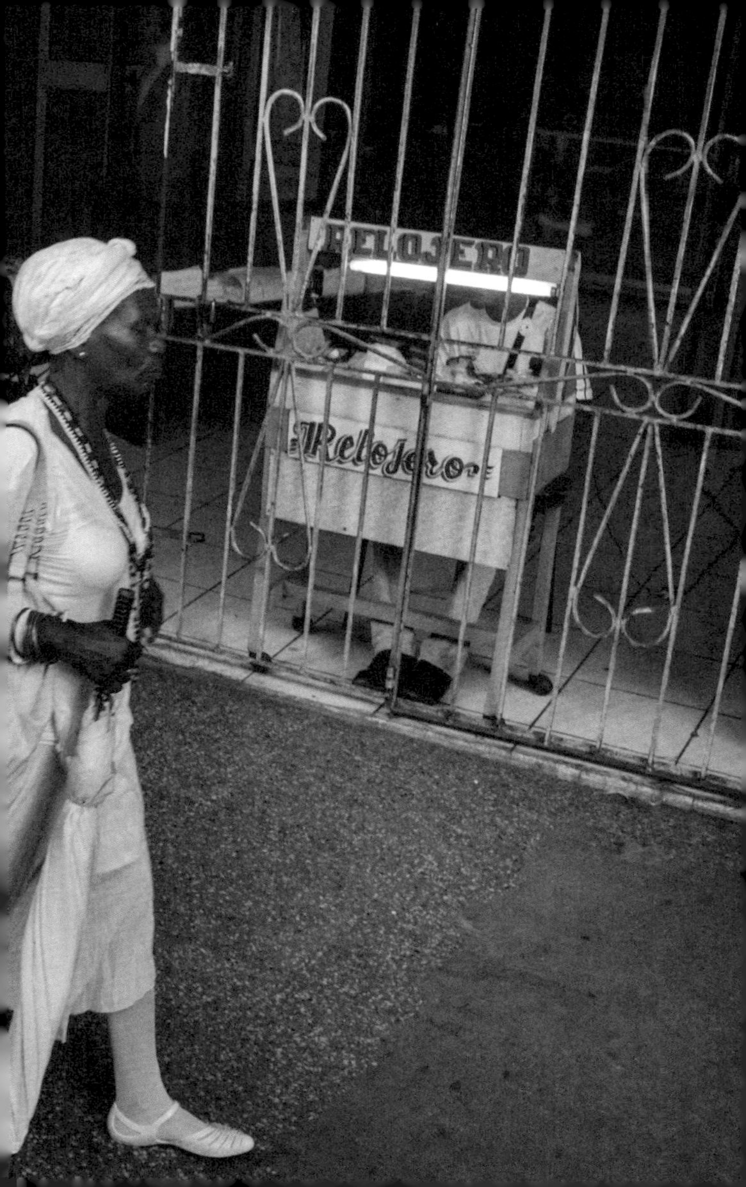
RELOJERO
Relojero

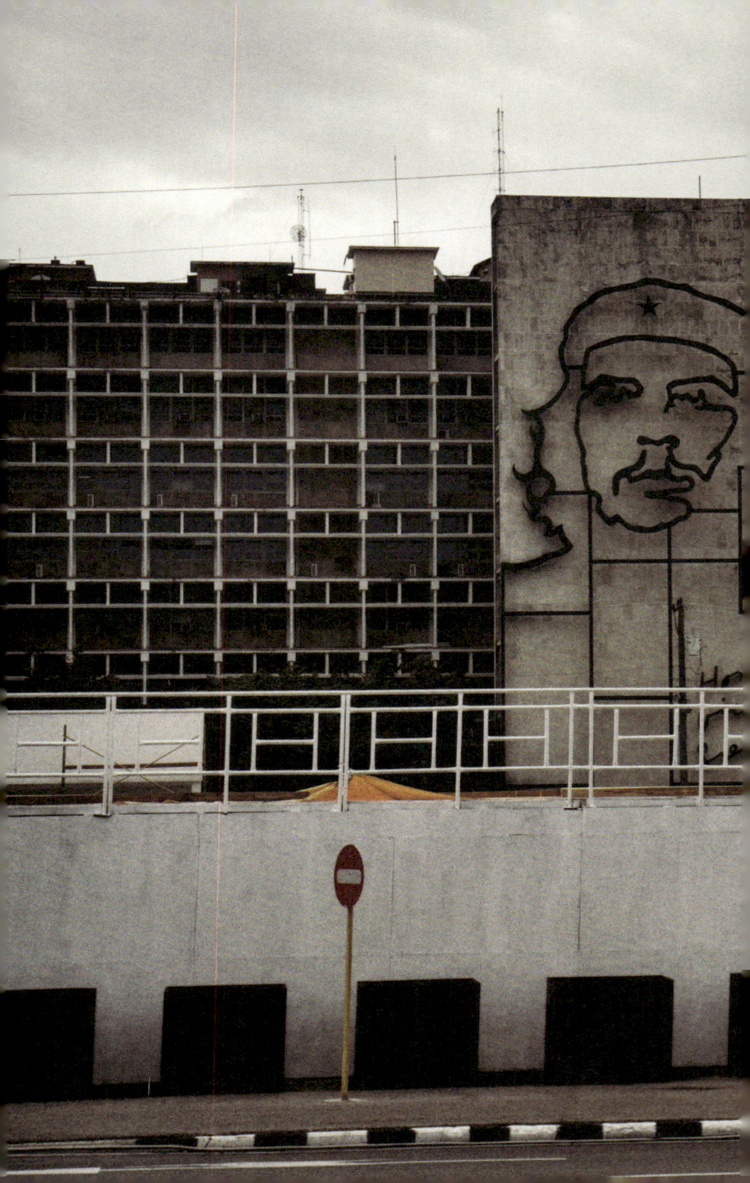

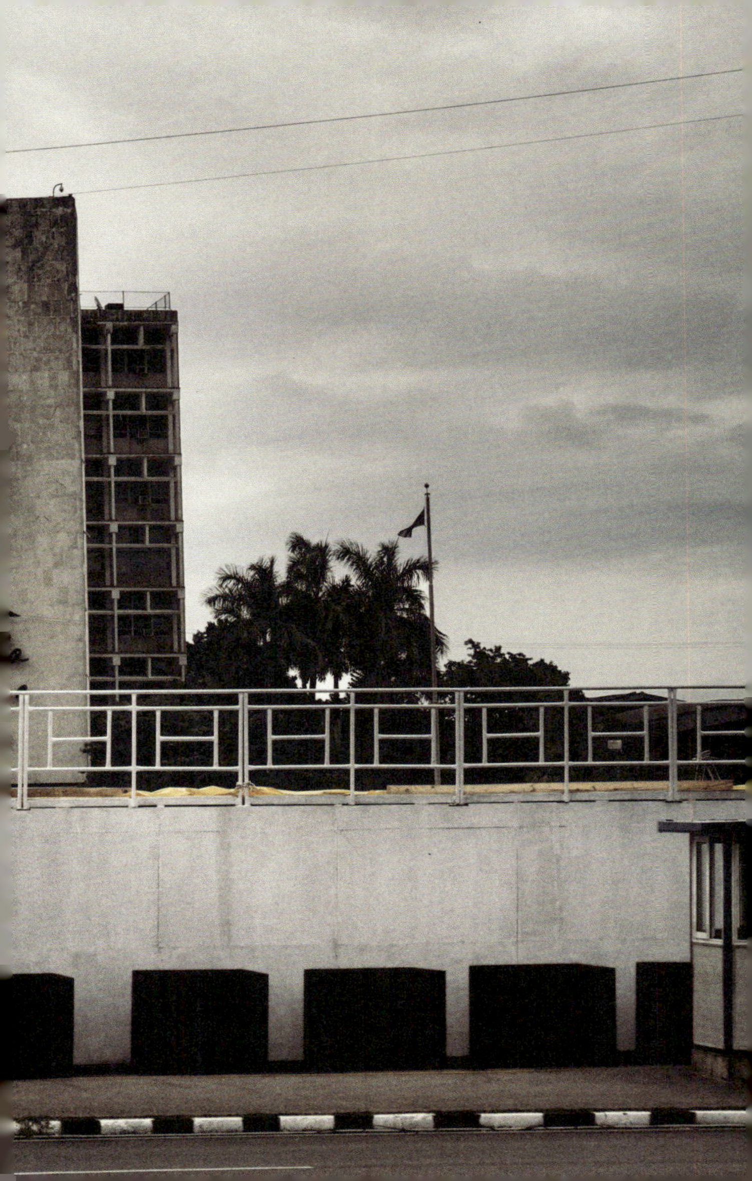

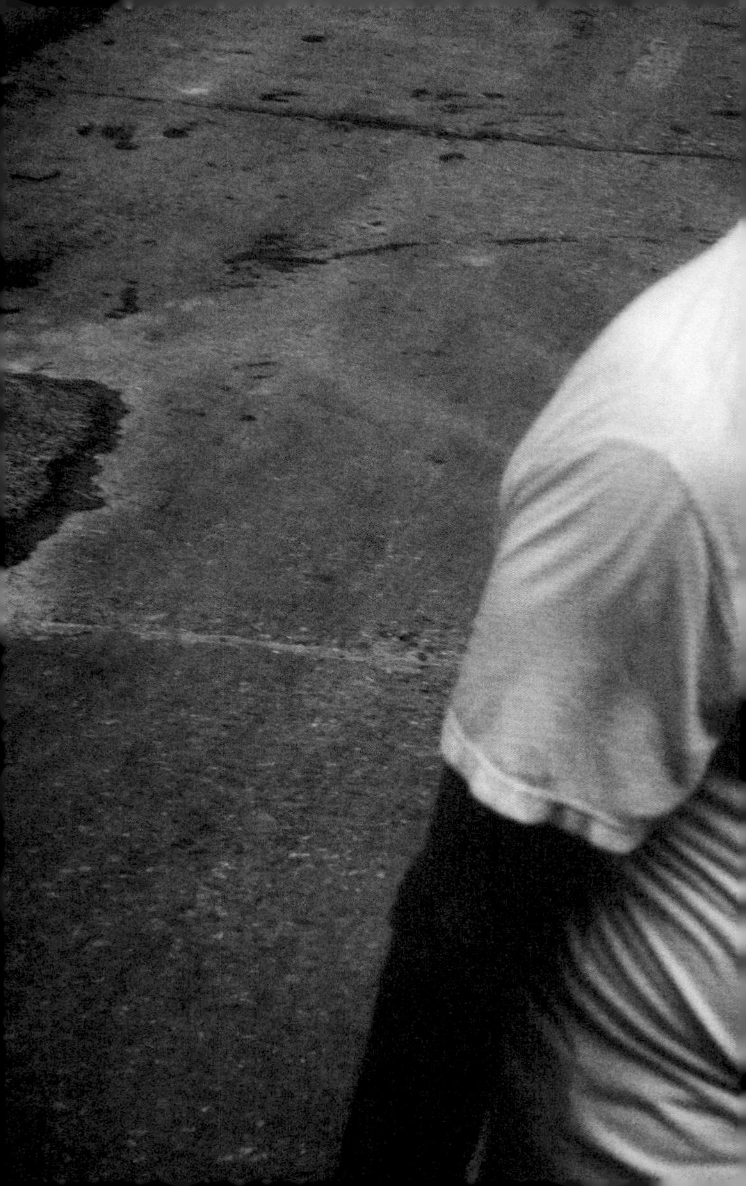

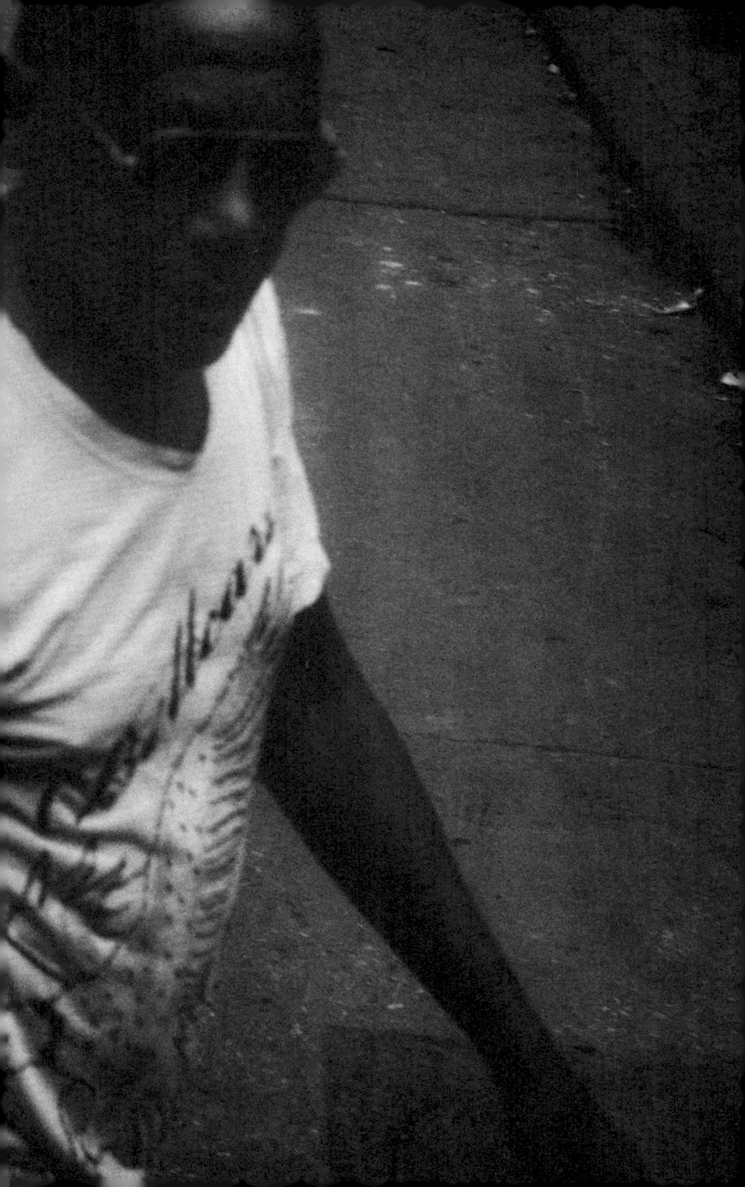

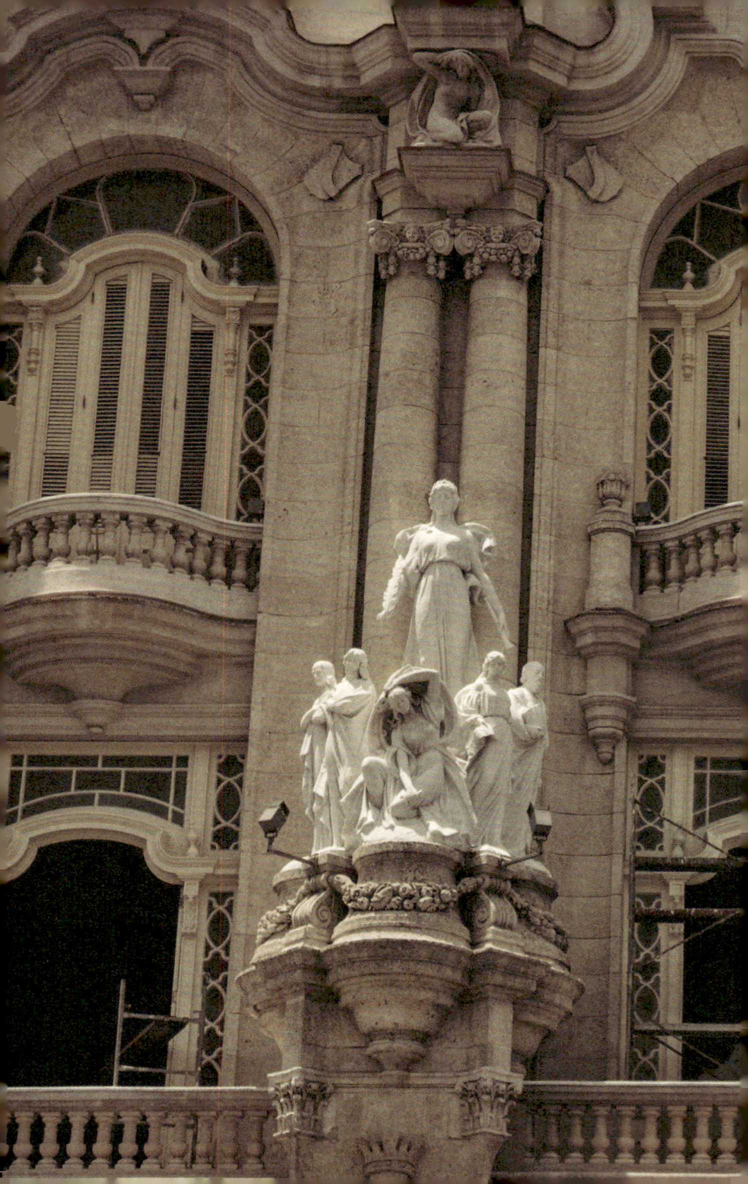

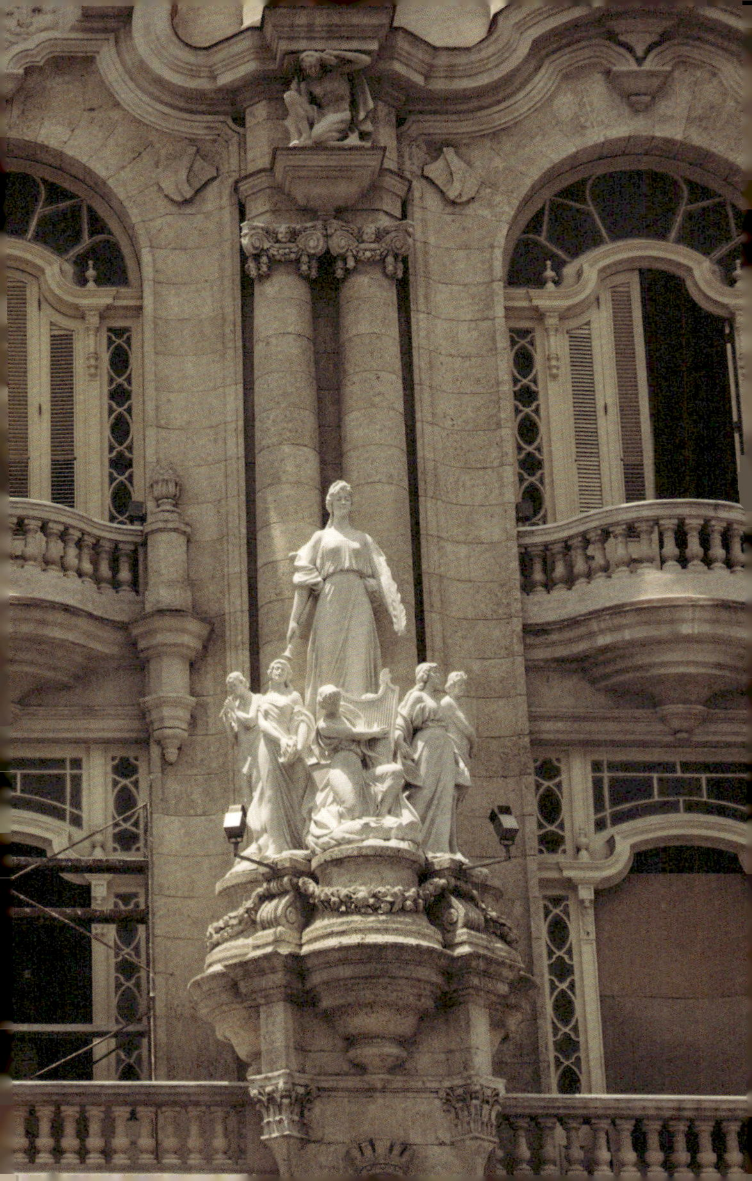

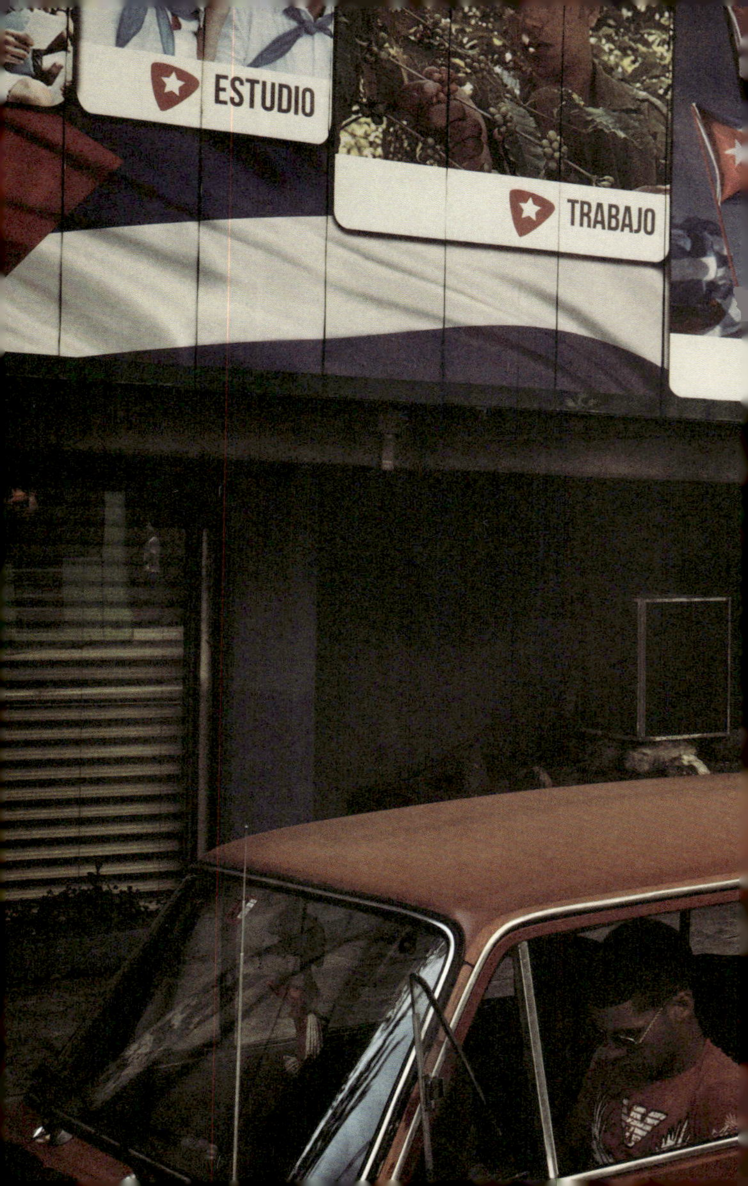
ESTUDIO
TRABAJO

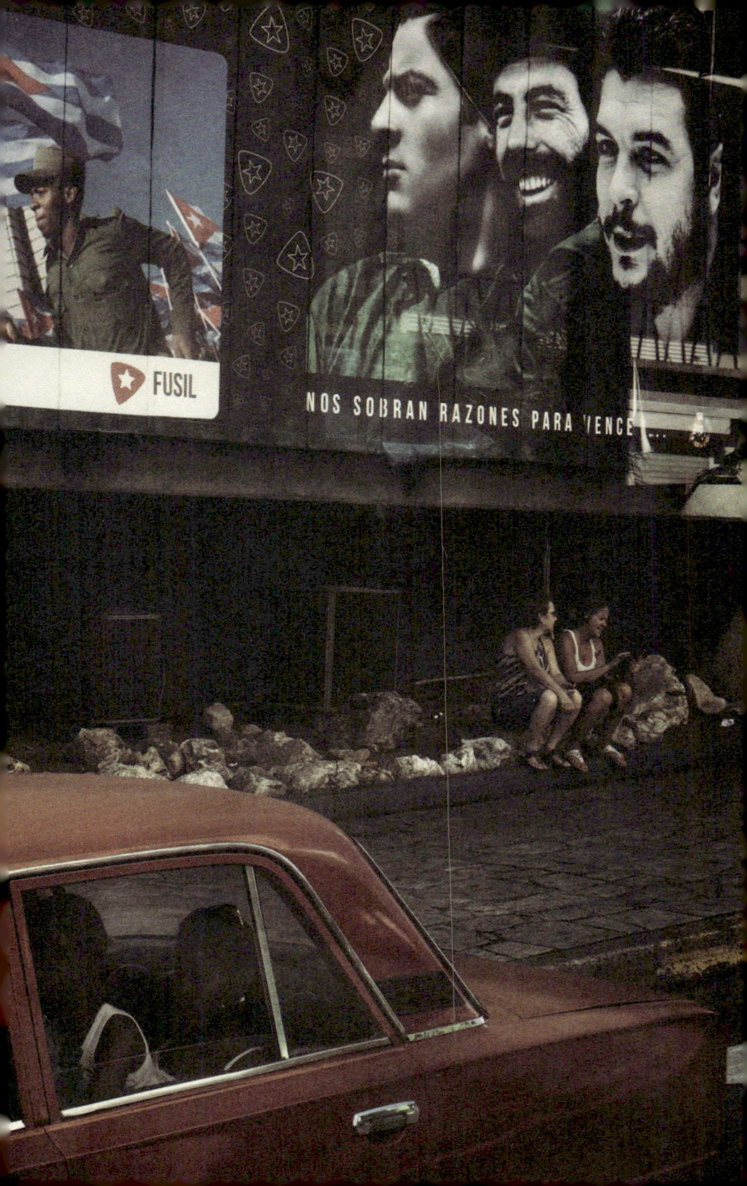
FUSIL
NOS SOBRAN RAZONES PARA VENCE

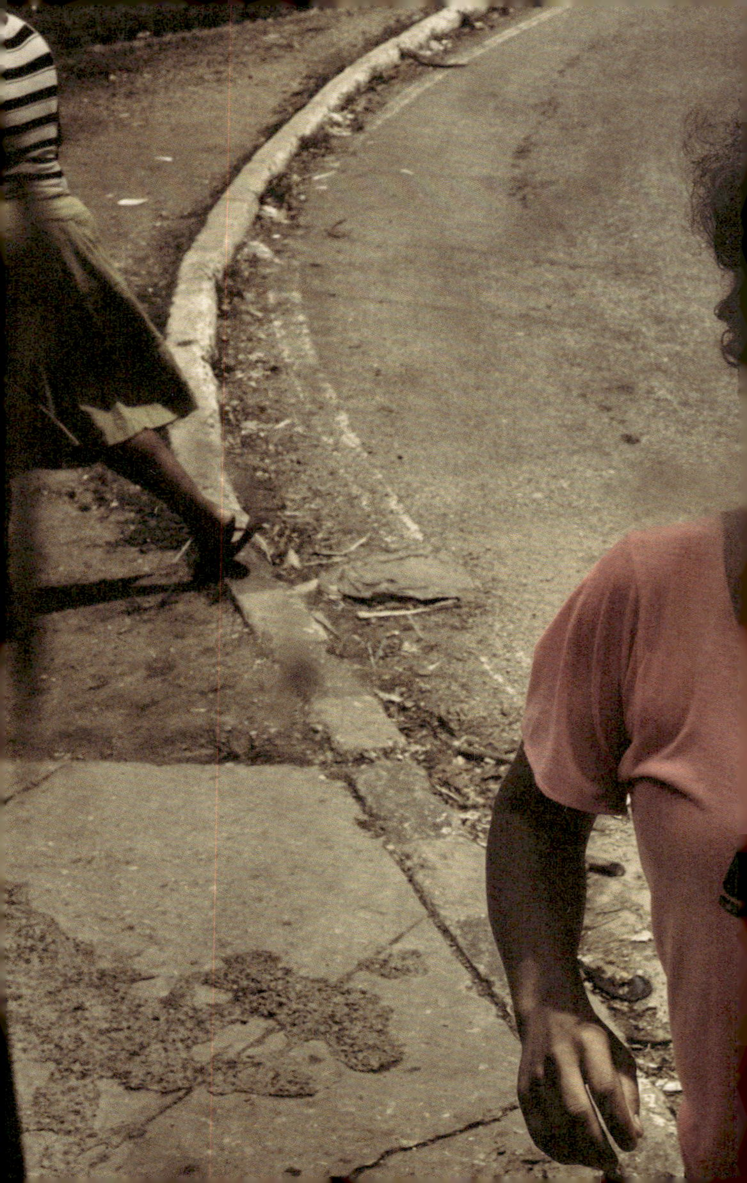

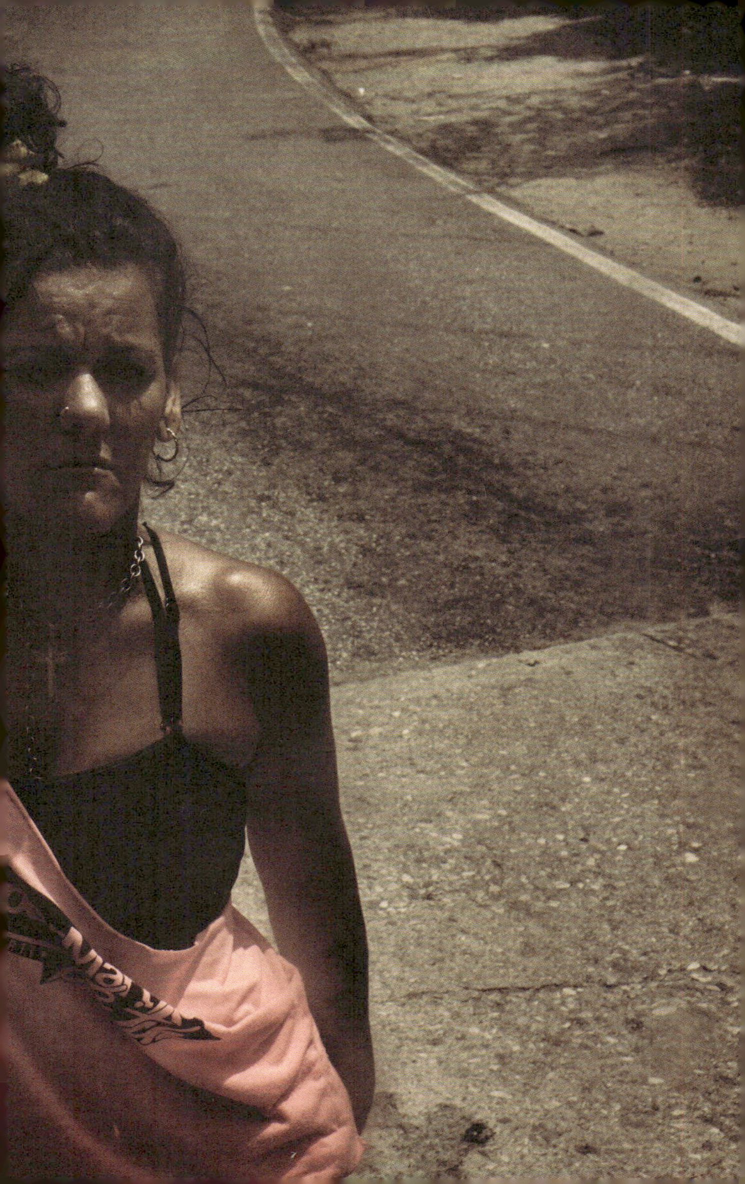

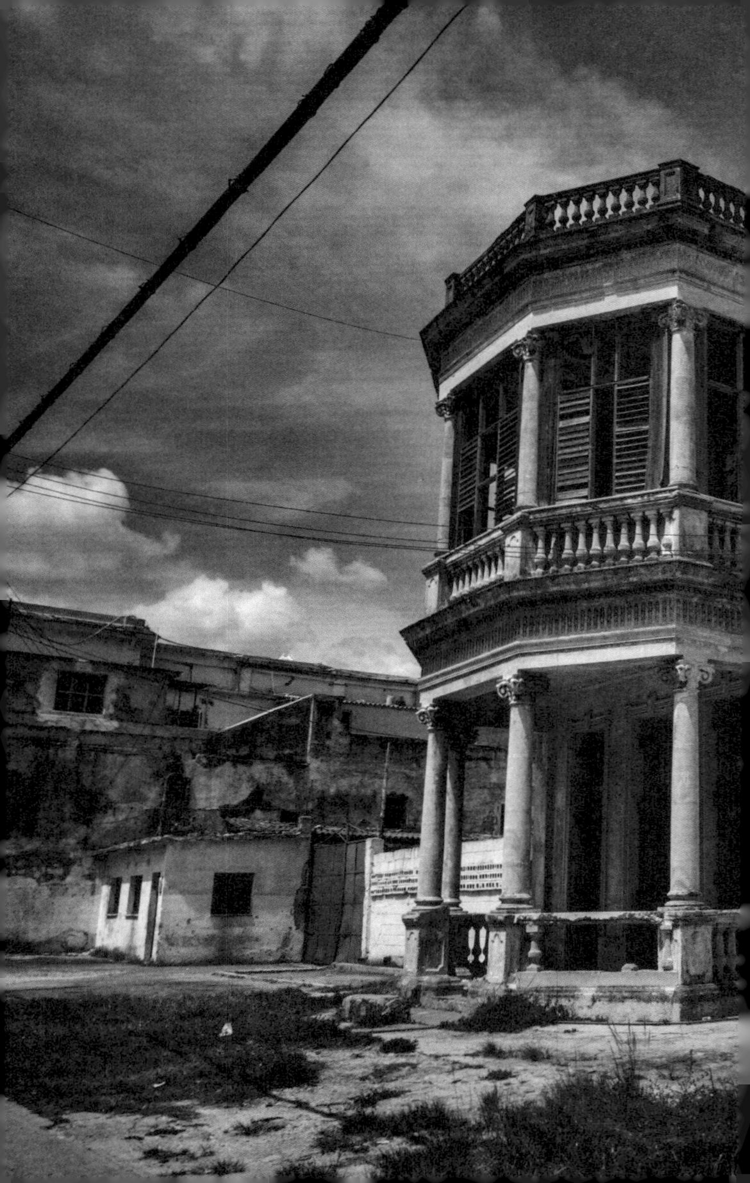

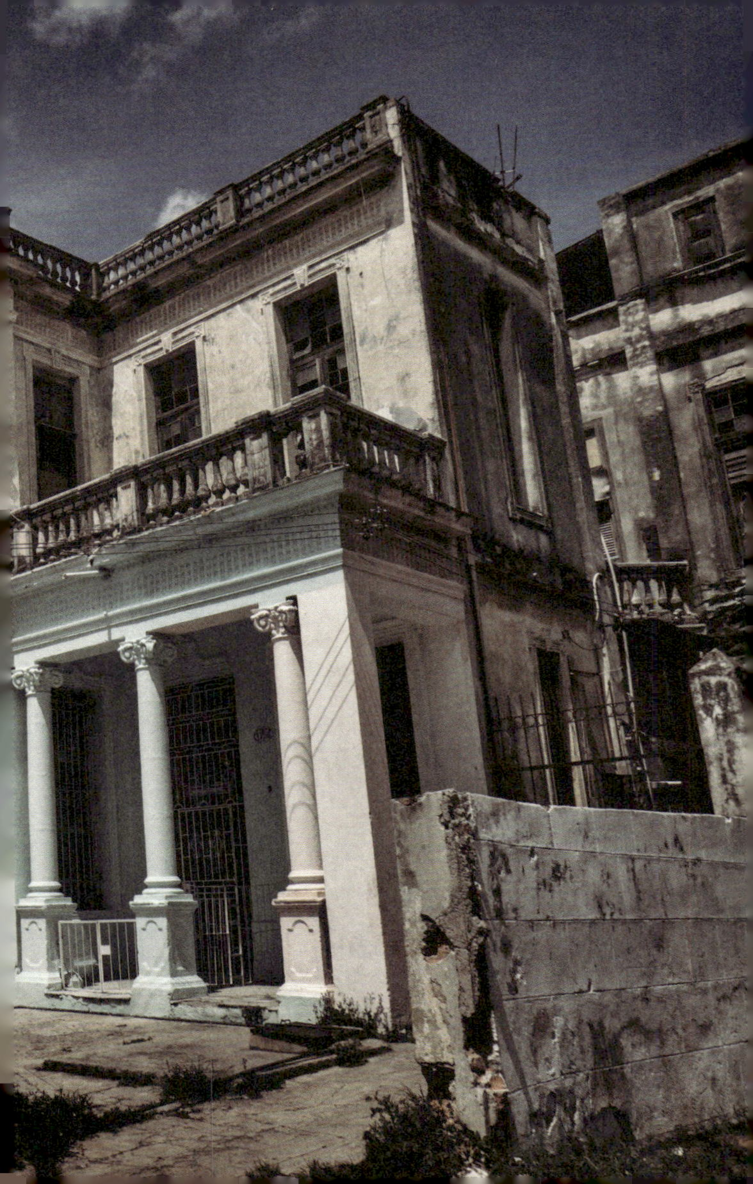

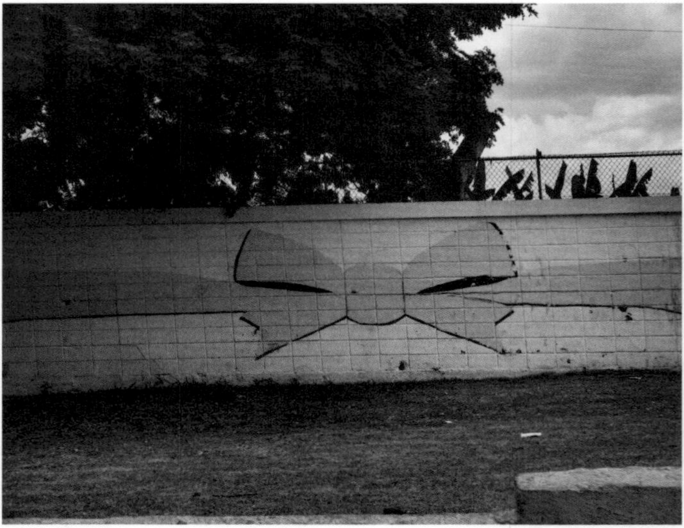

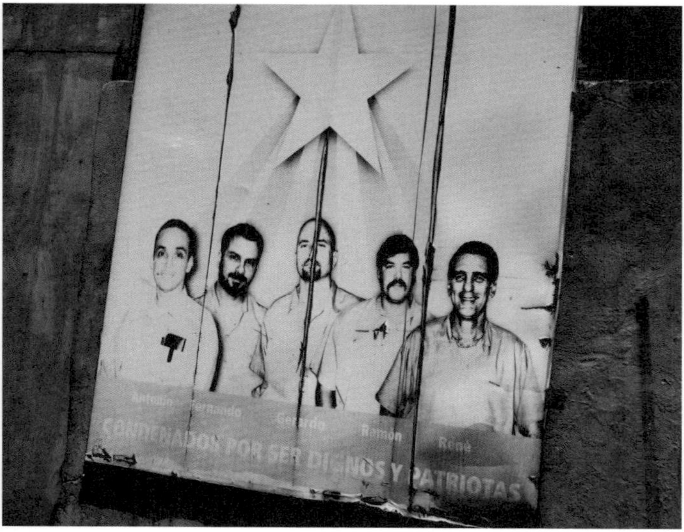
Gerardo
Ramón
René
CONDENADOS POR SER
NOS Y PATRIOTAS

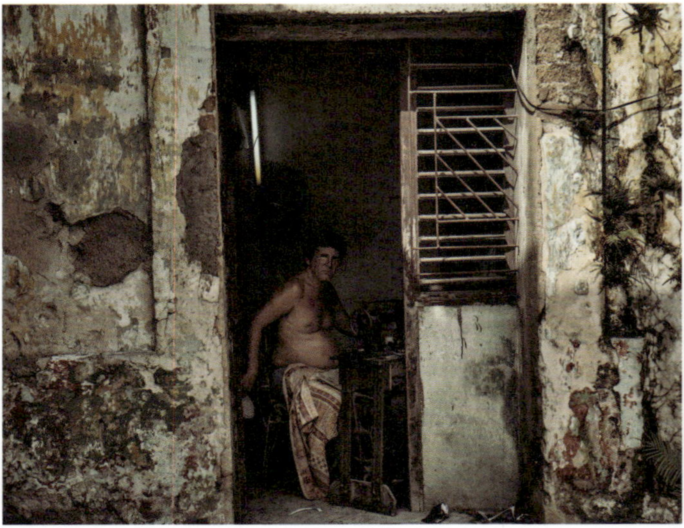

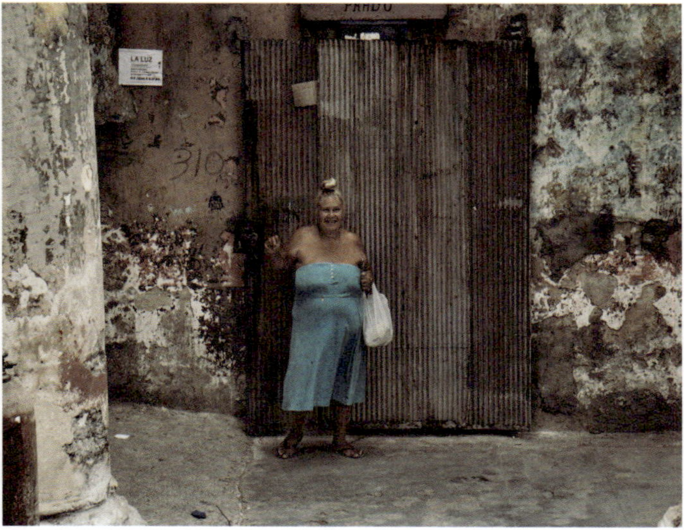
LA LUZ
310

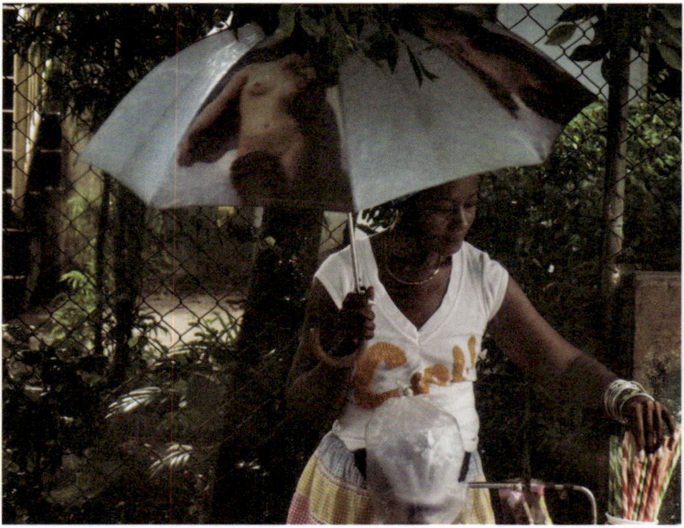

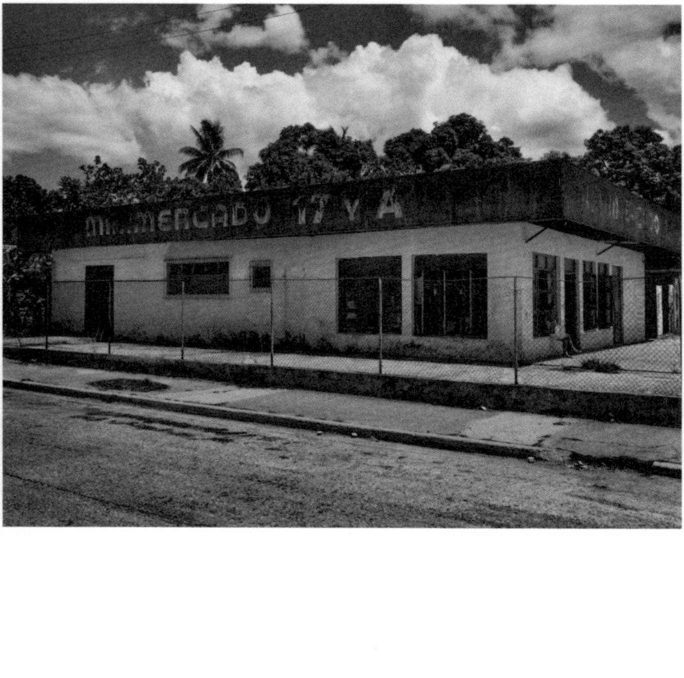
MERCADO 17 Y A

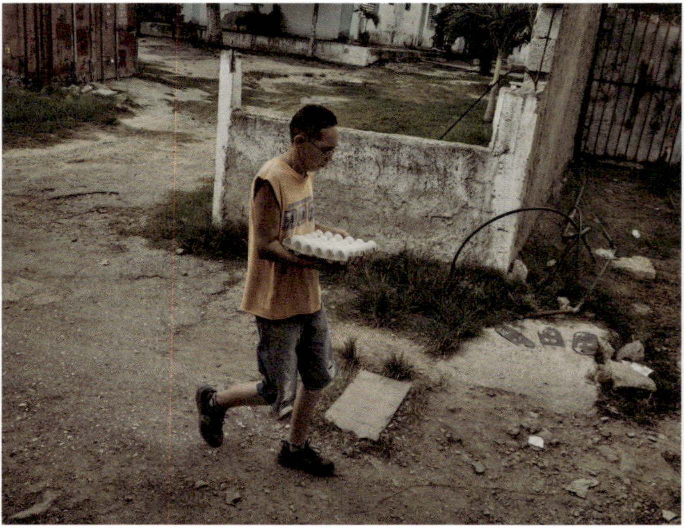

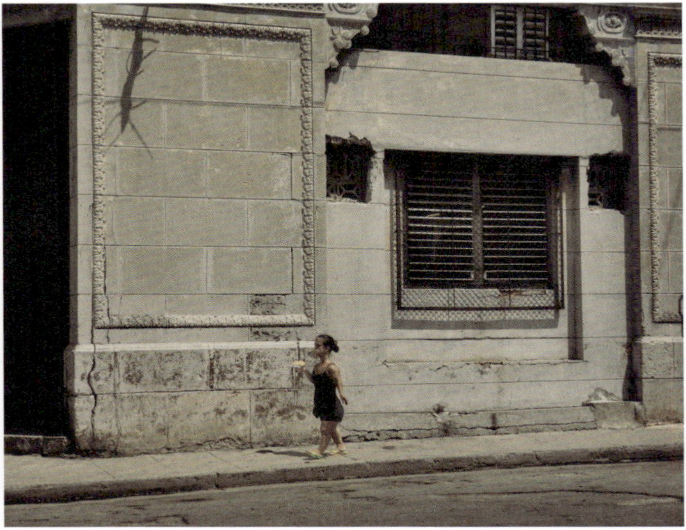

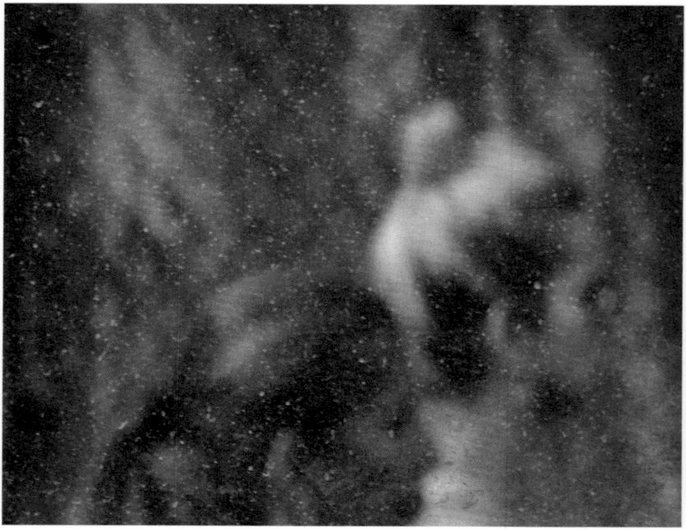

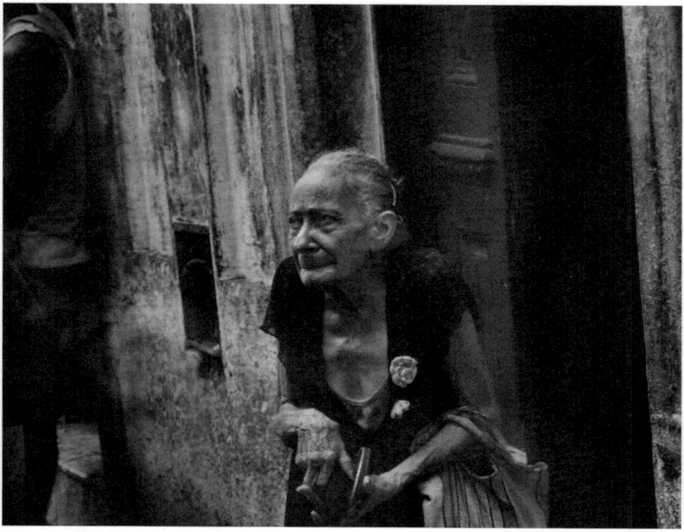

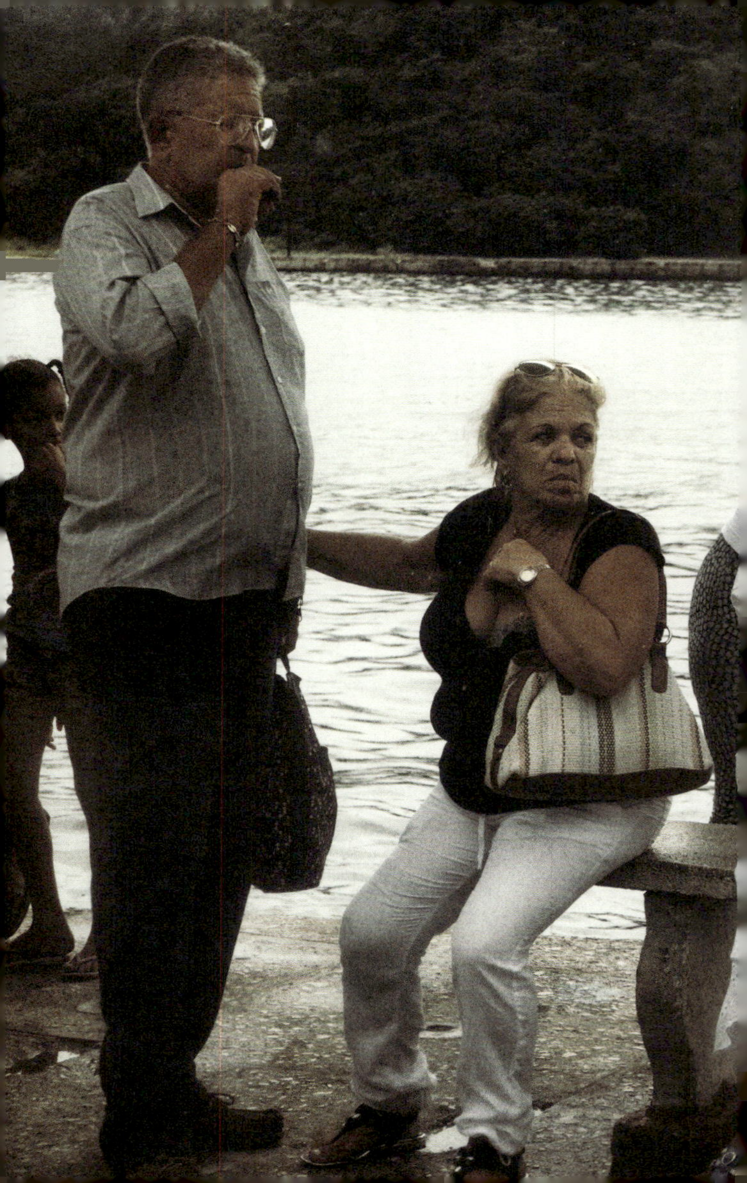

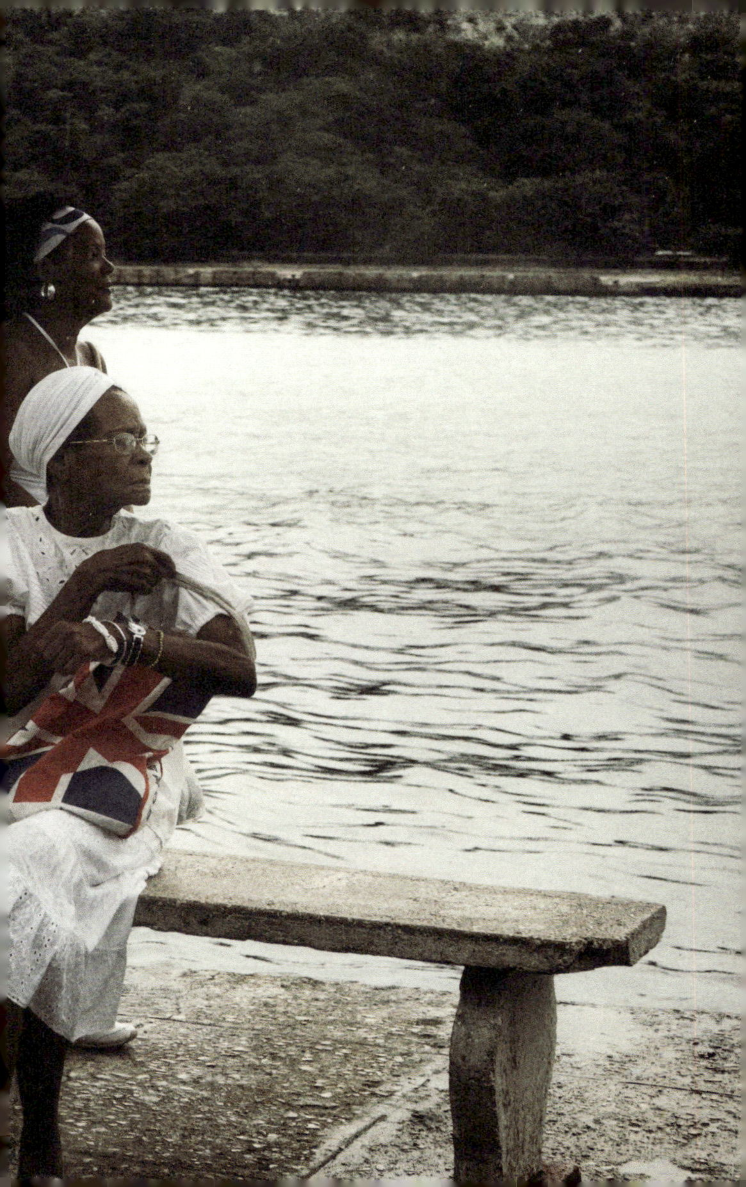

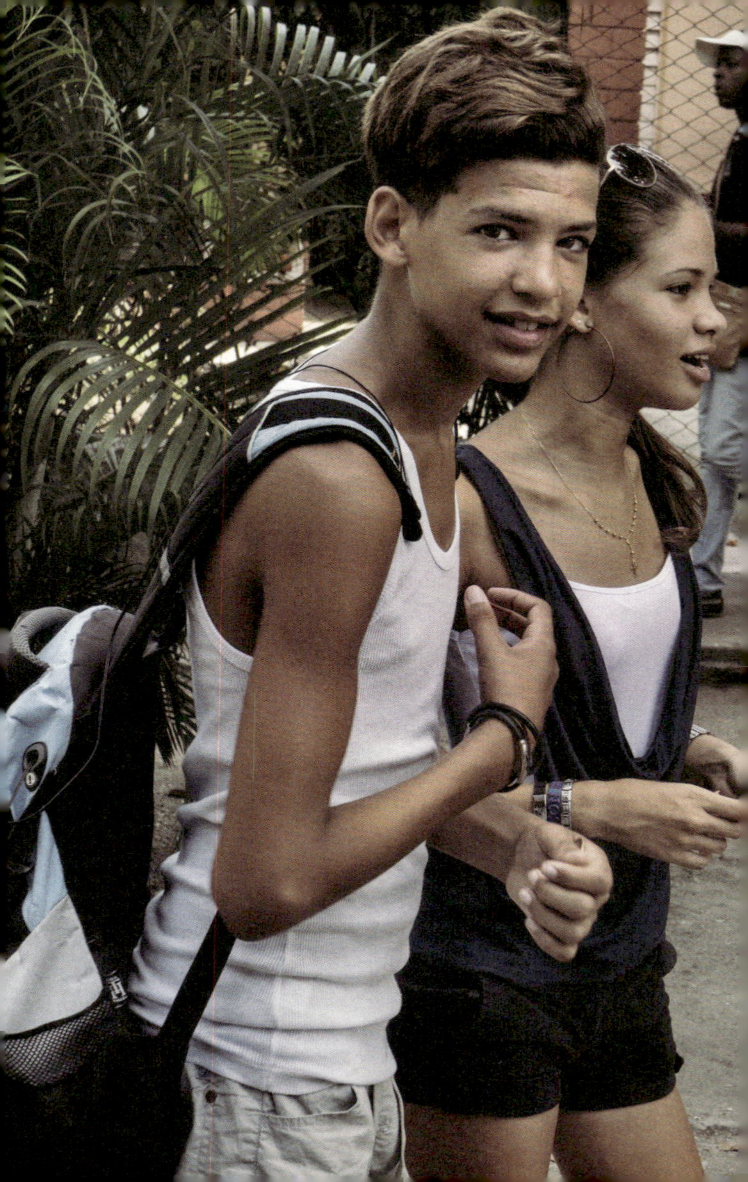

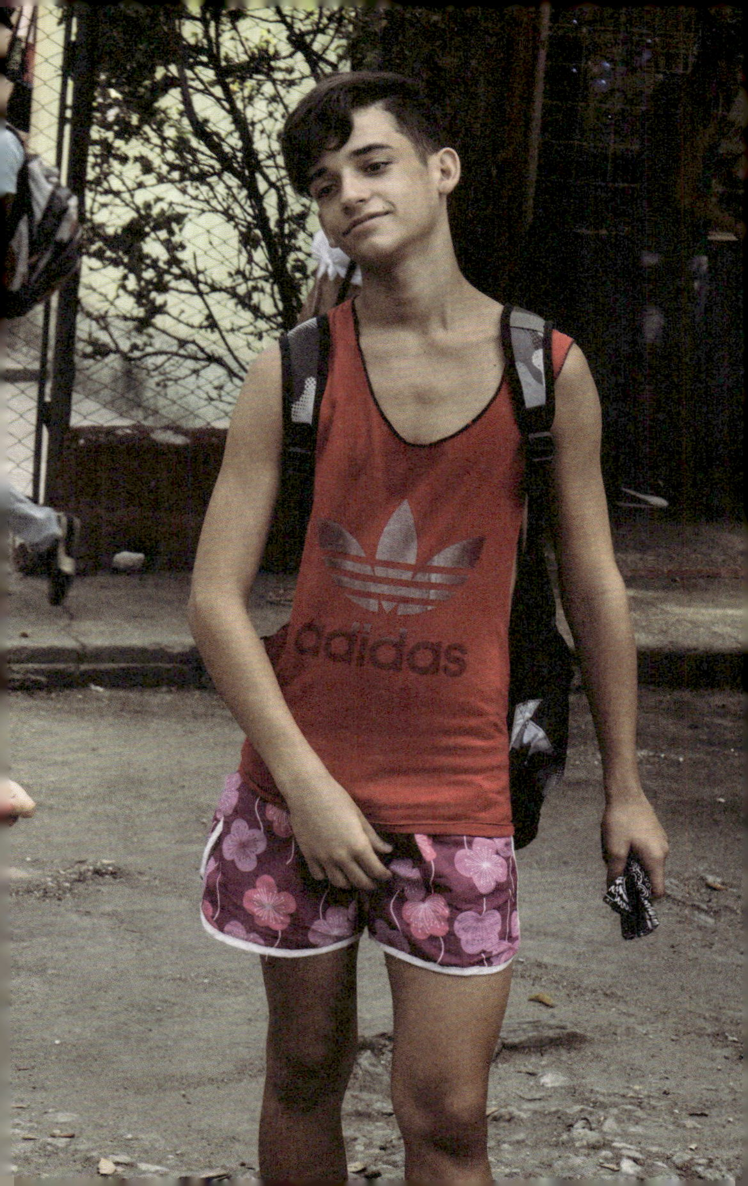
adidas

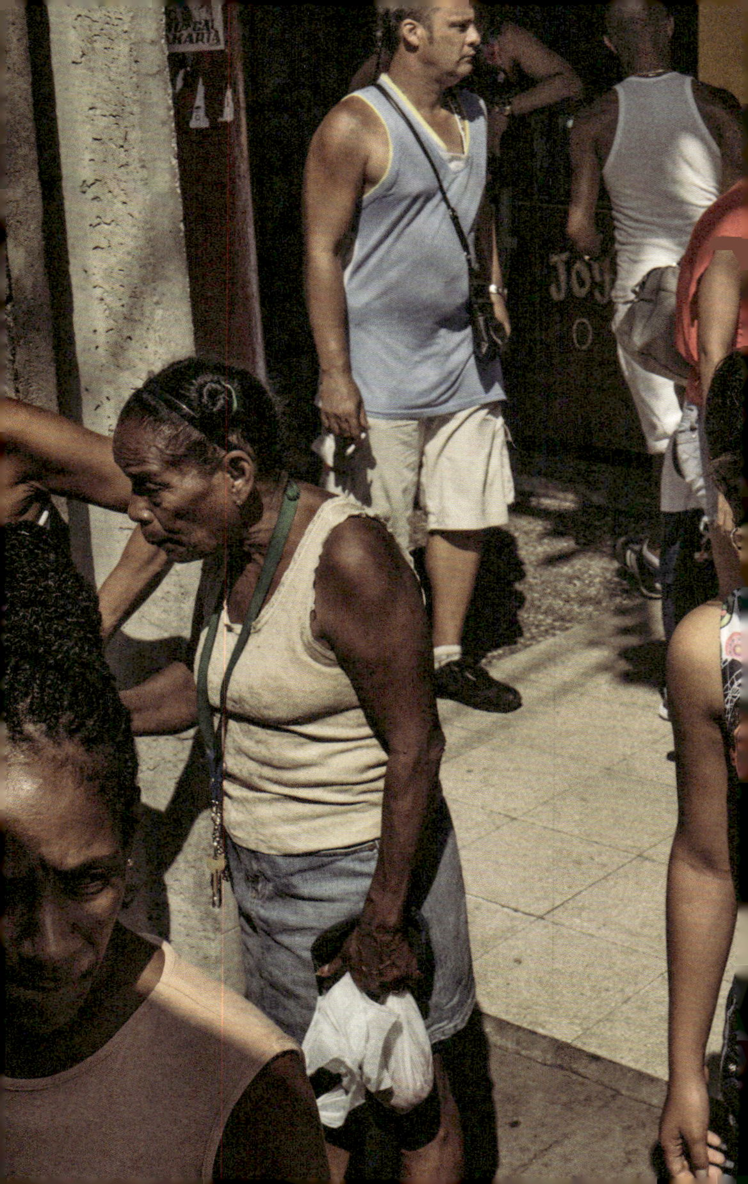

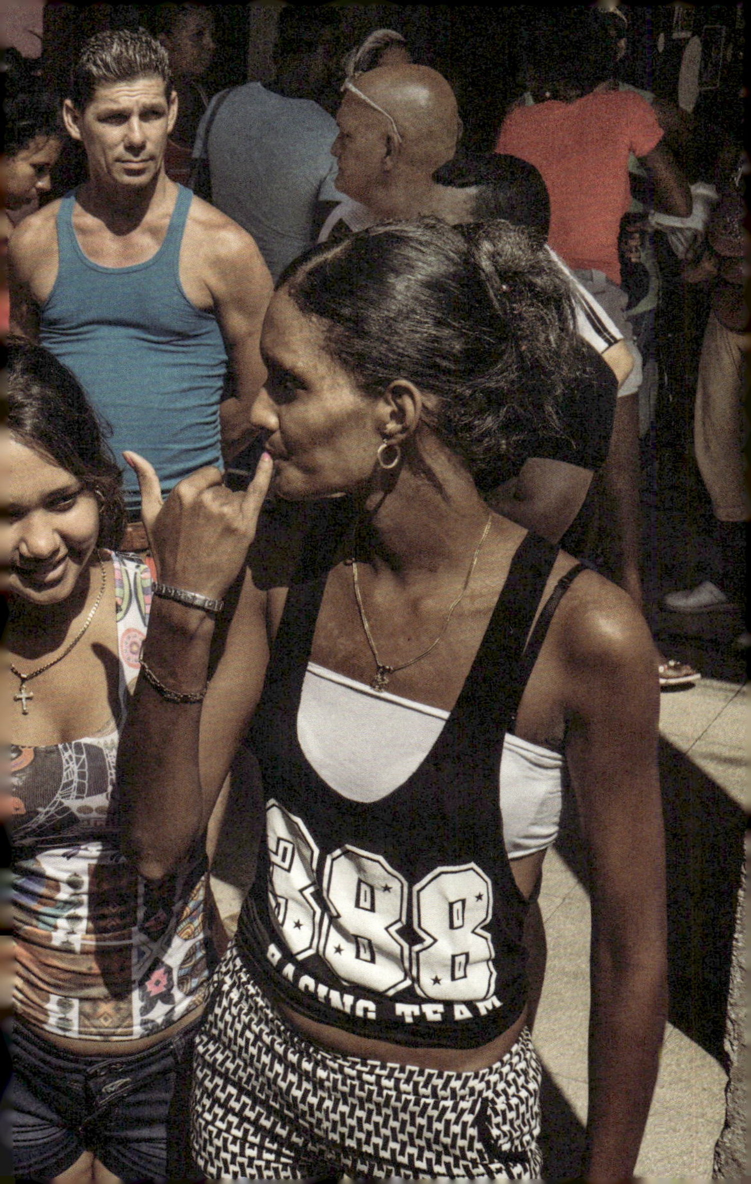

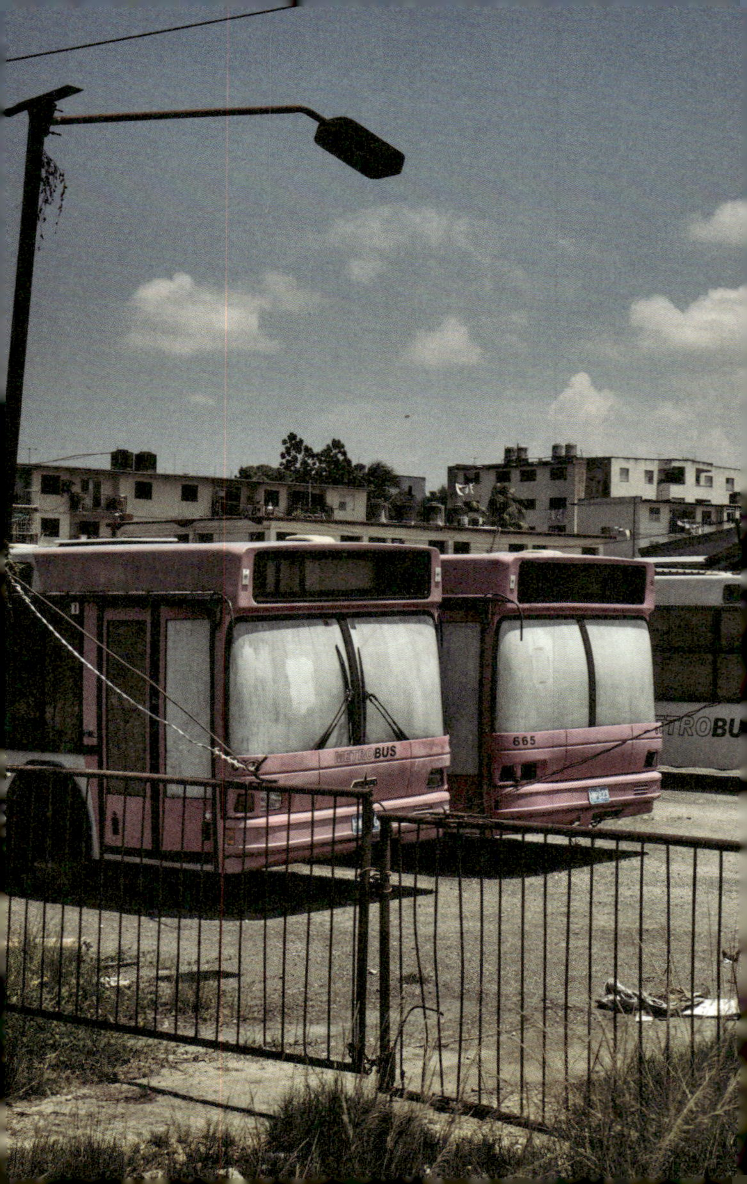
METROBUS
665
TROBU

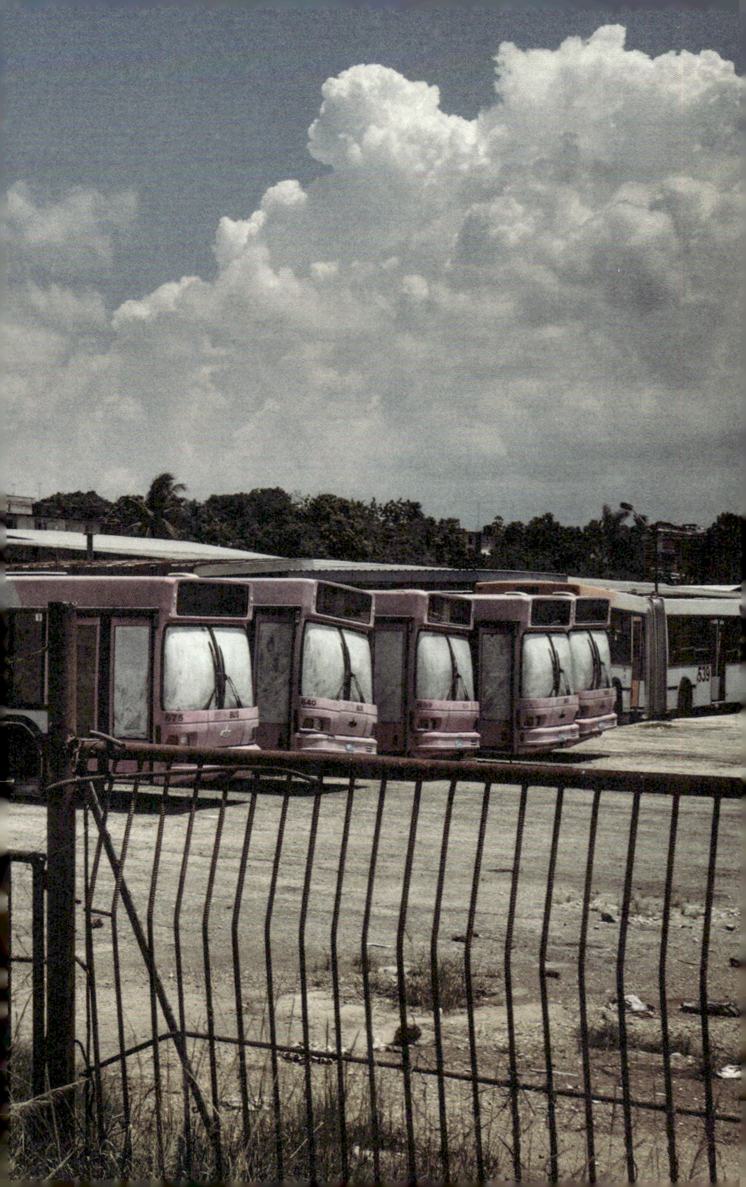
639

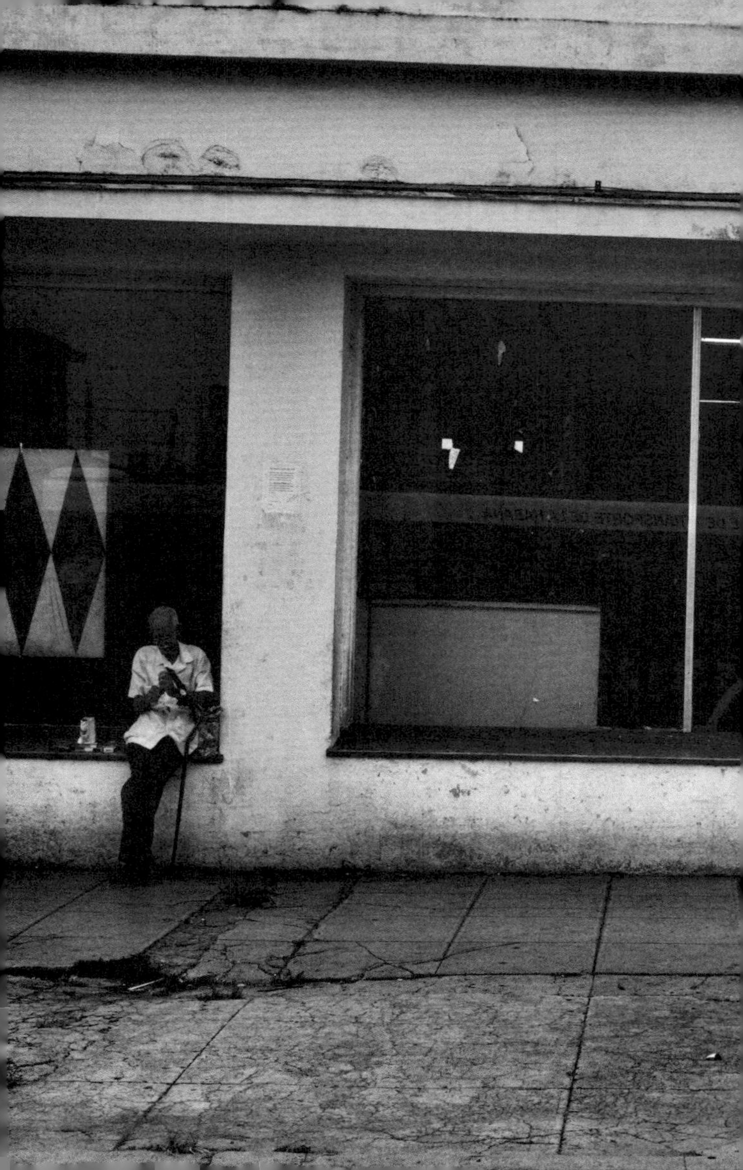

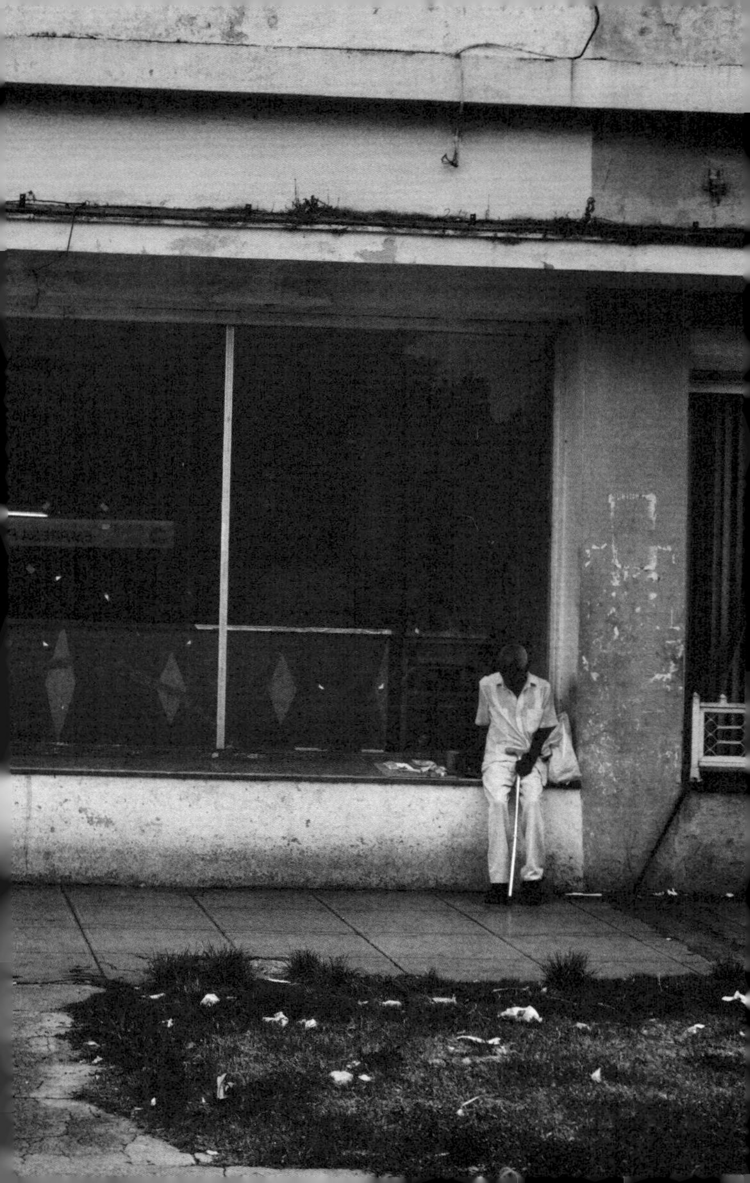

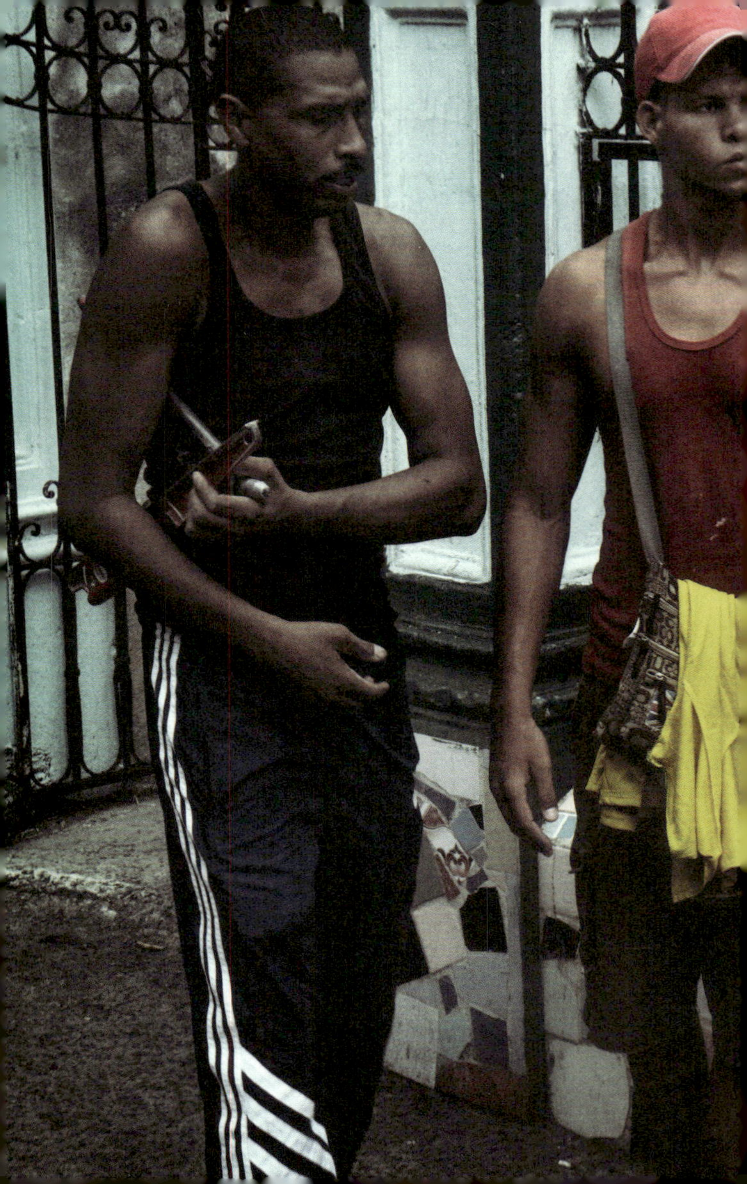

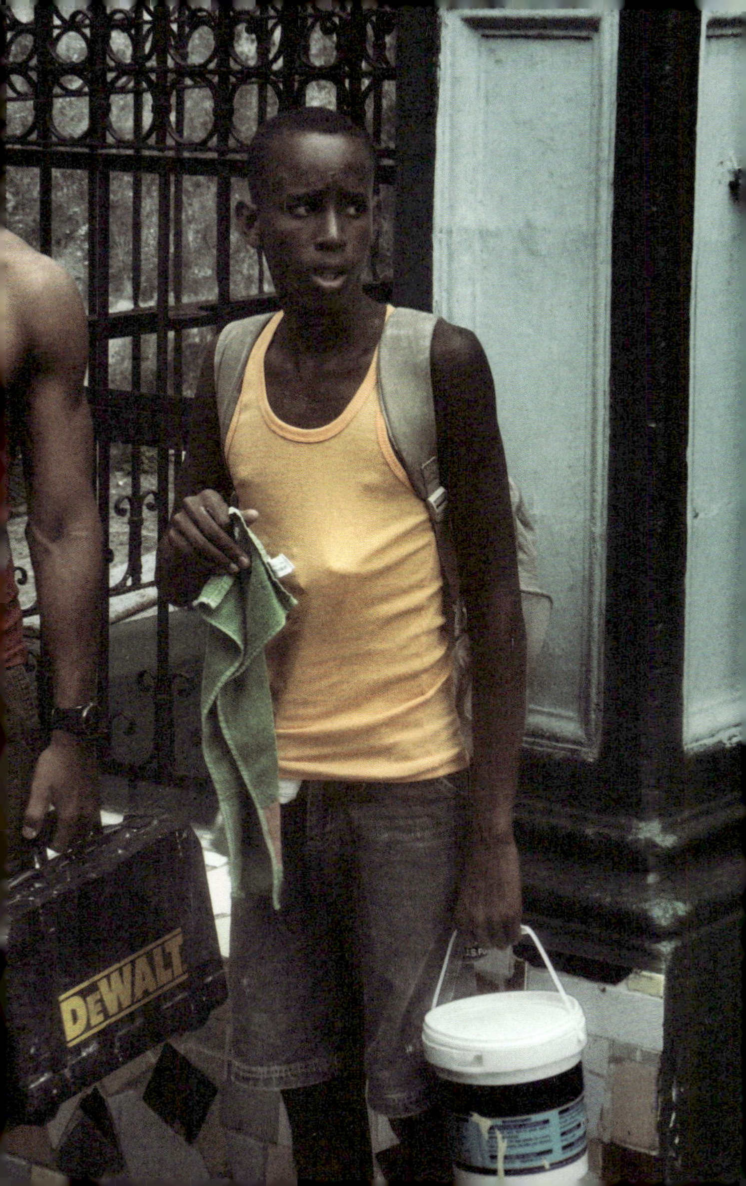
DEWALT

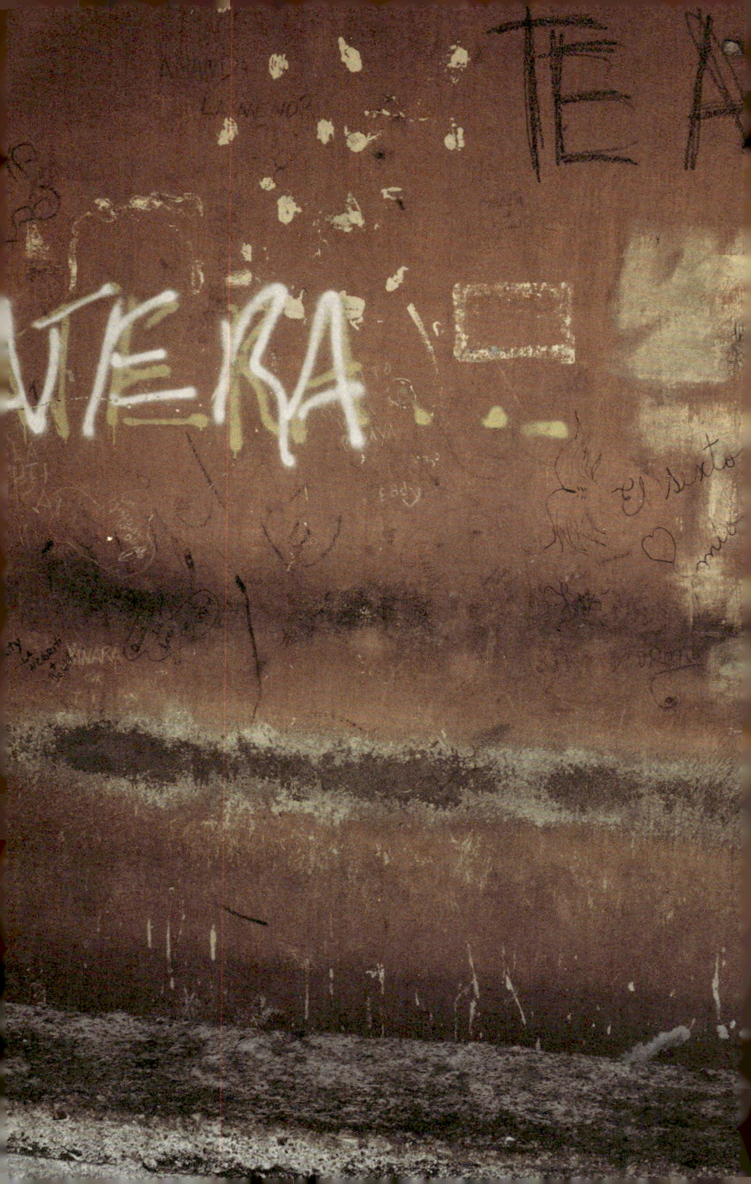
VERA

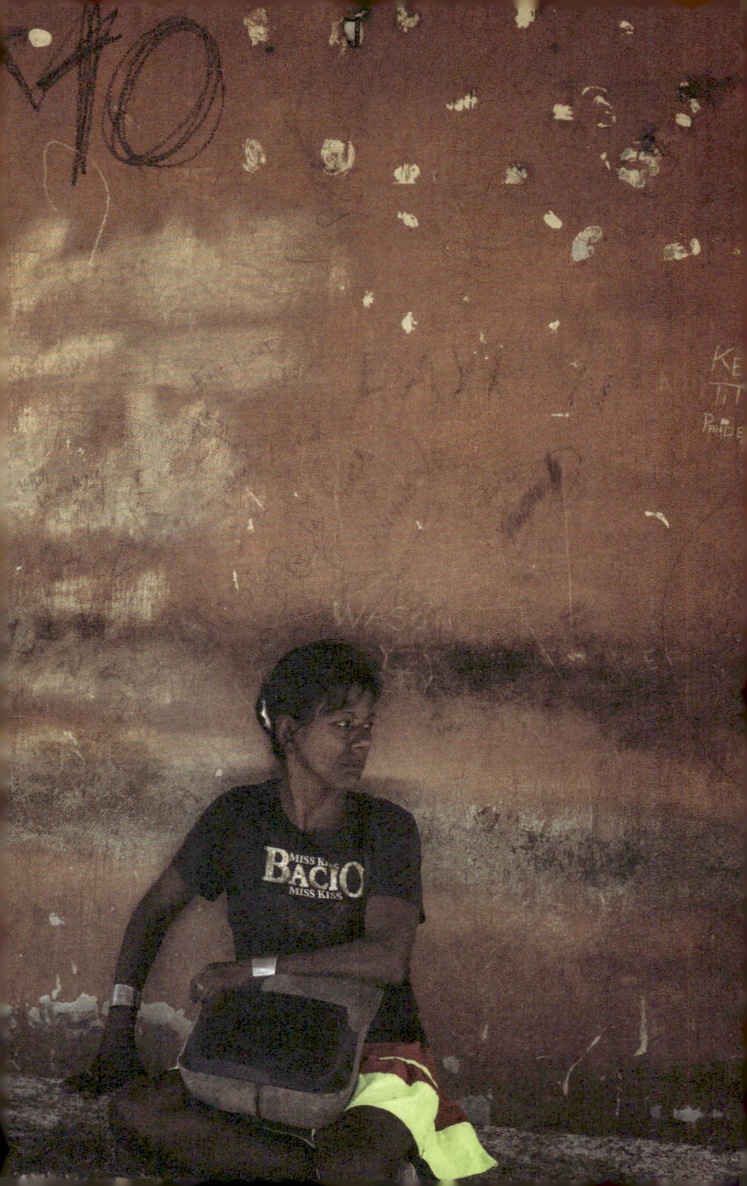
BACIO
MISS KISS

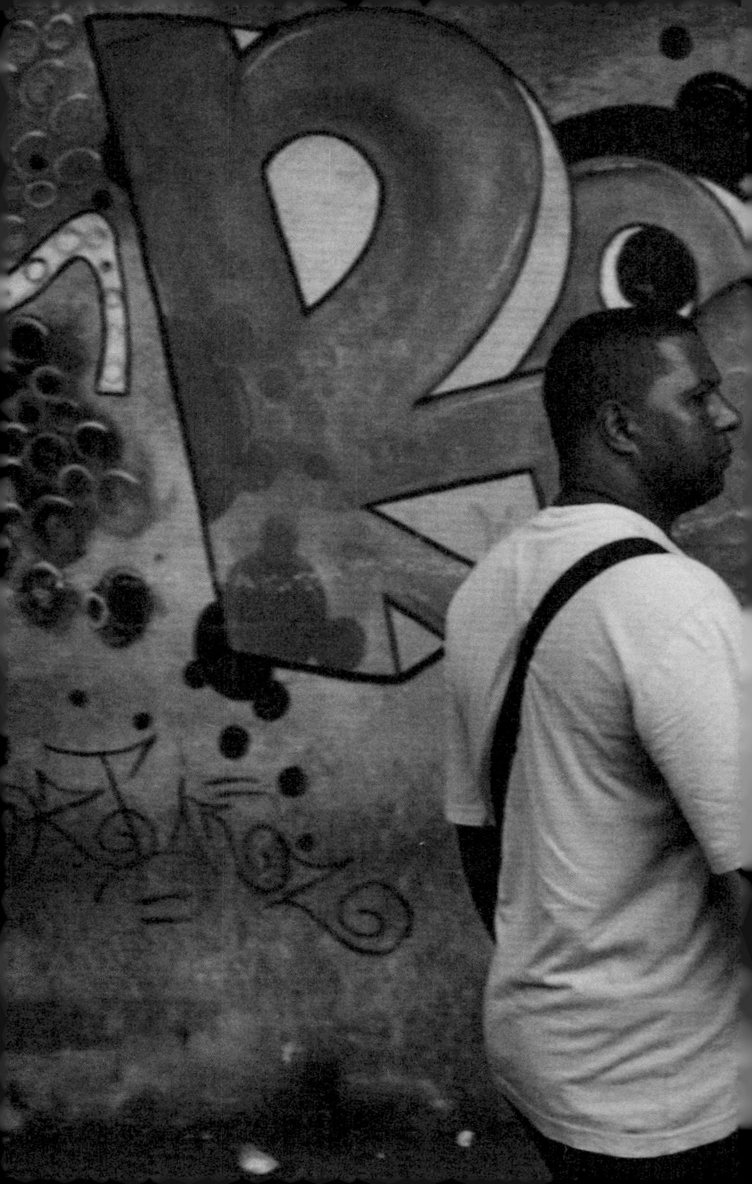

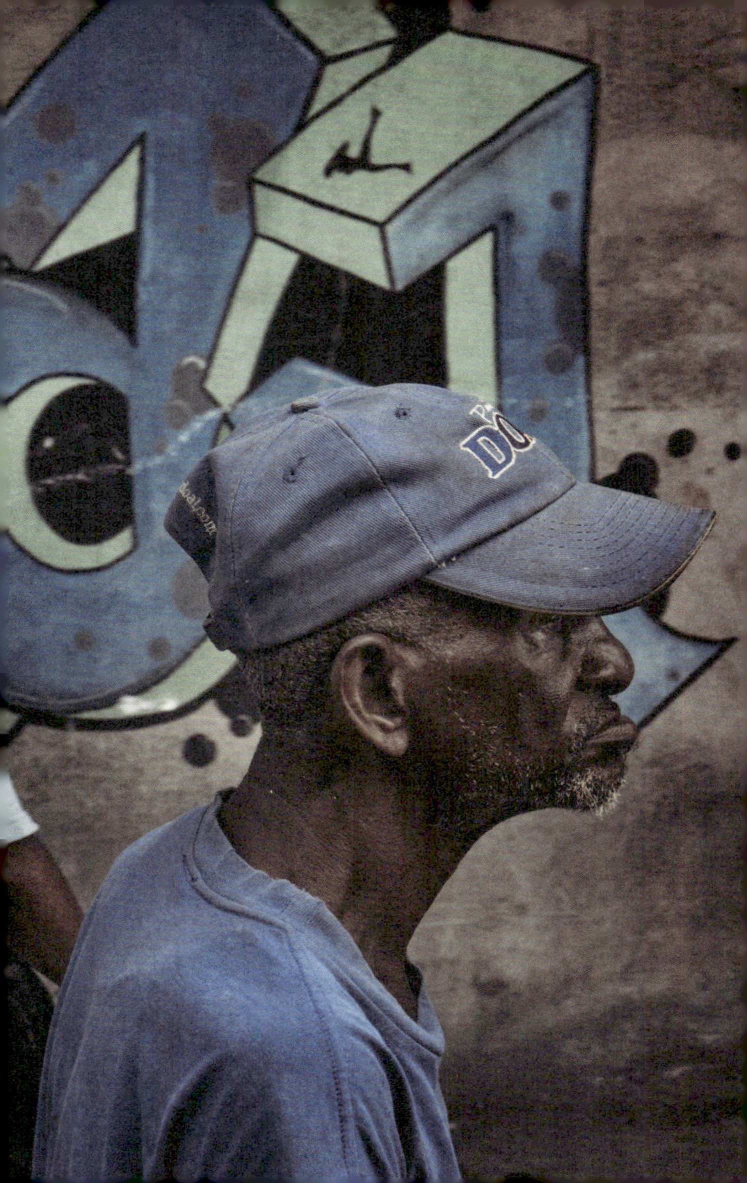

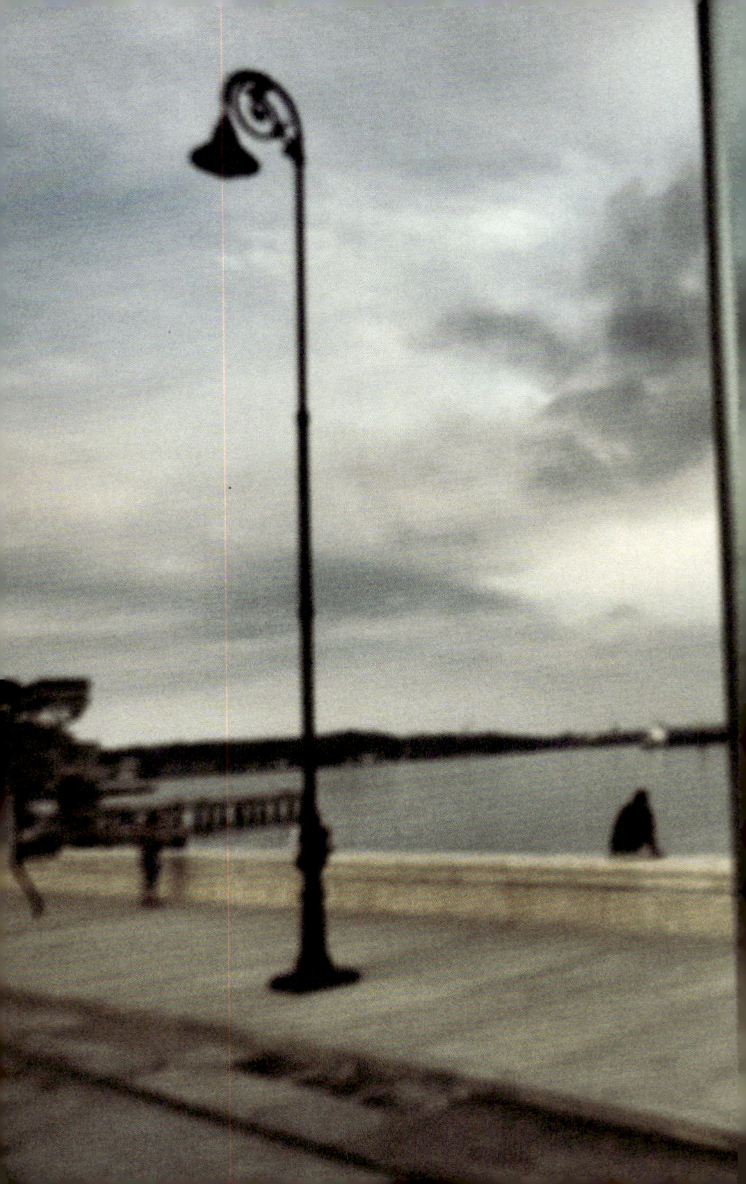

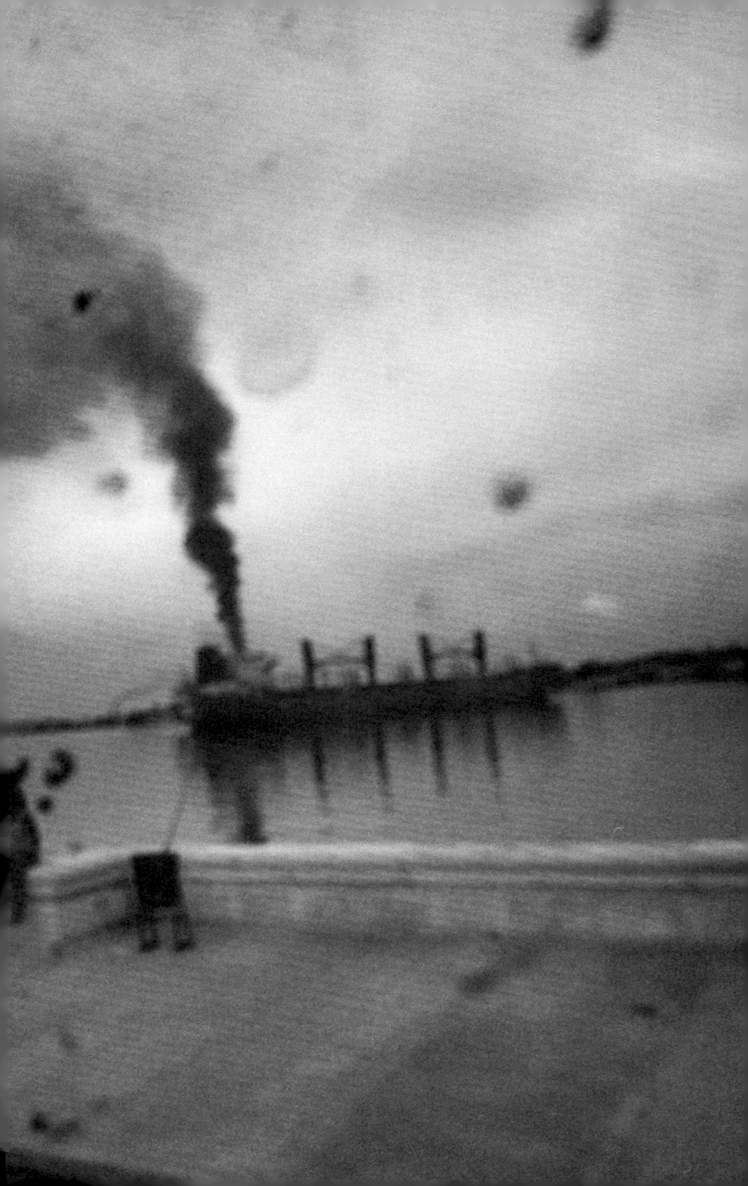

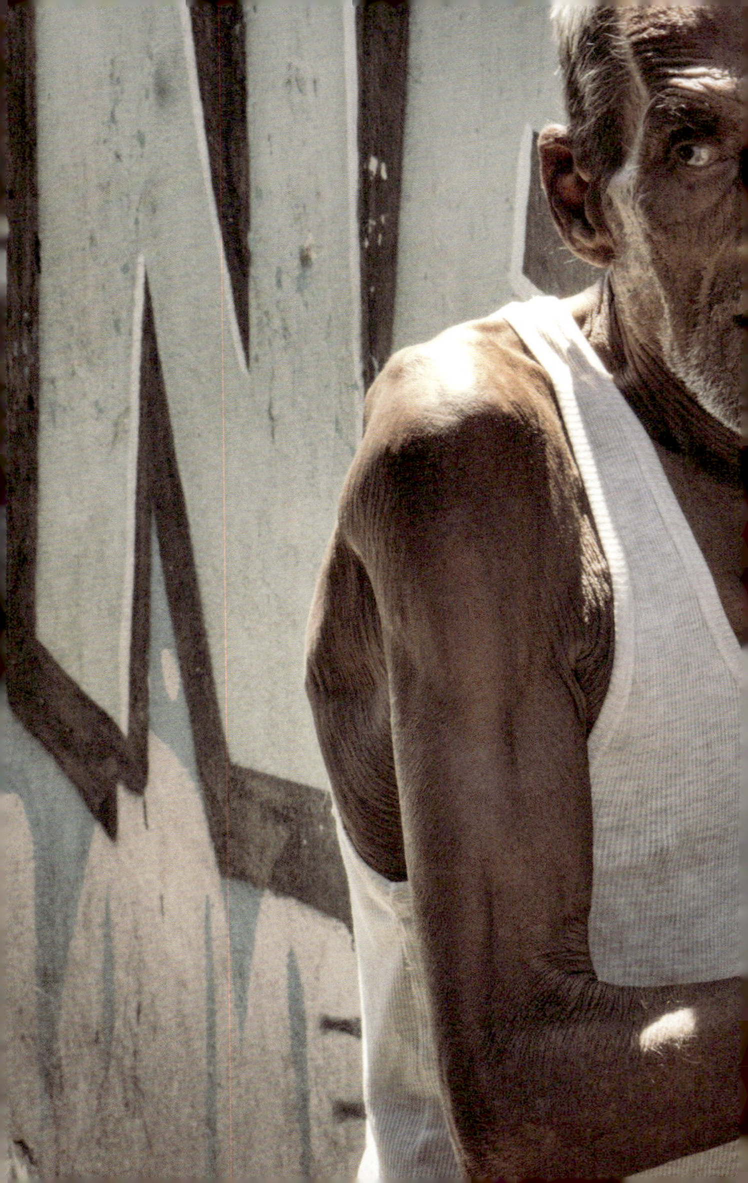

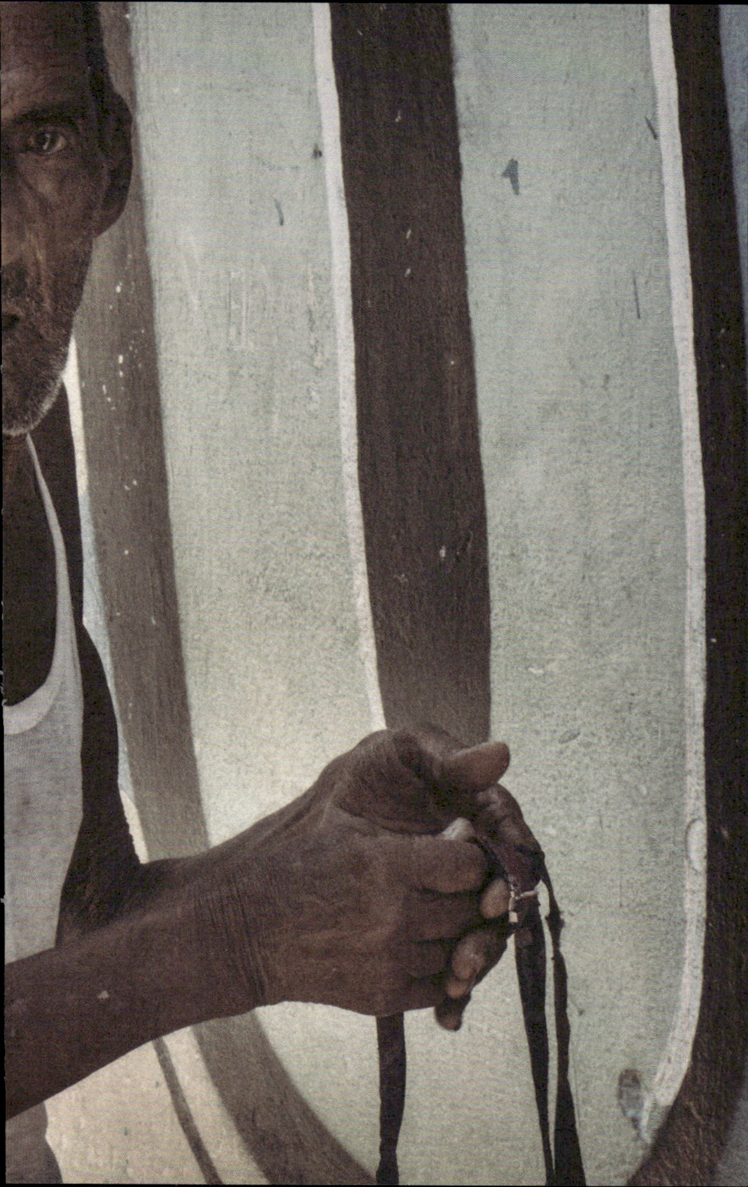

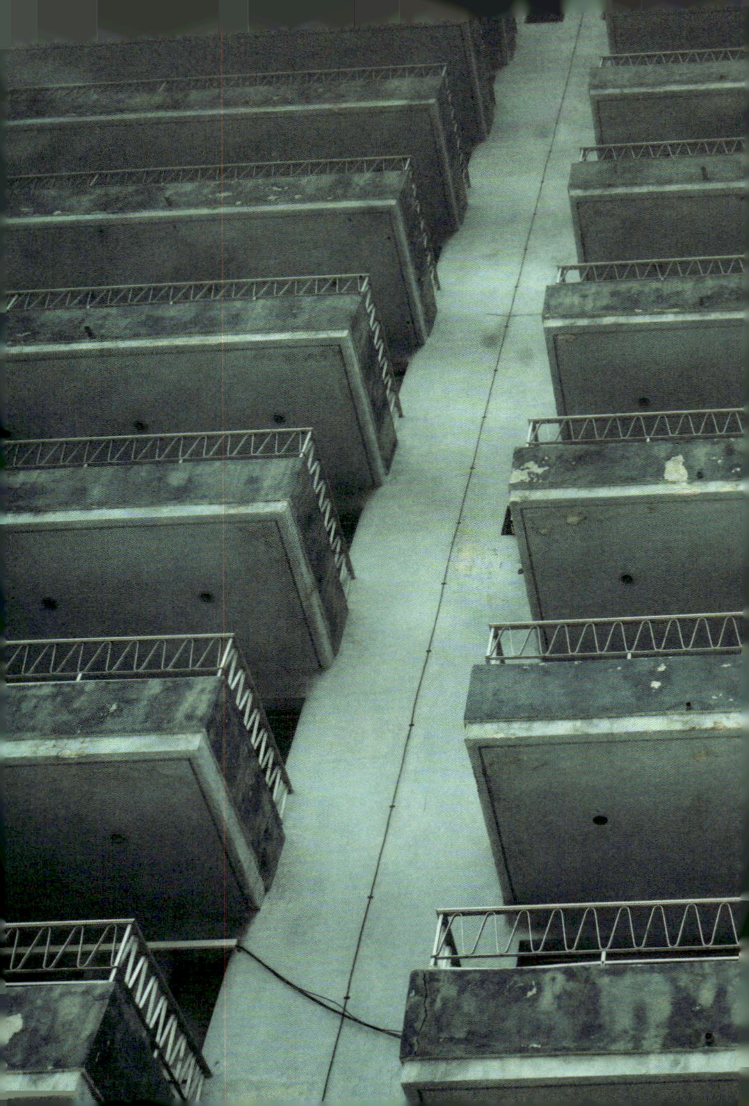

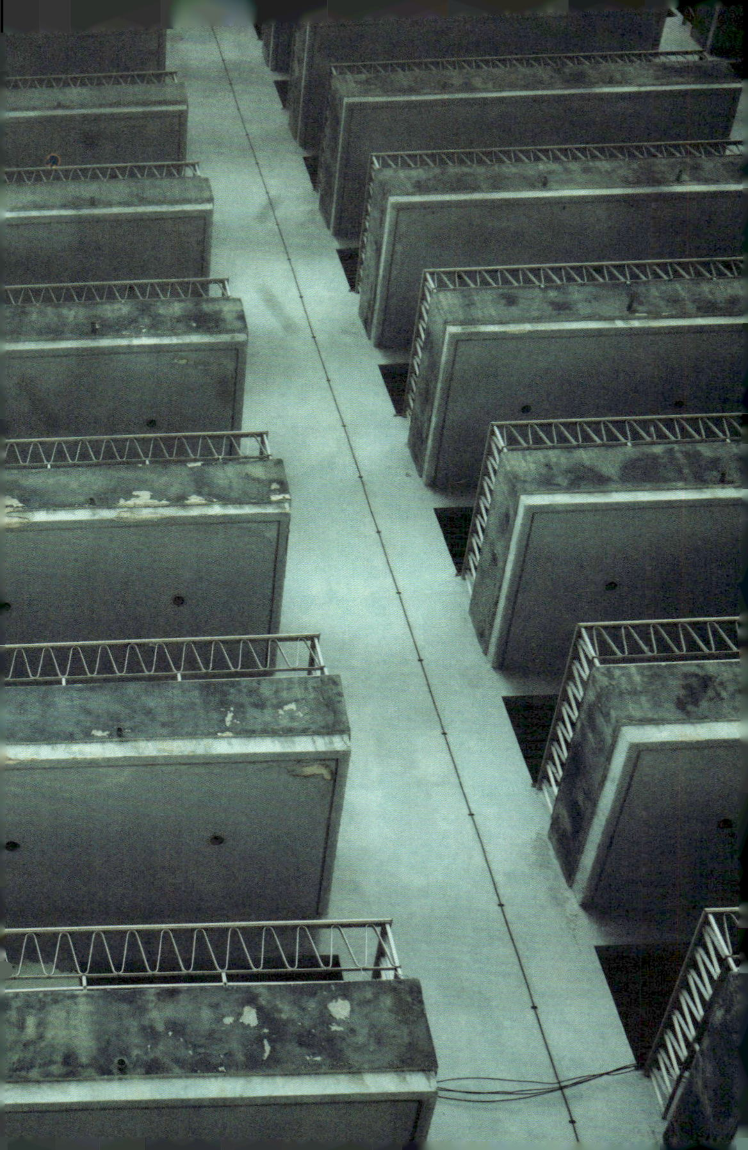

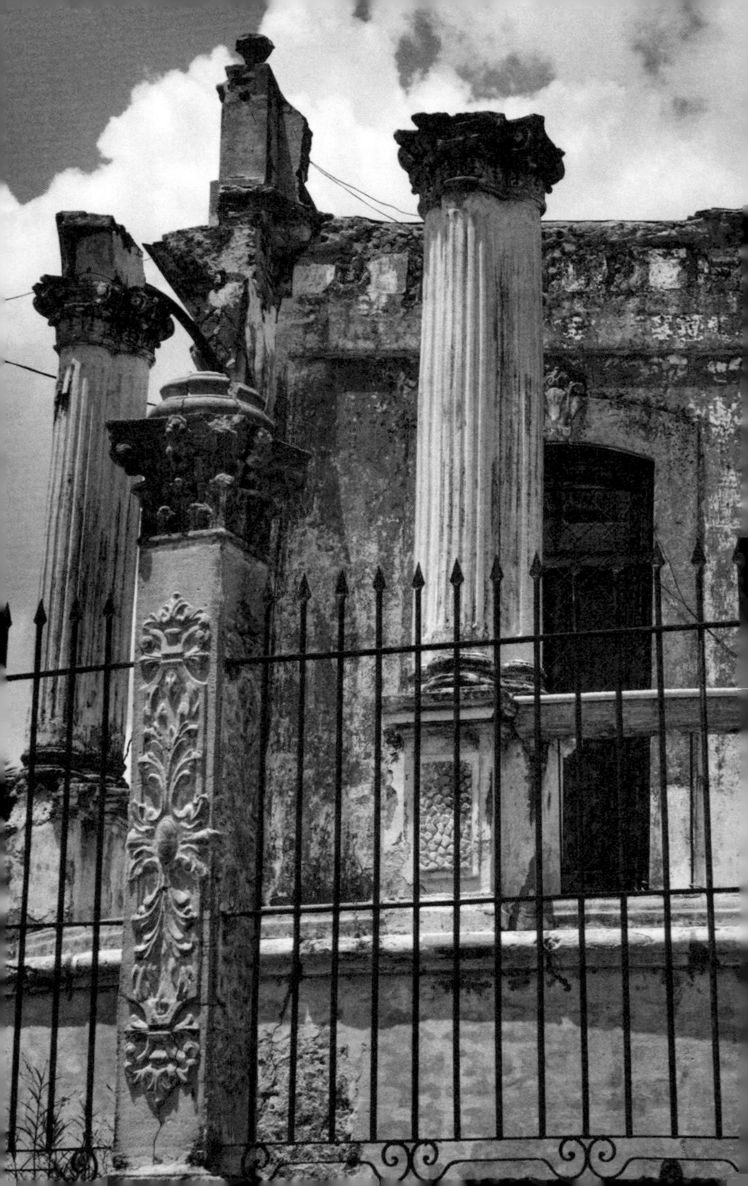

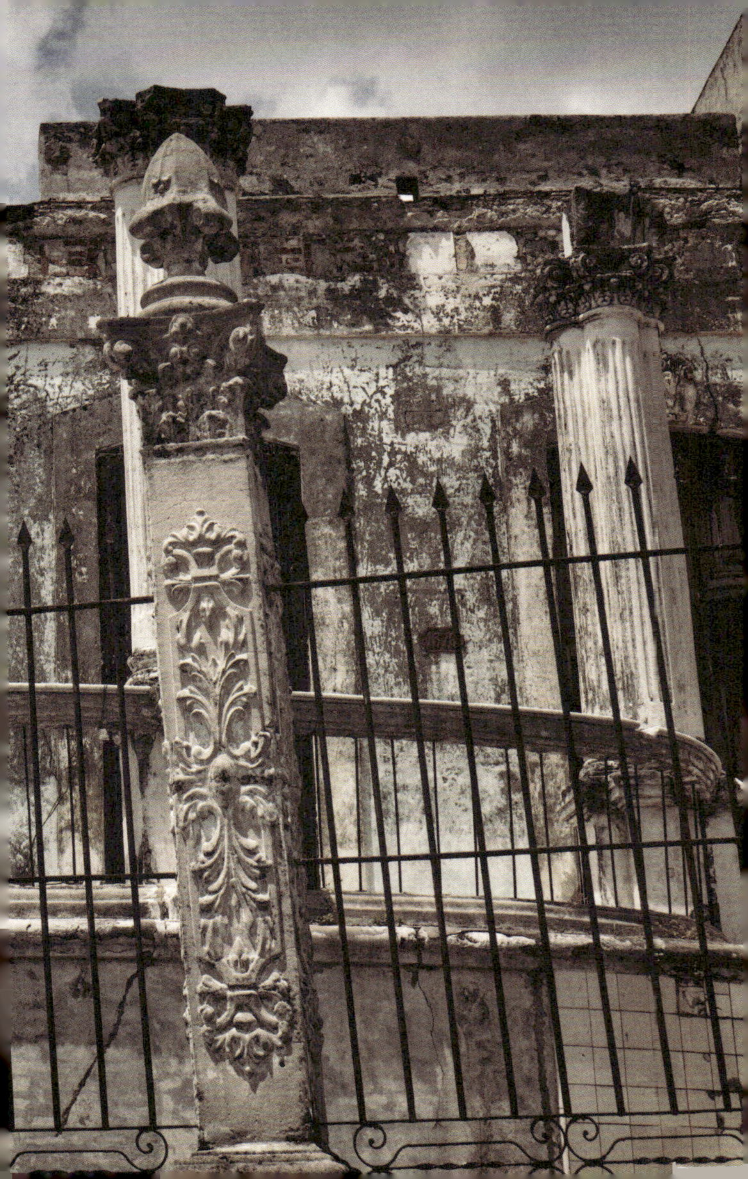

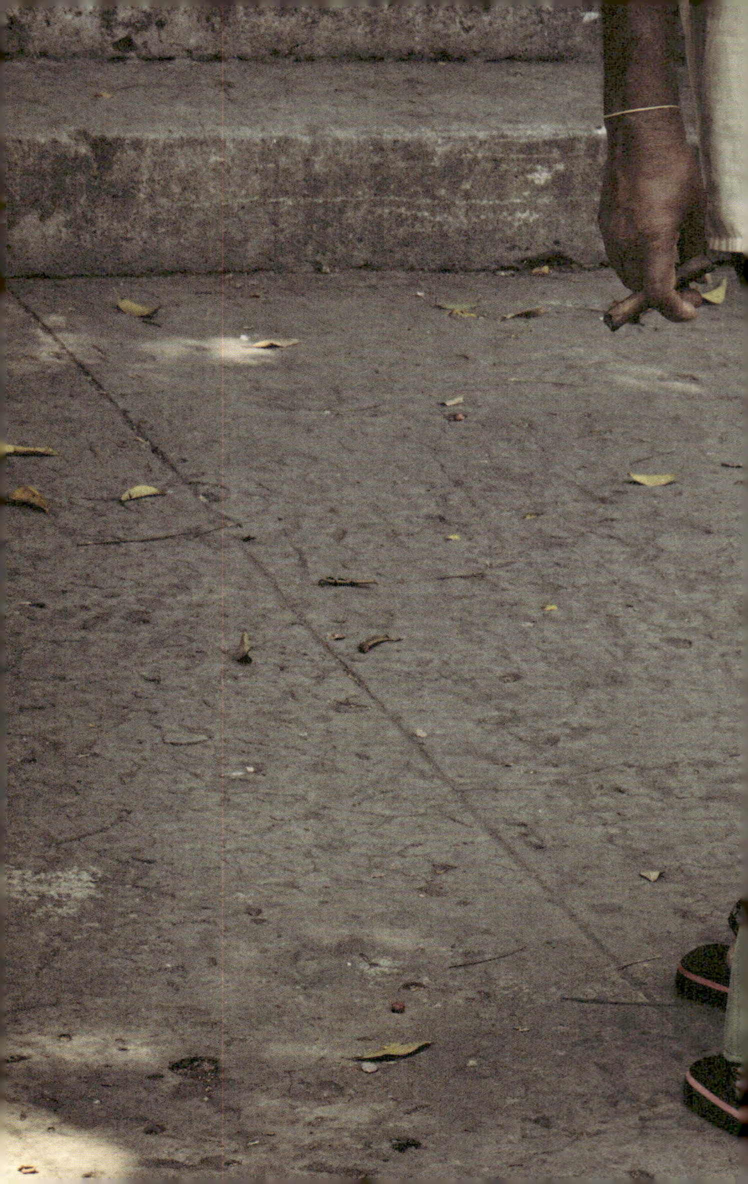

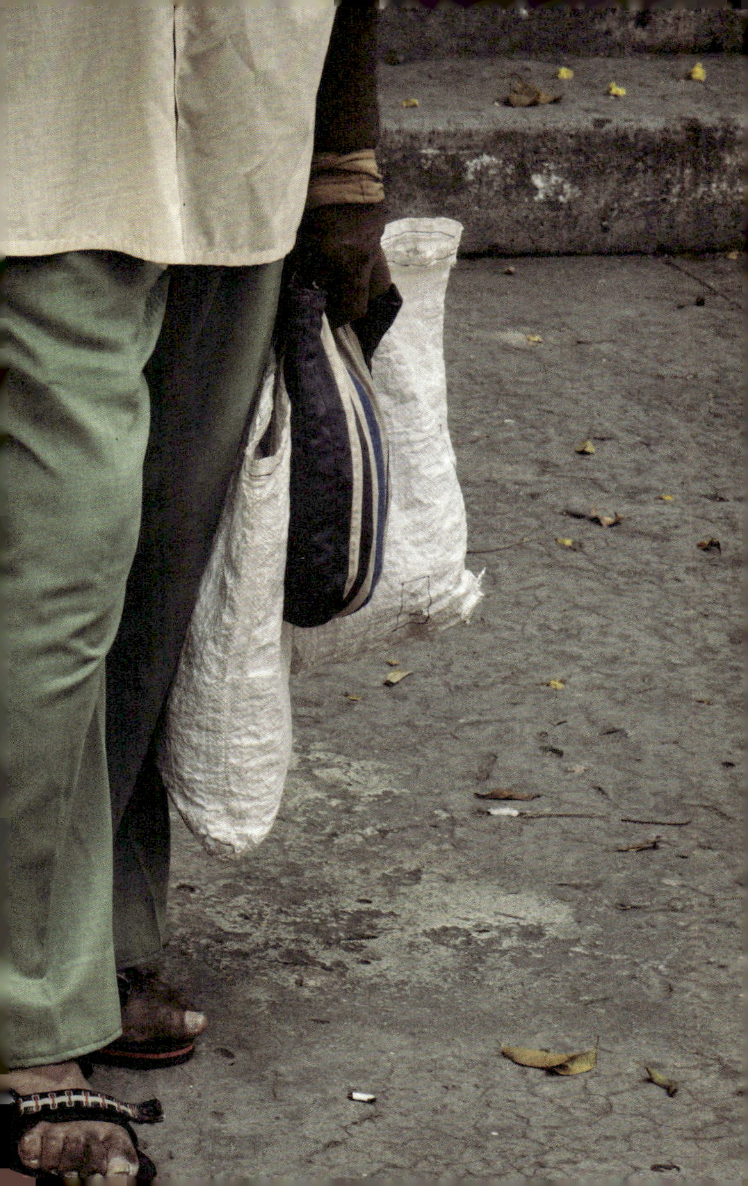

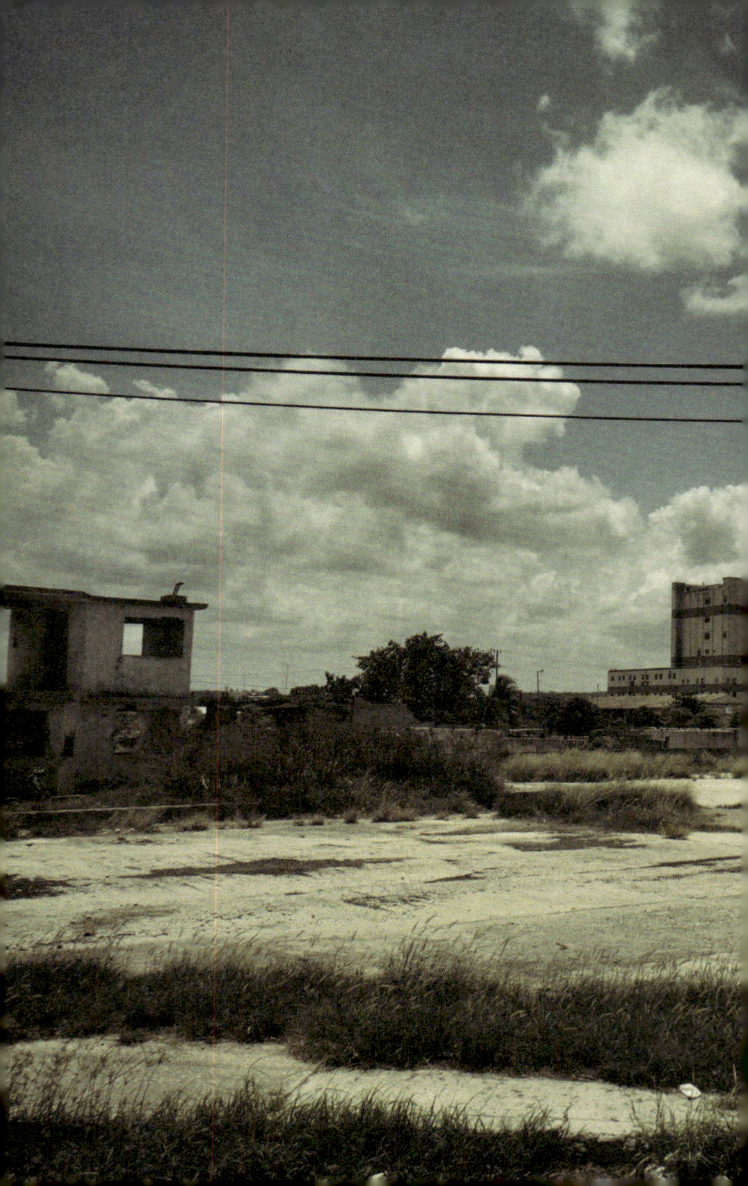

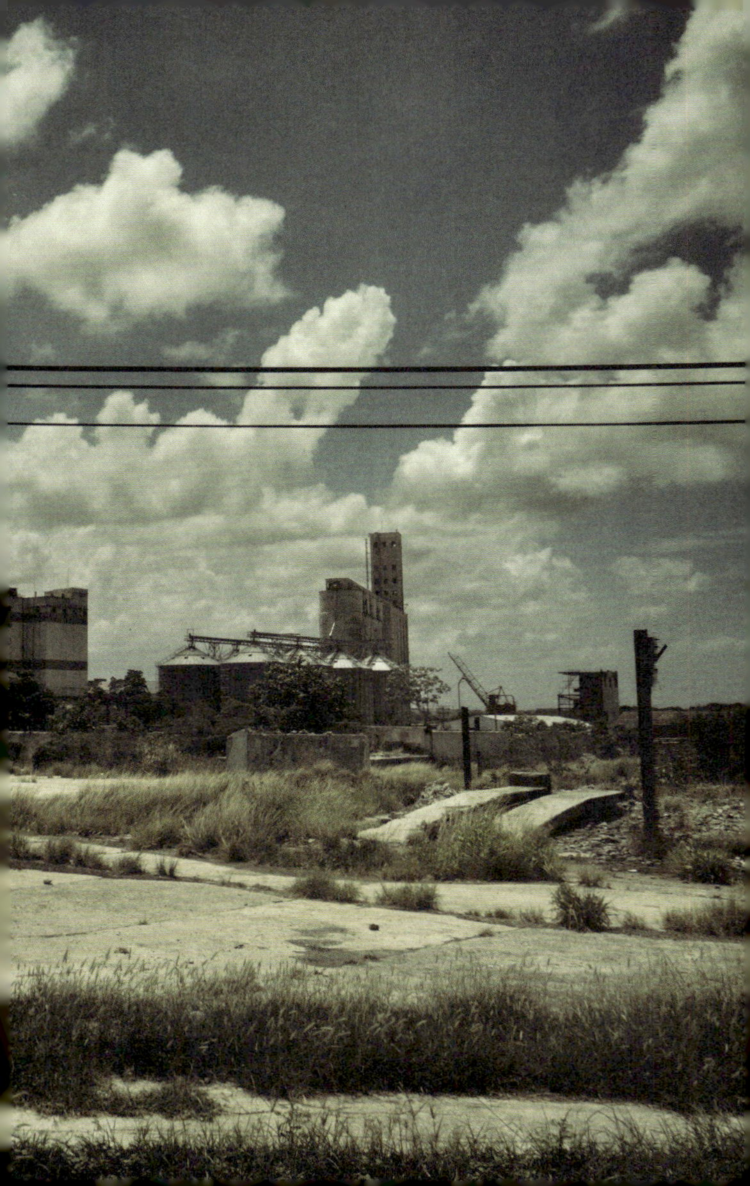

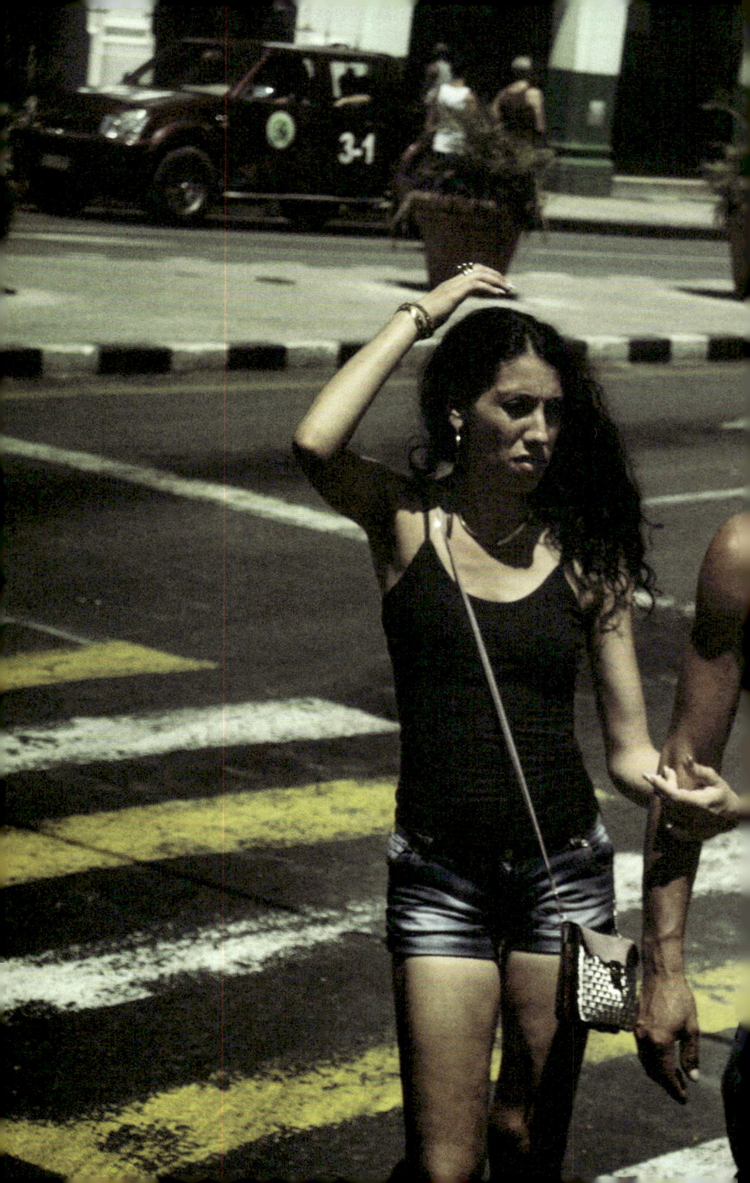
3-1

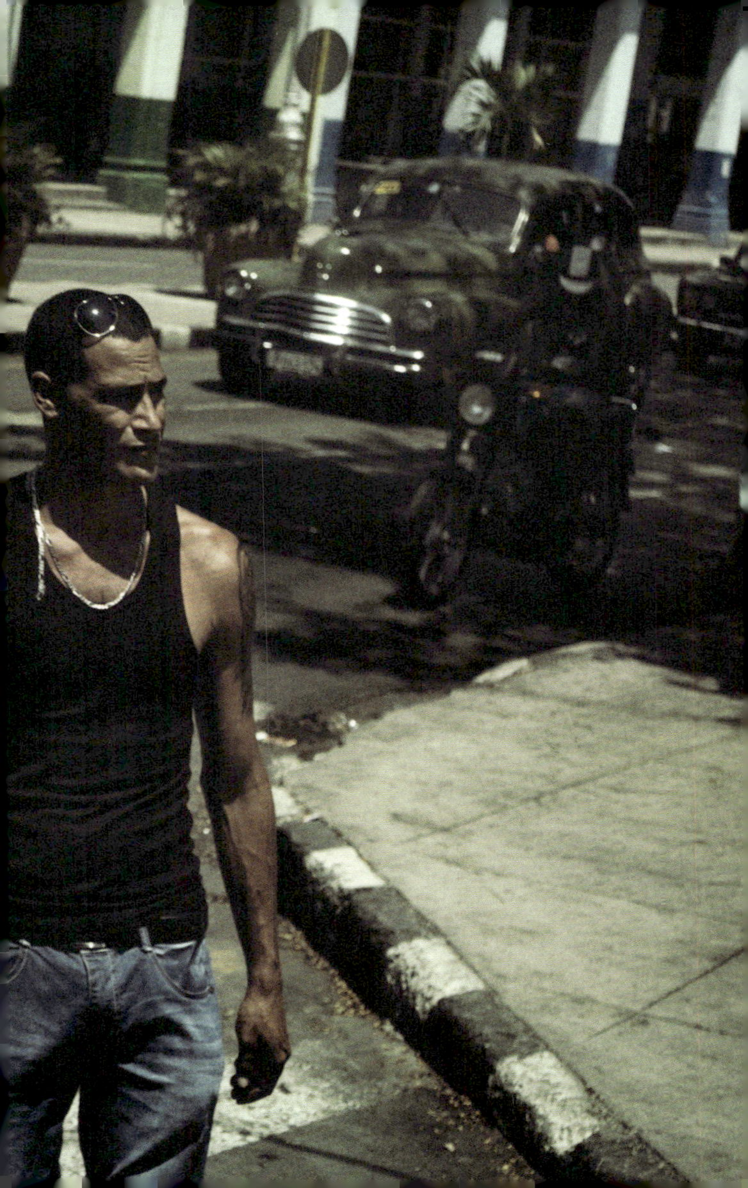

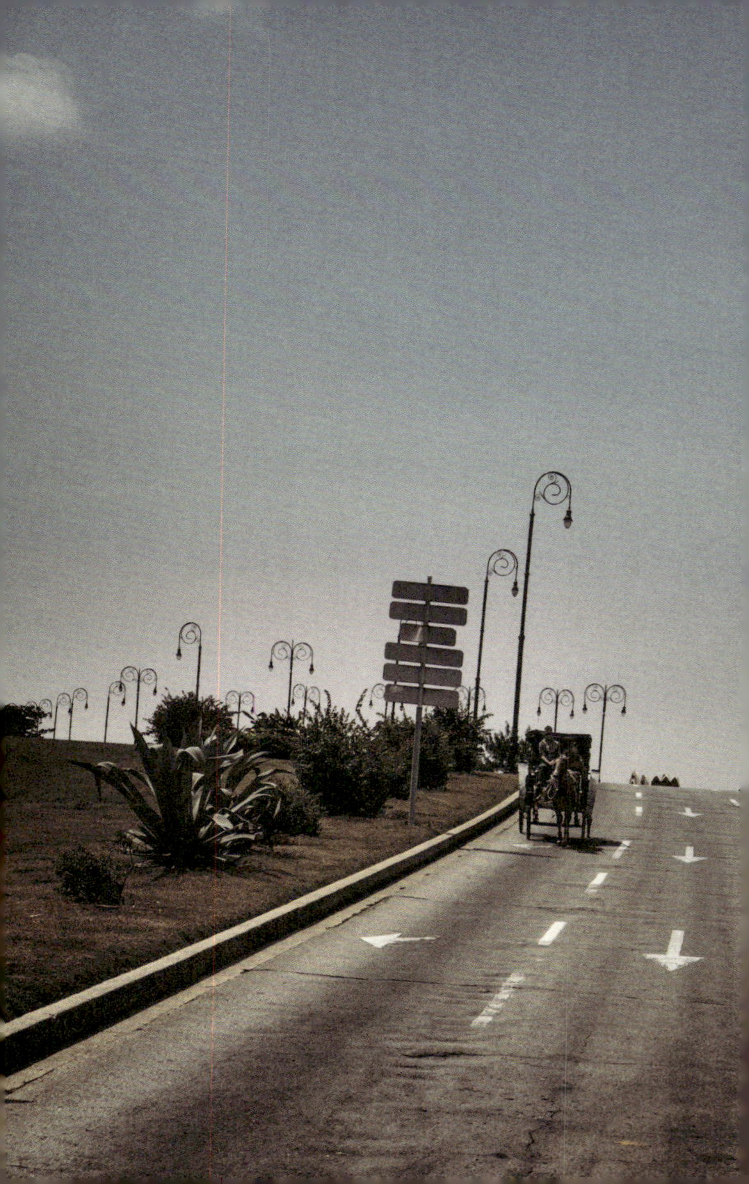

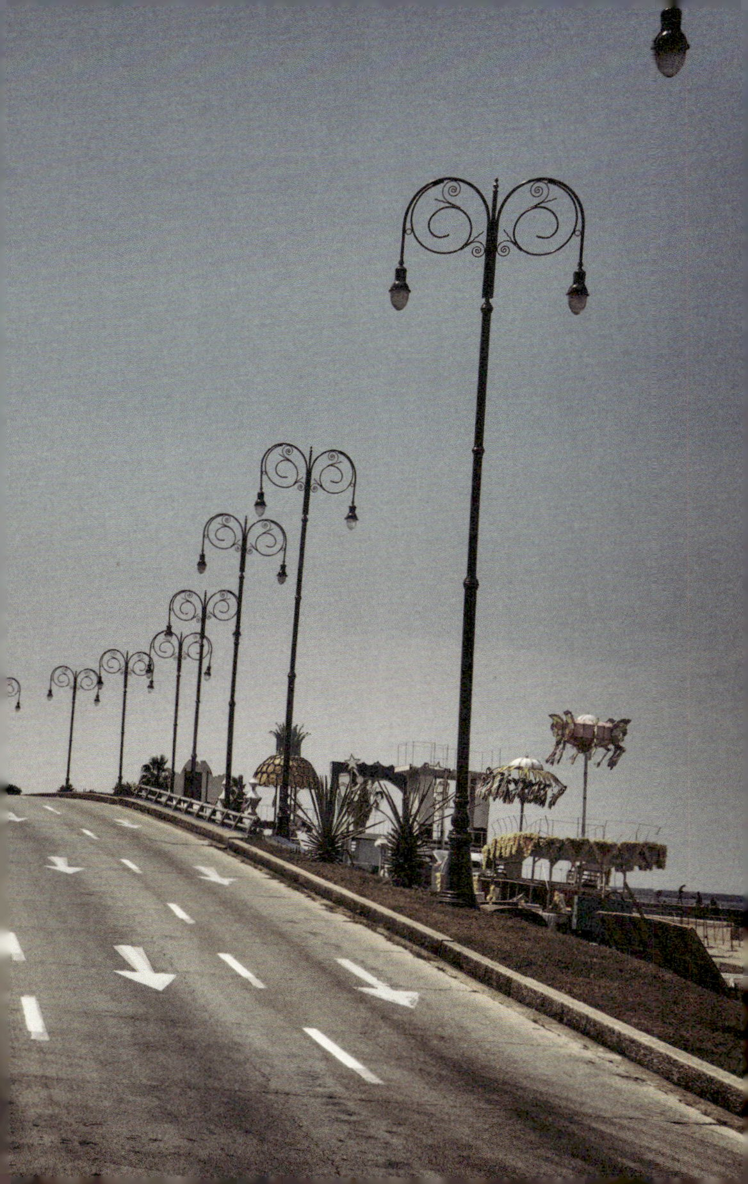

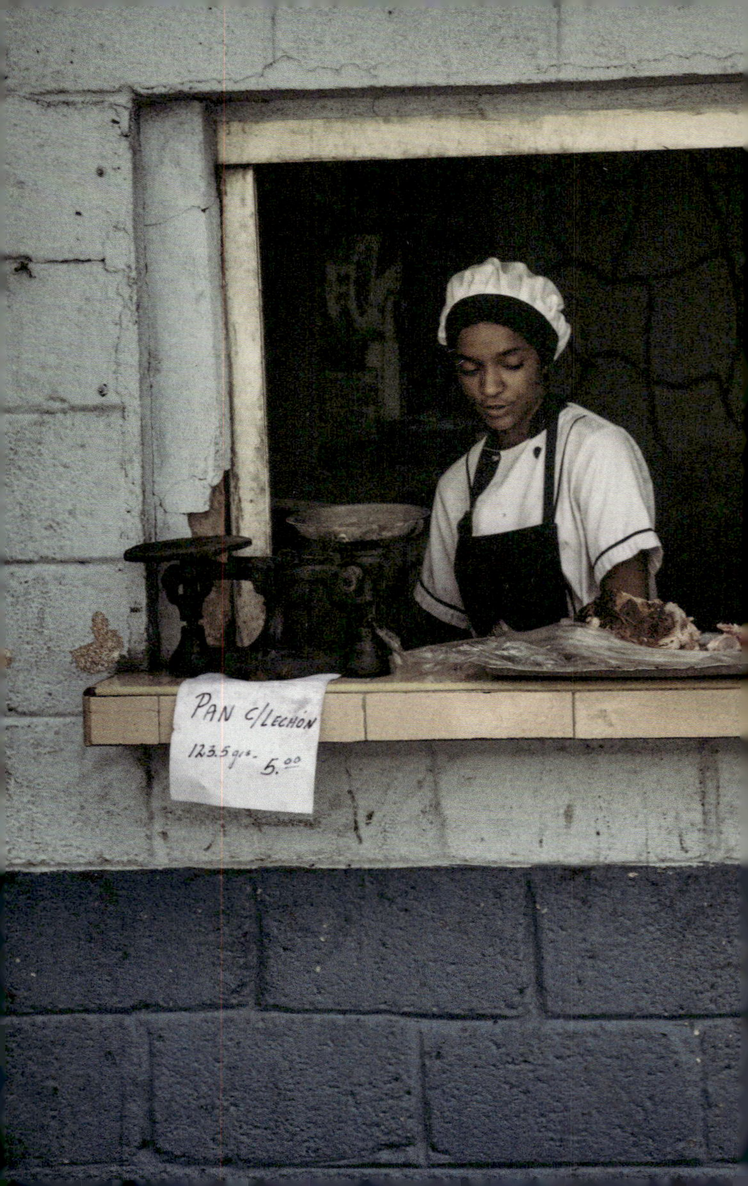
PAN C/LECHÓN
123.5 grs. 5.00

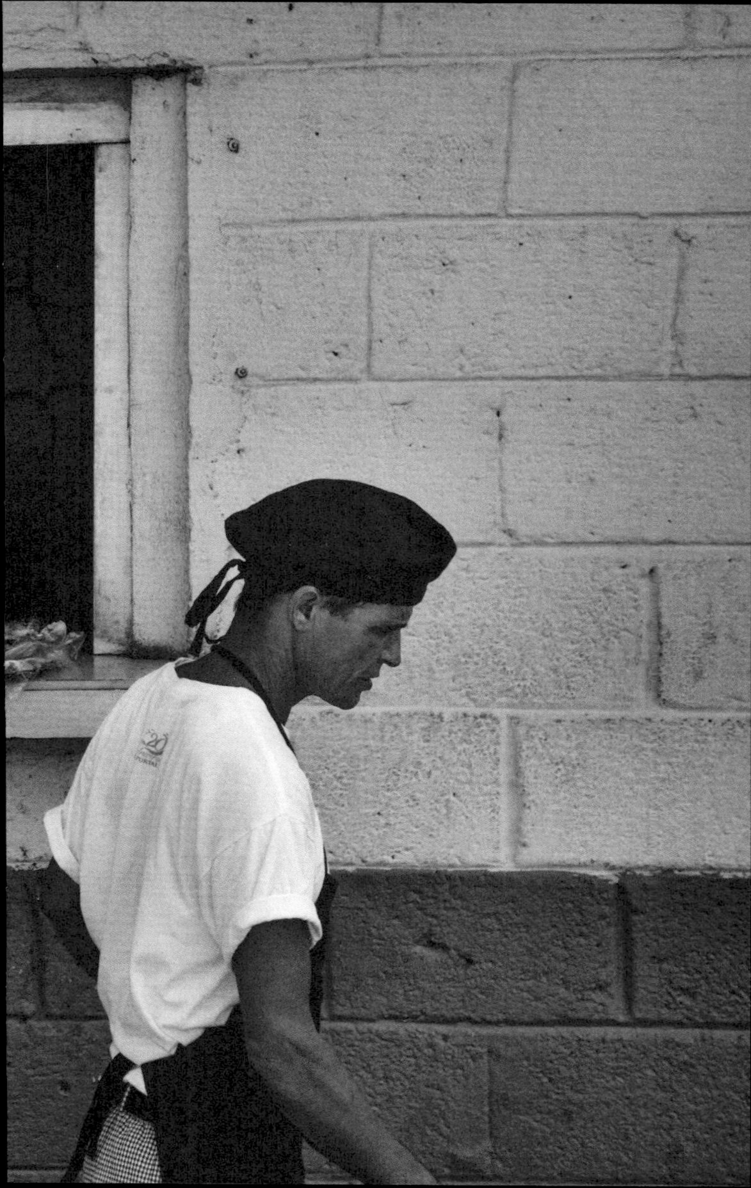

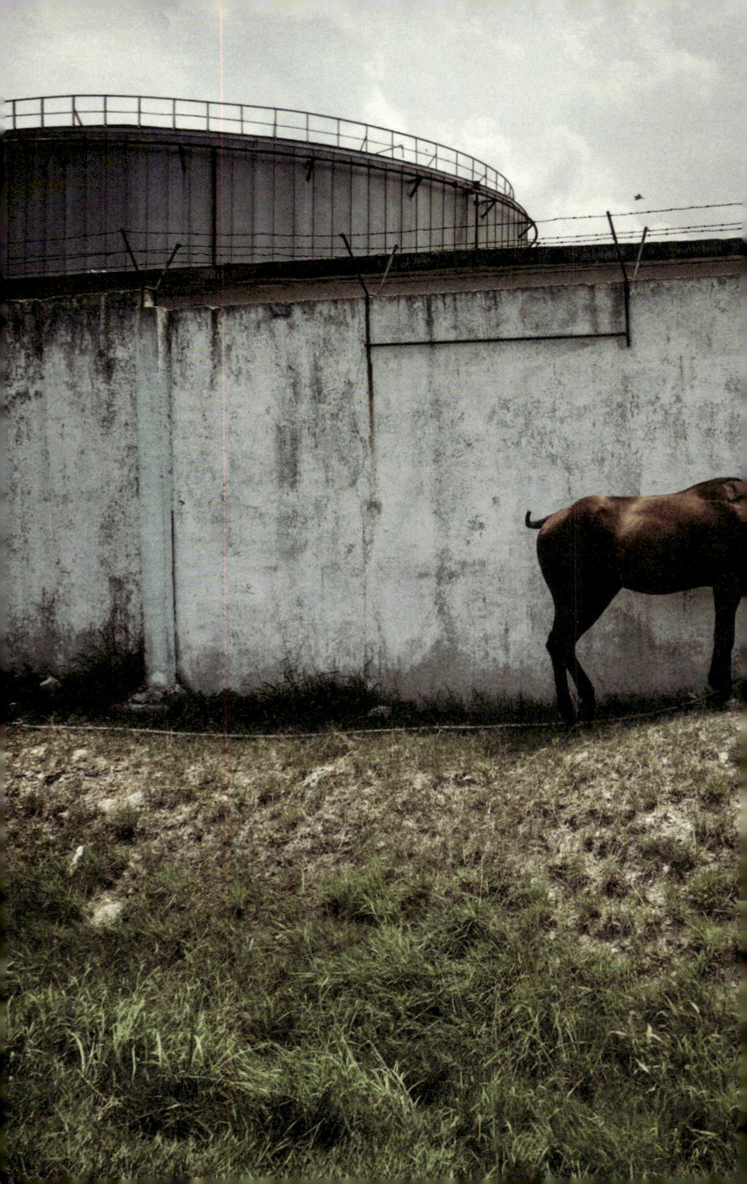

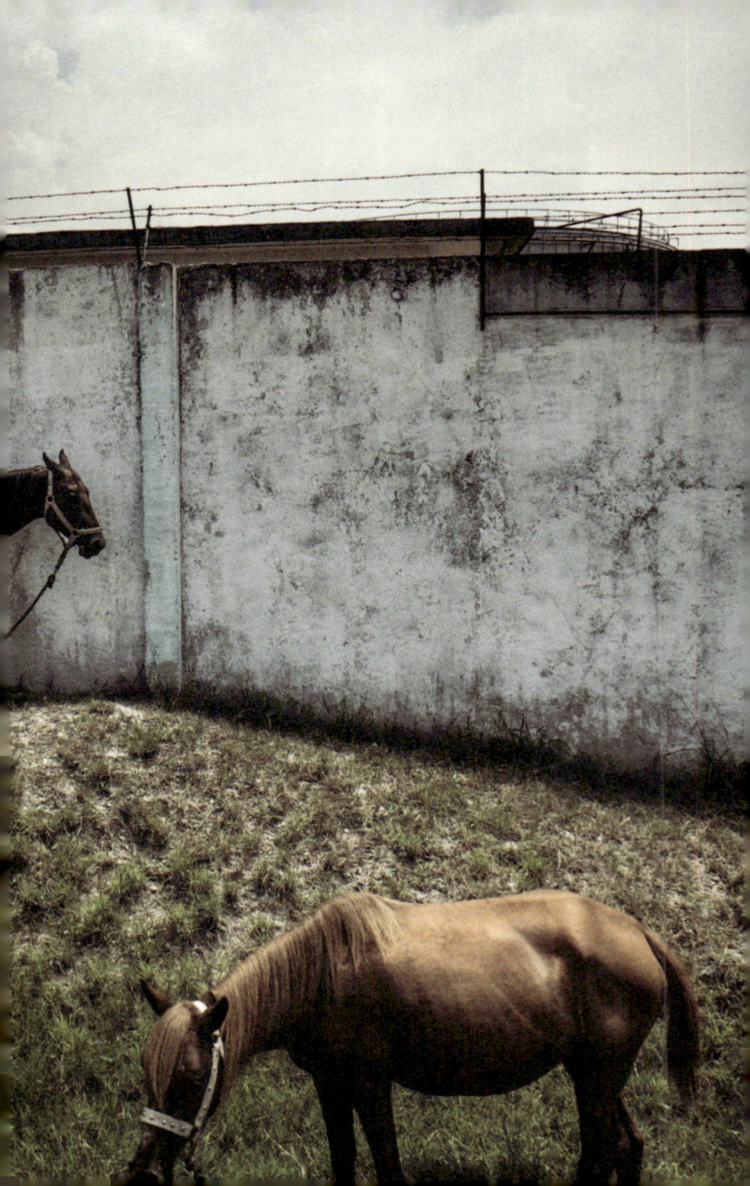

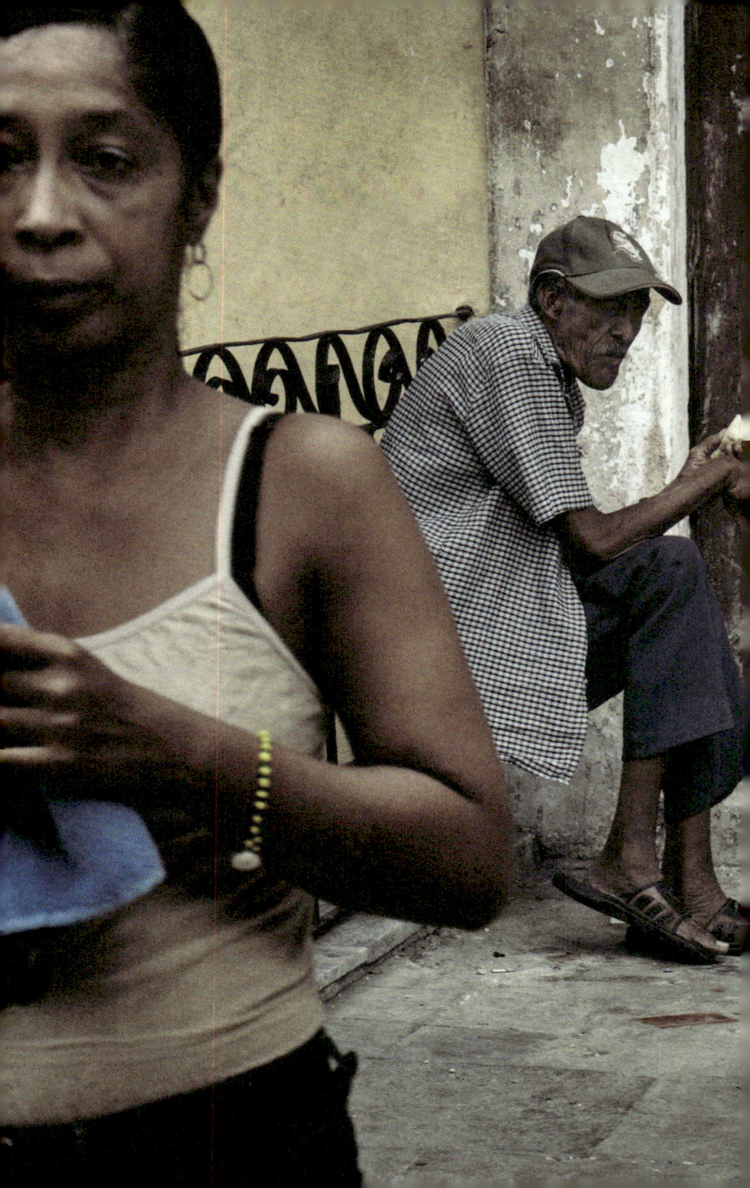

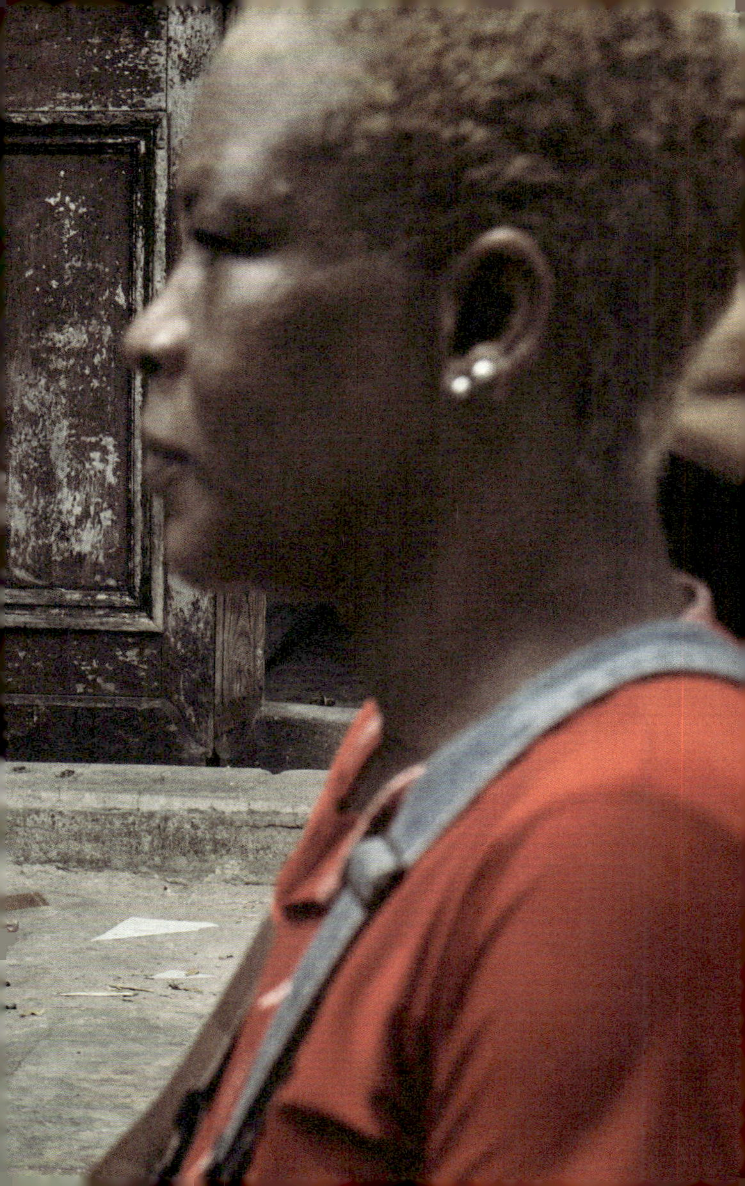

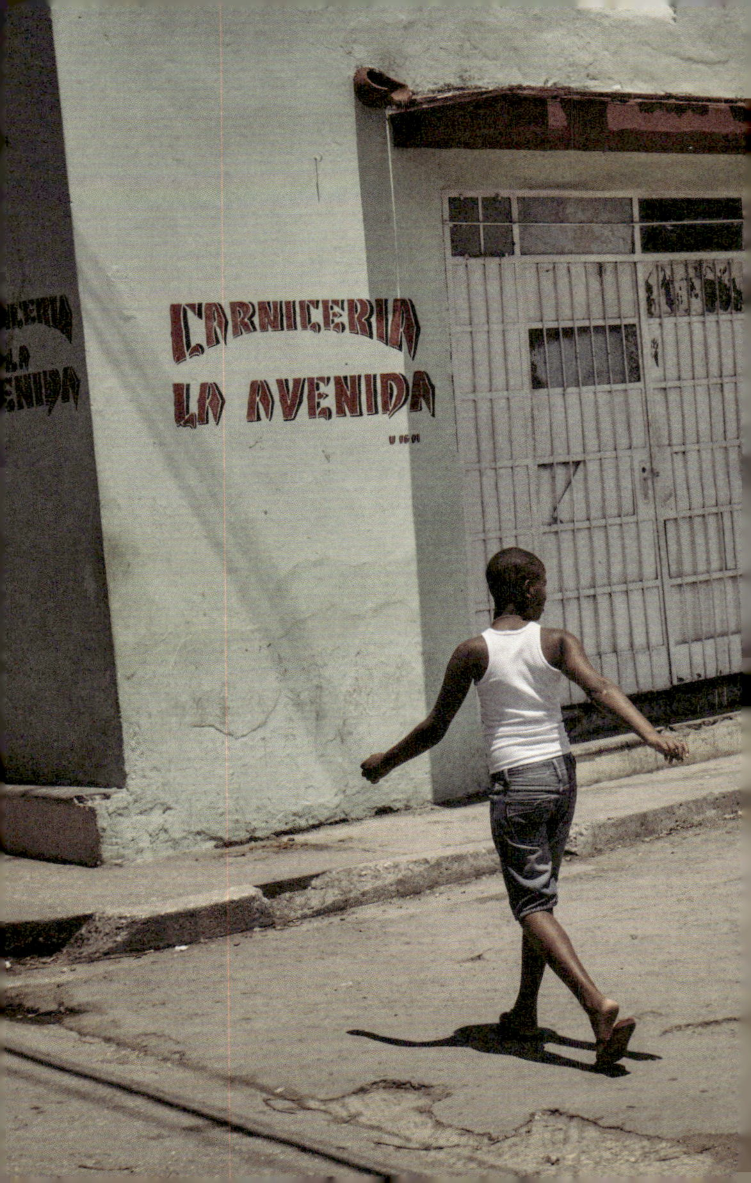
CARNICERIA
LA AVENIDA

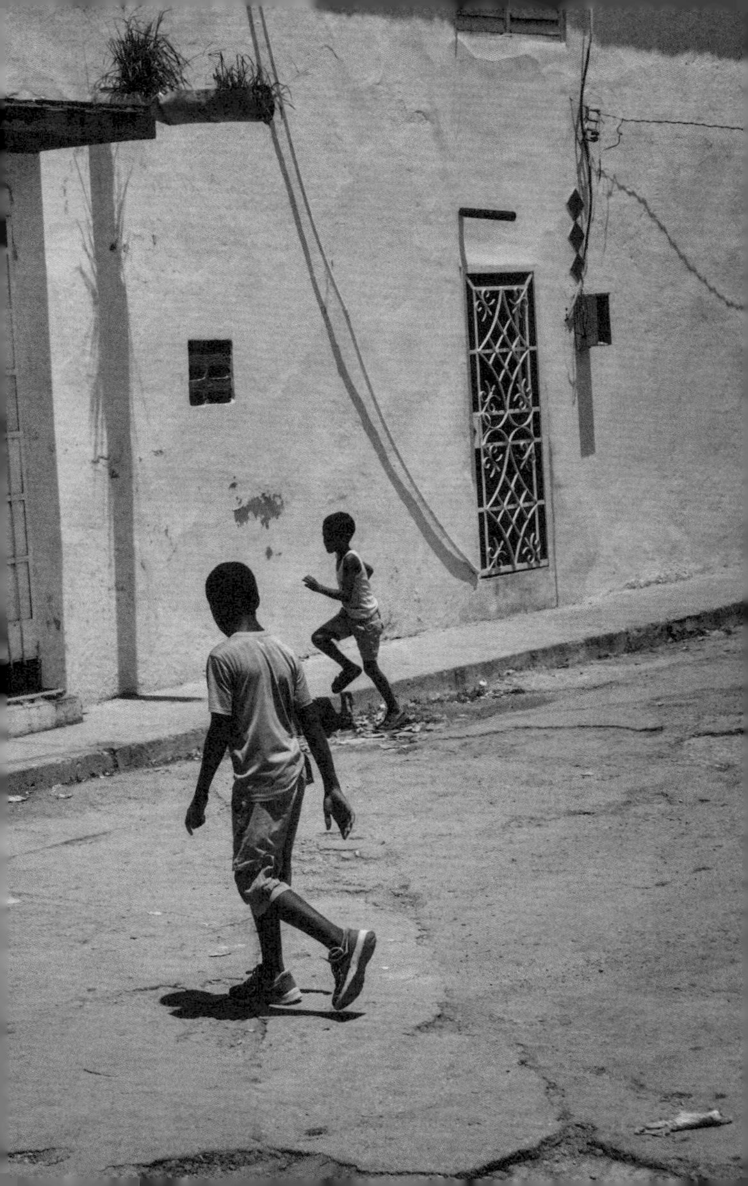

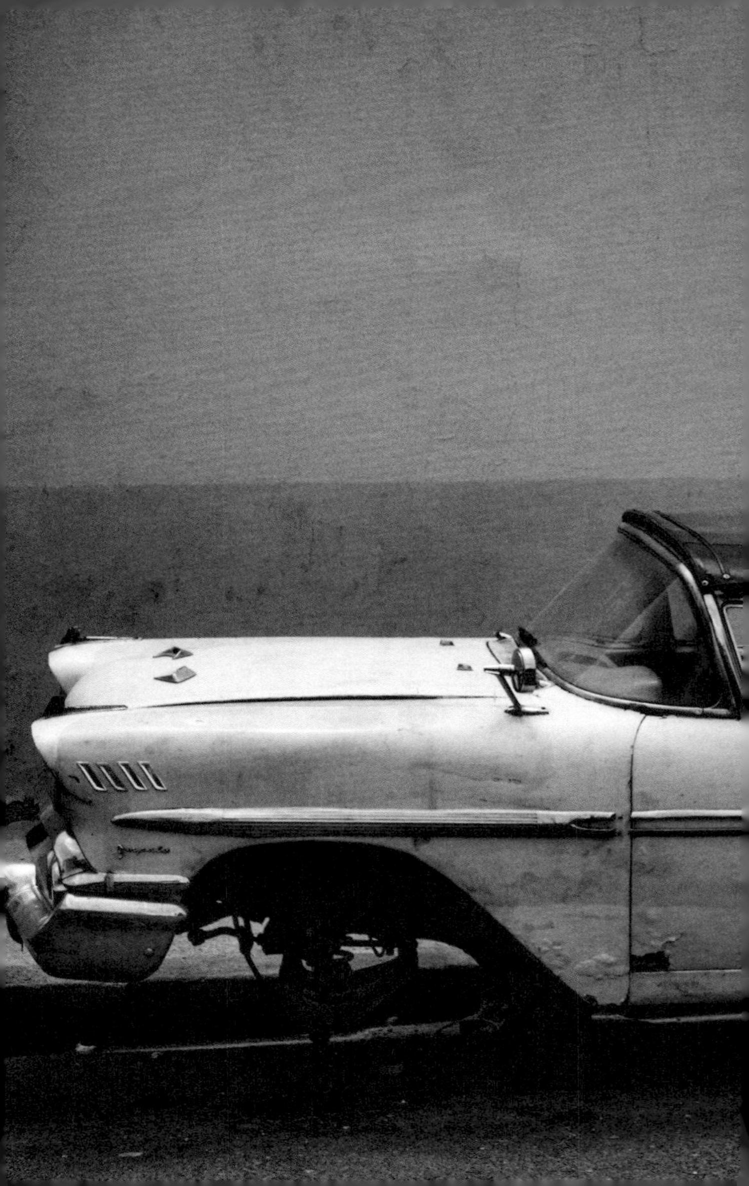

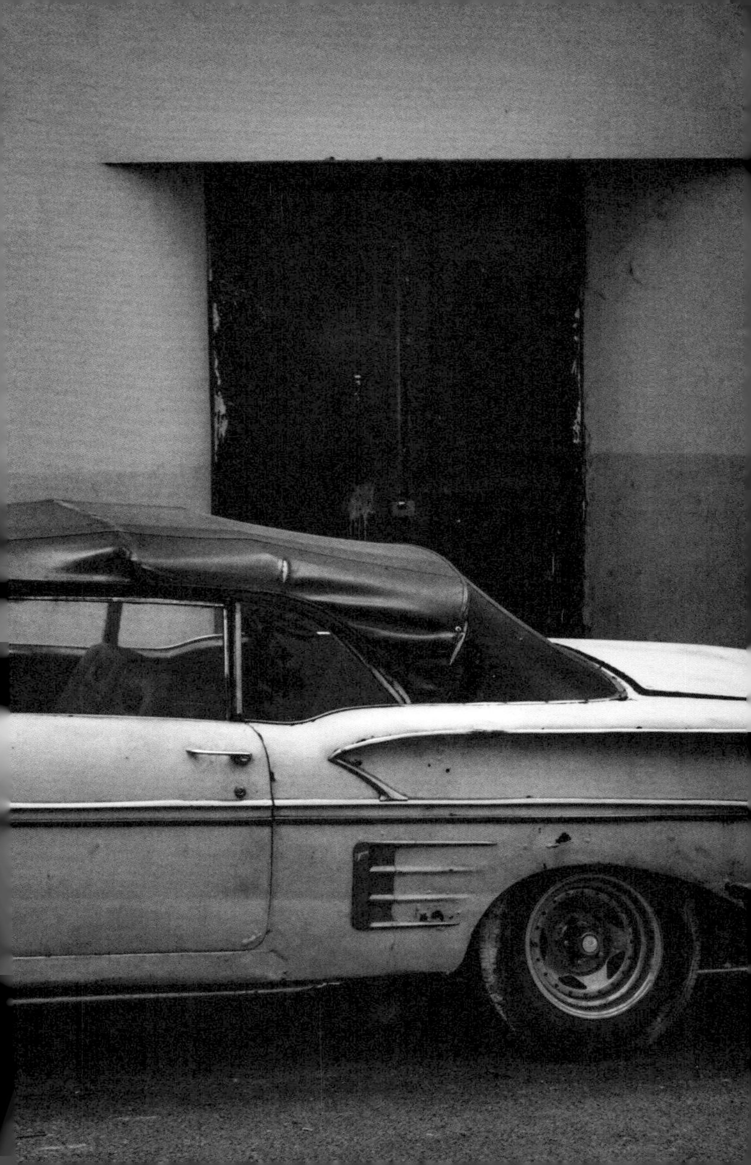

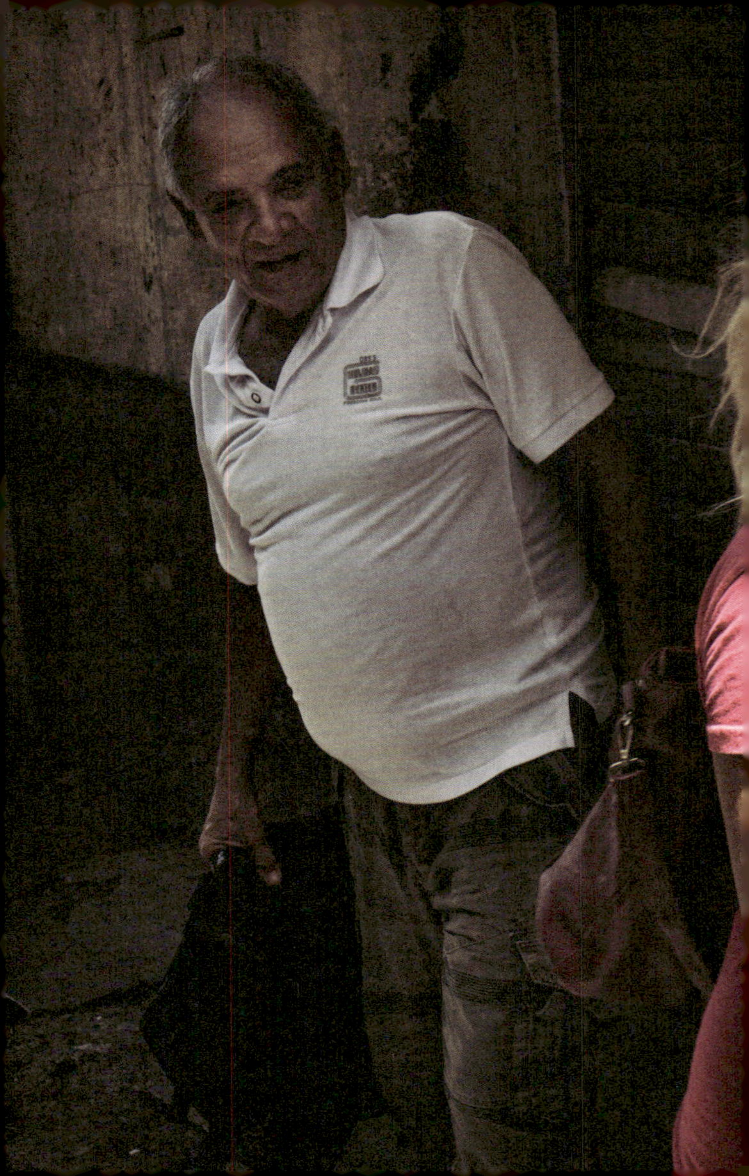

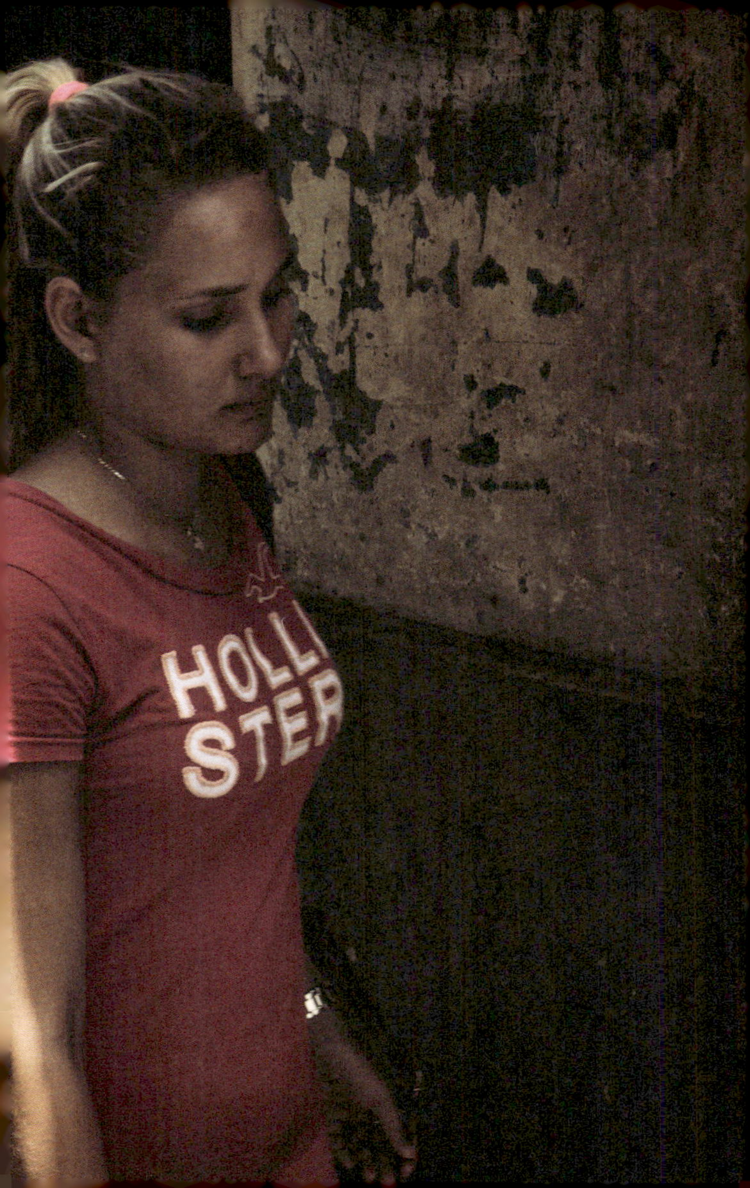
HOLLI
STER

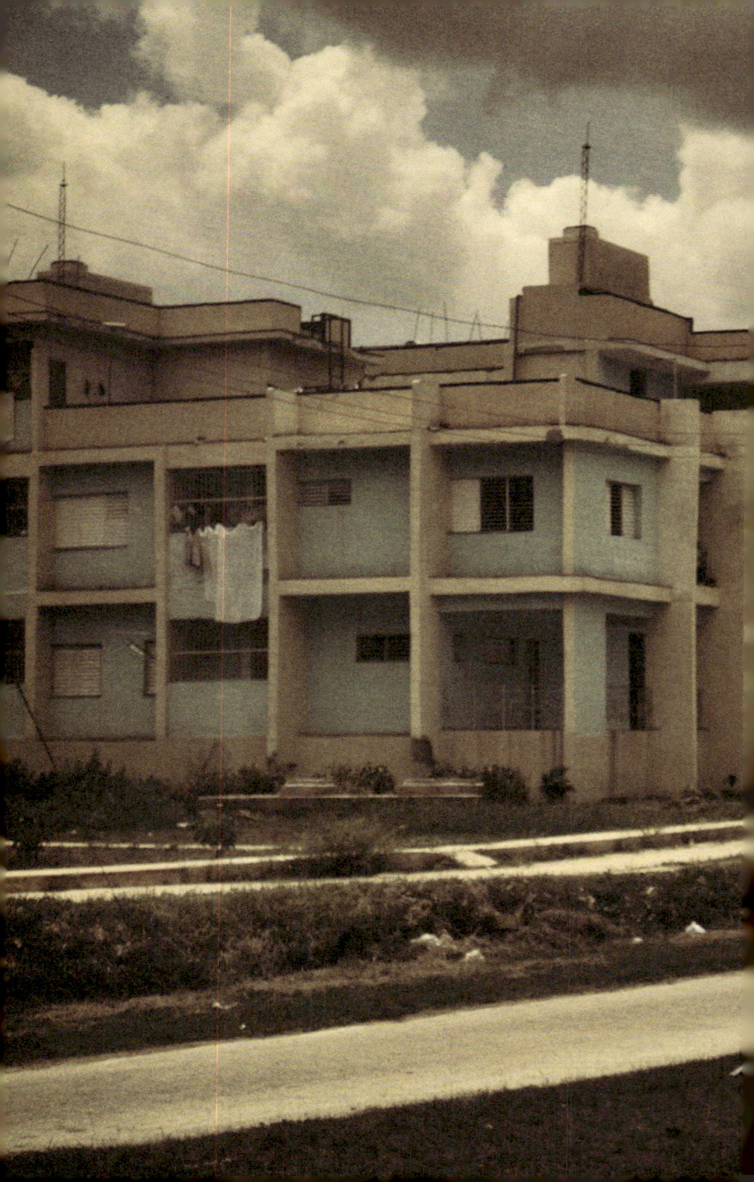

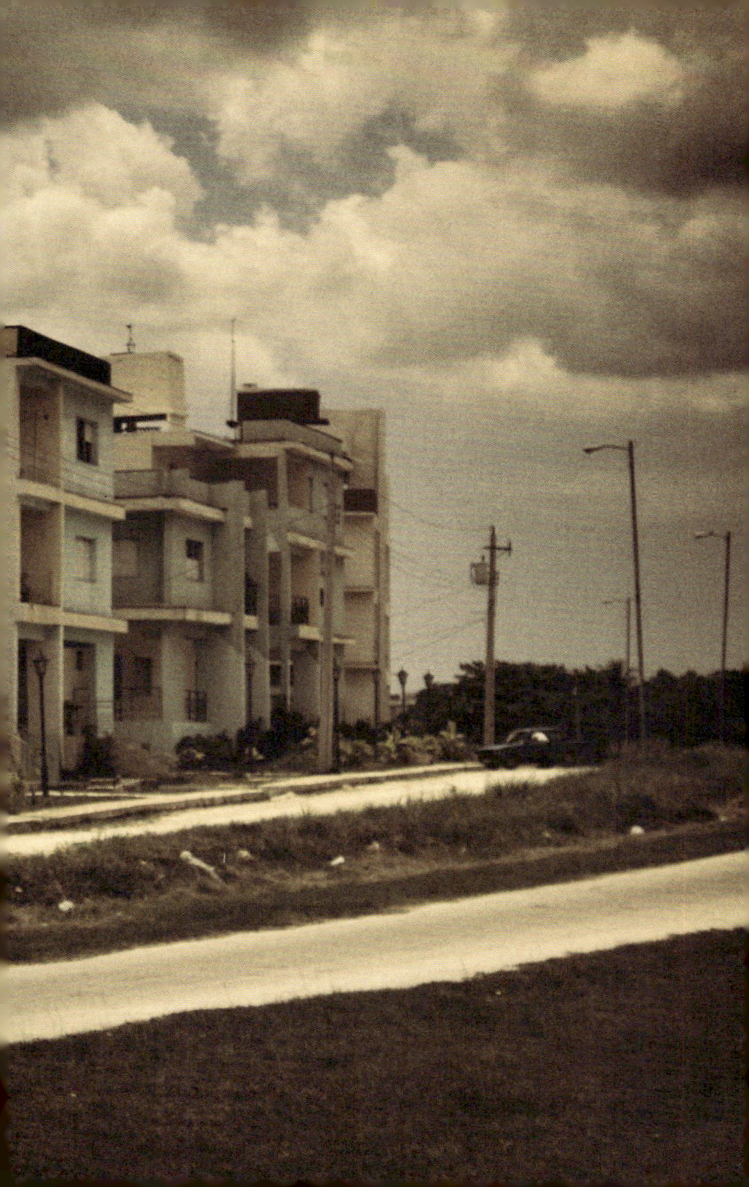

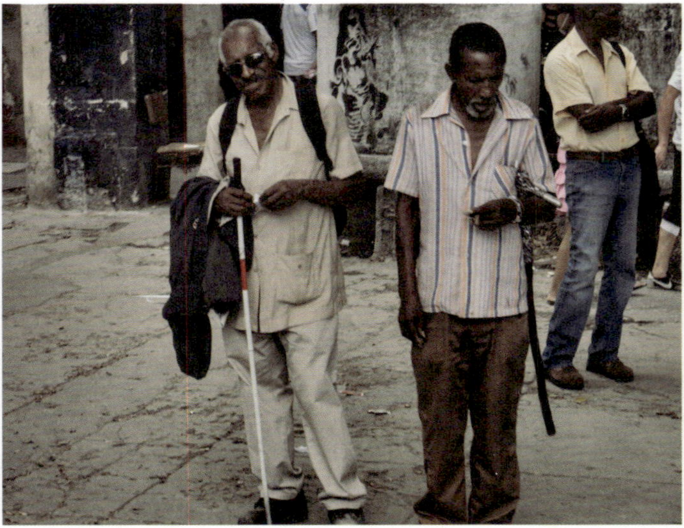

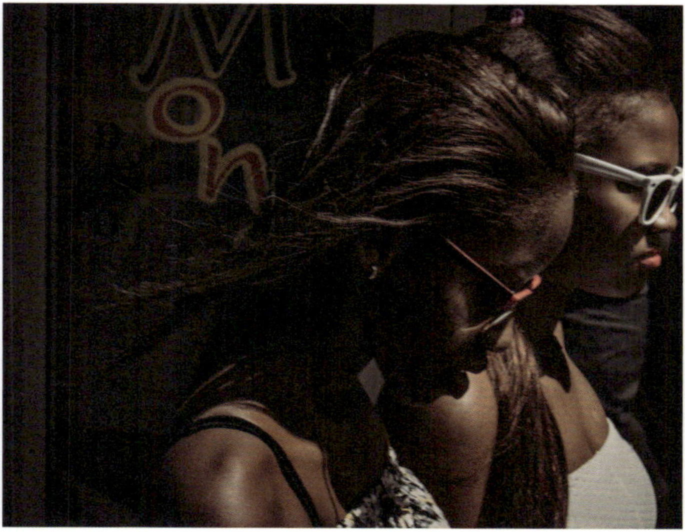
M
on

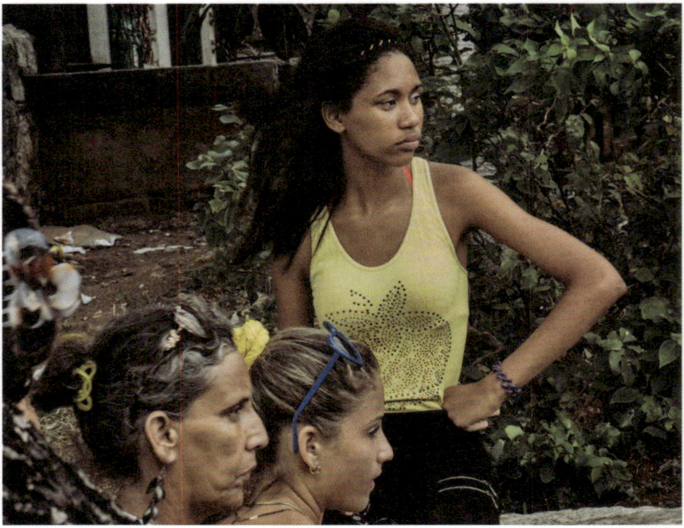

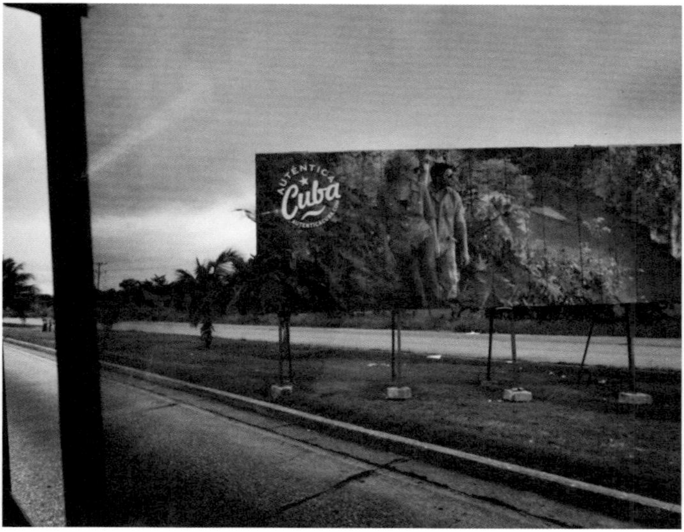
AUTENTICA
Cuba

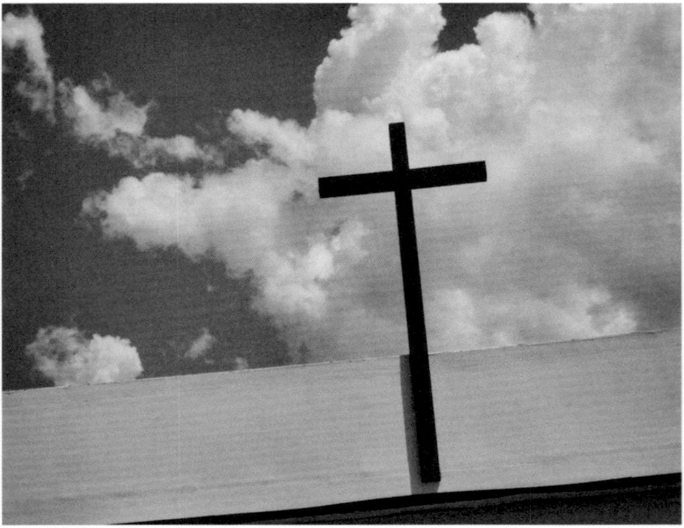

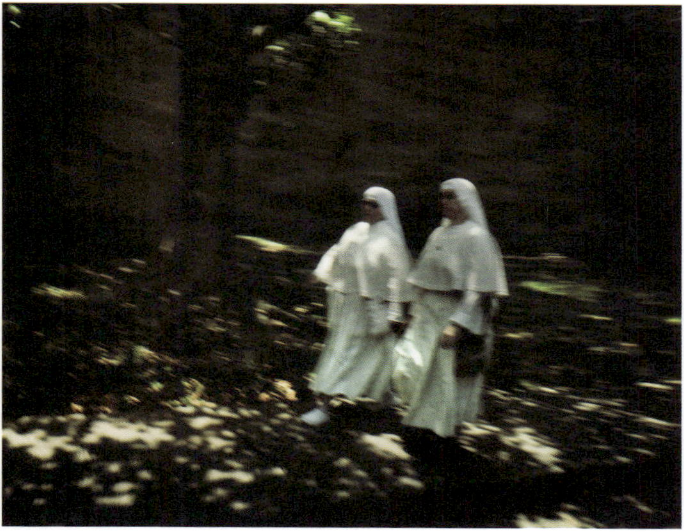

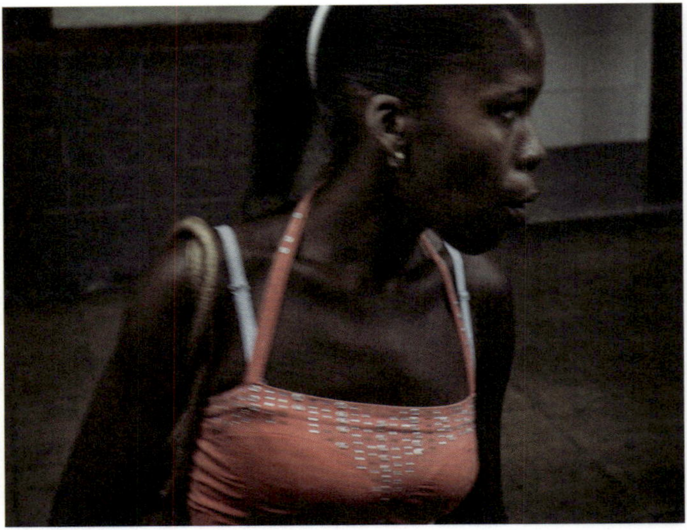

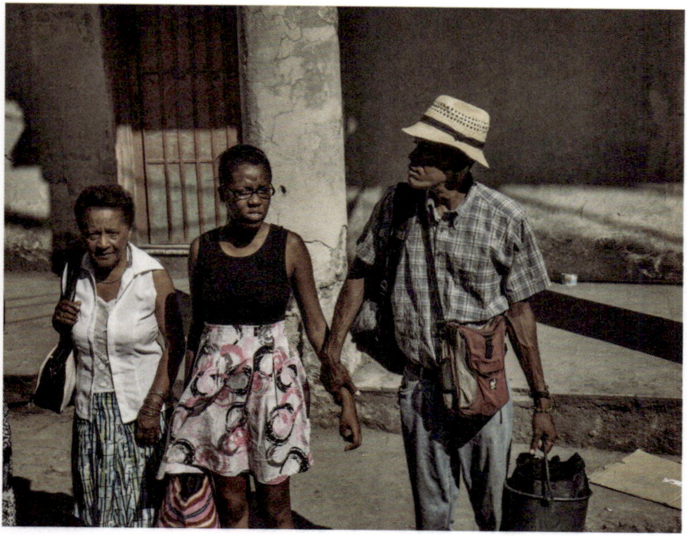

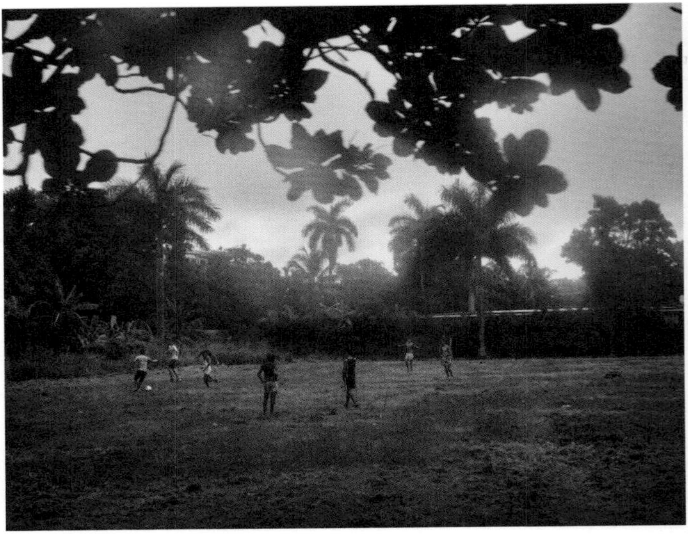

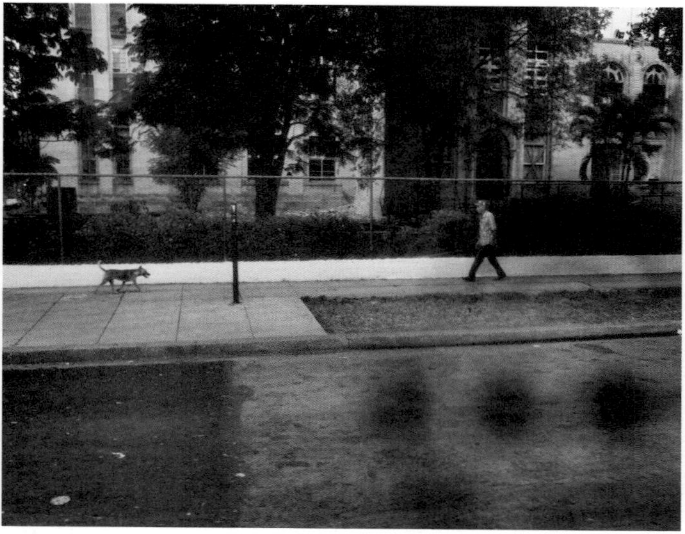

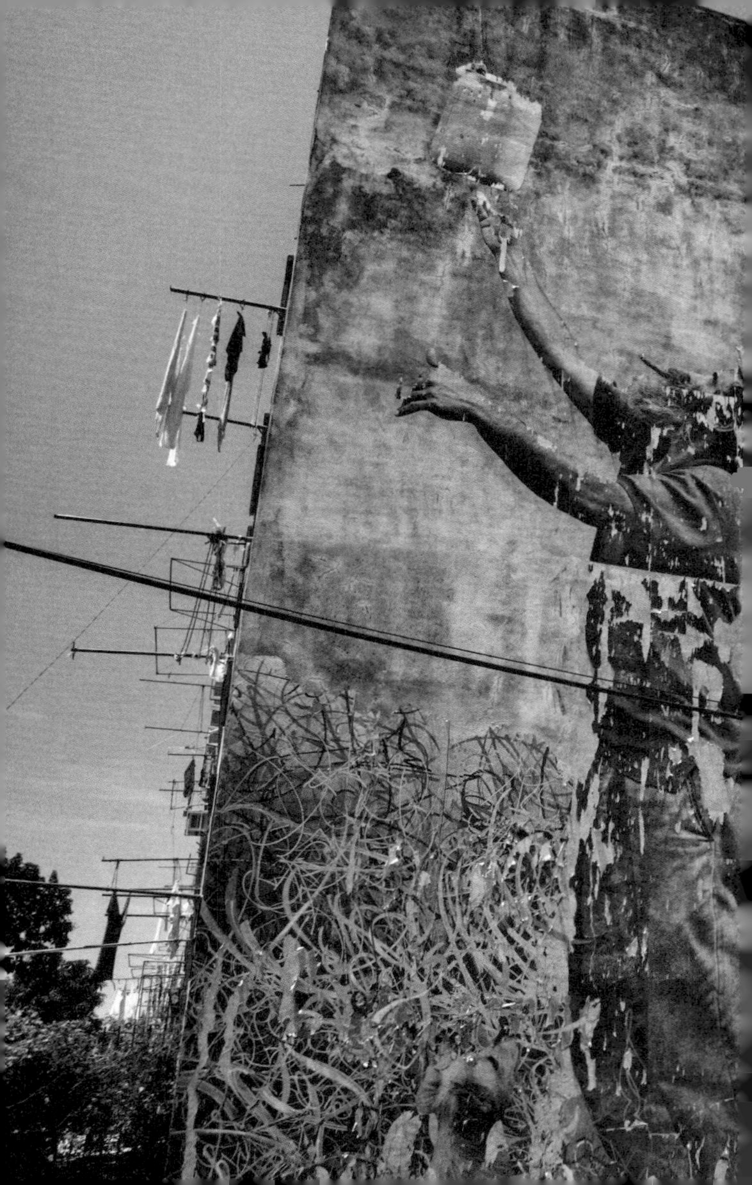

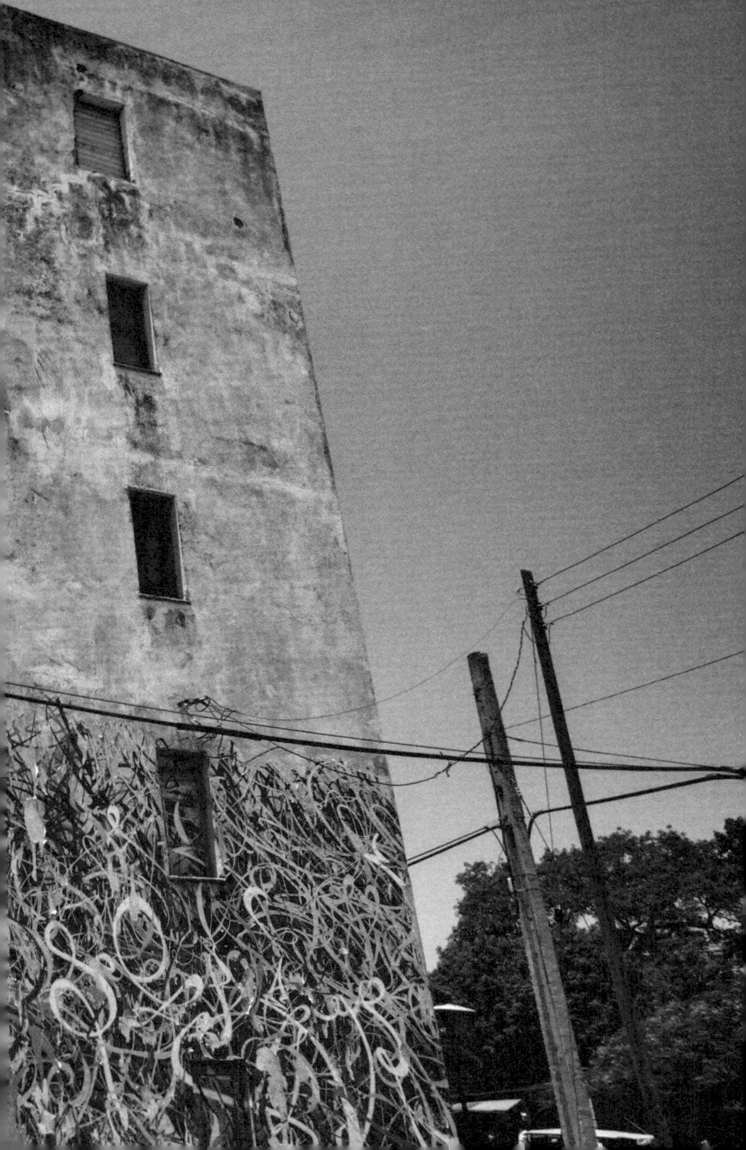

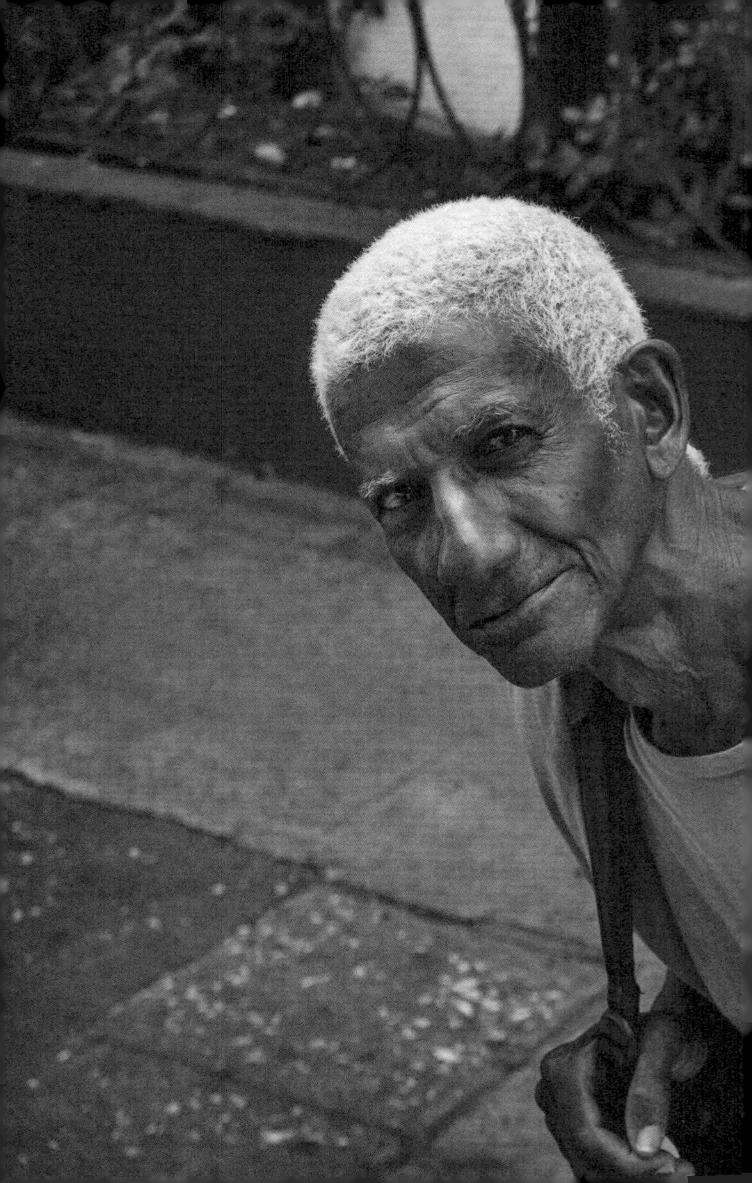

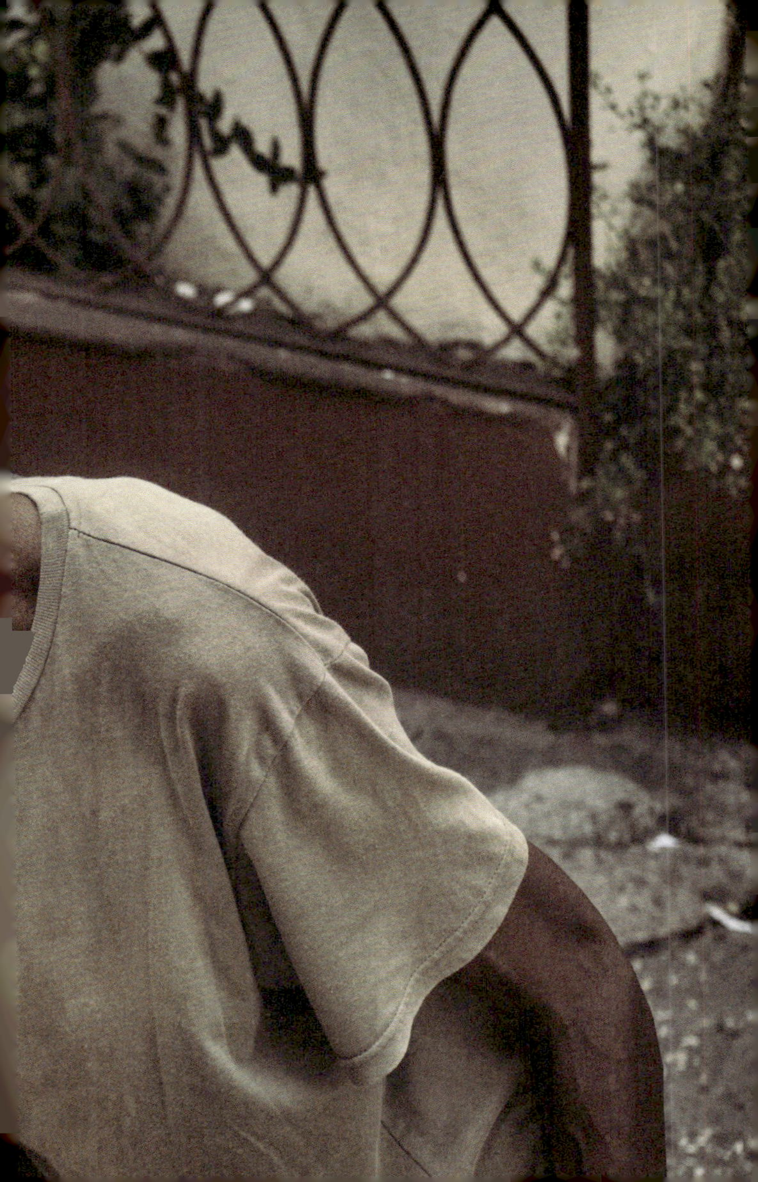

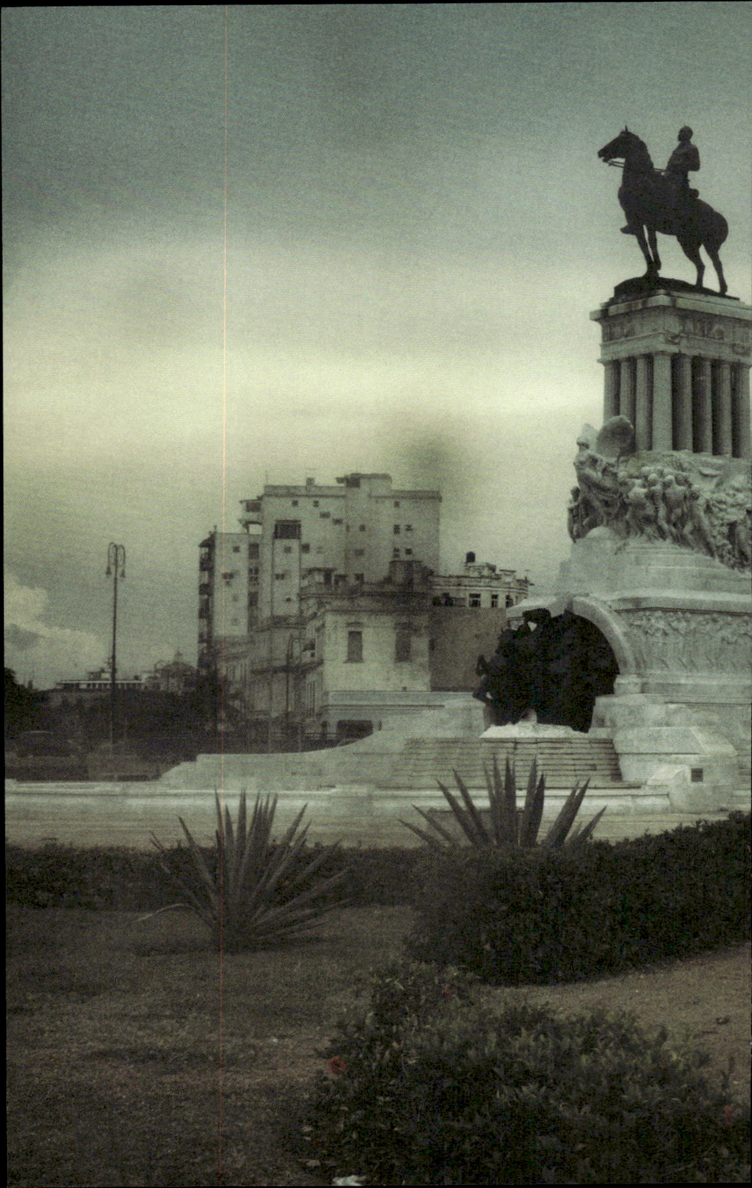

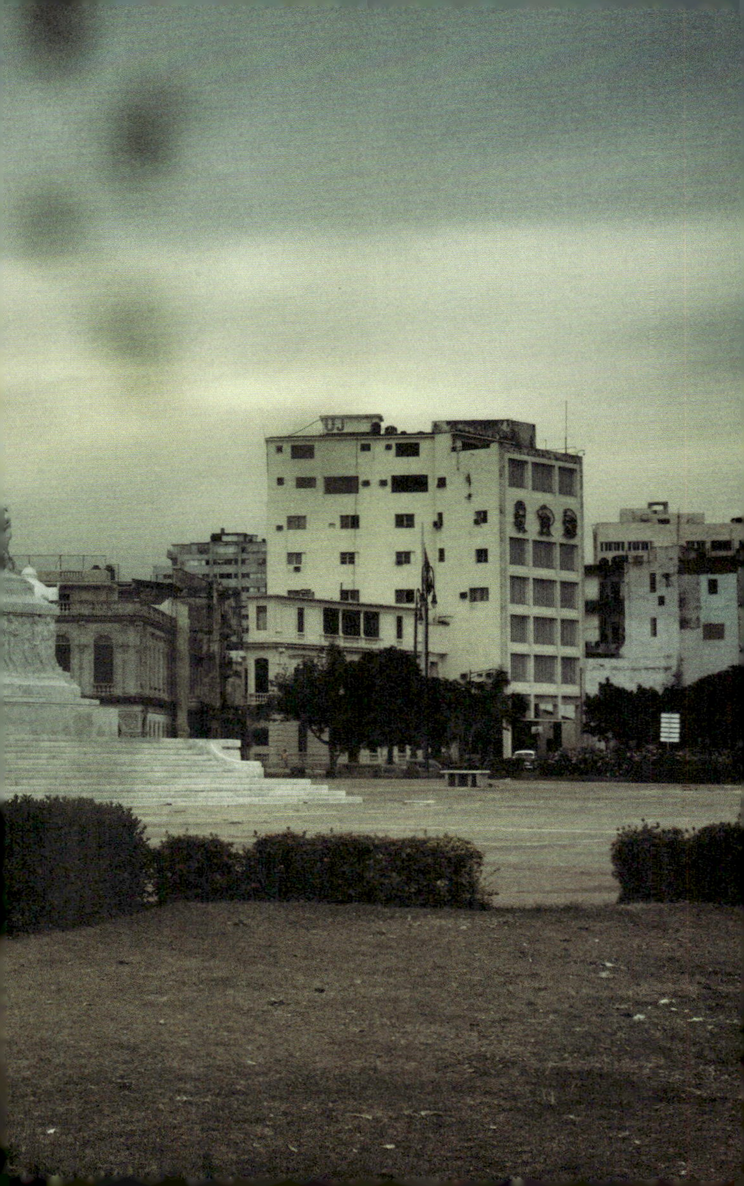
UJ

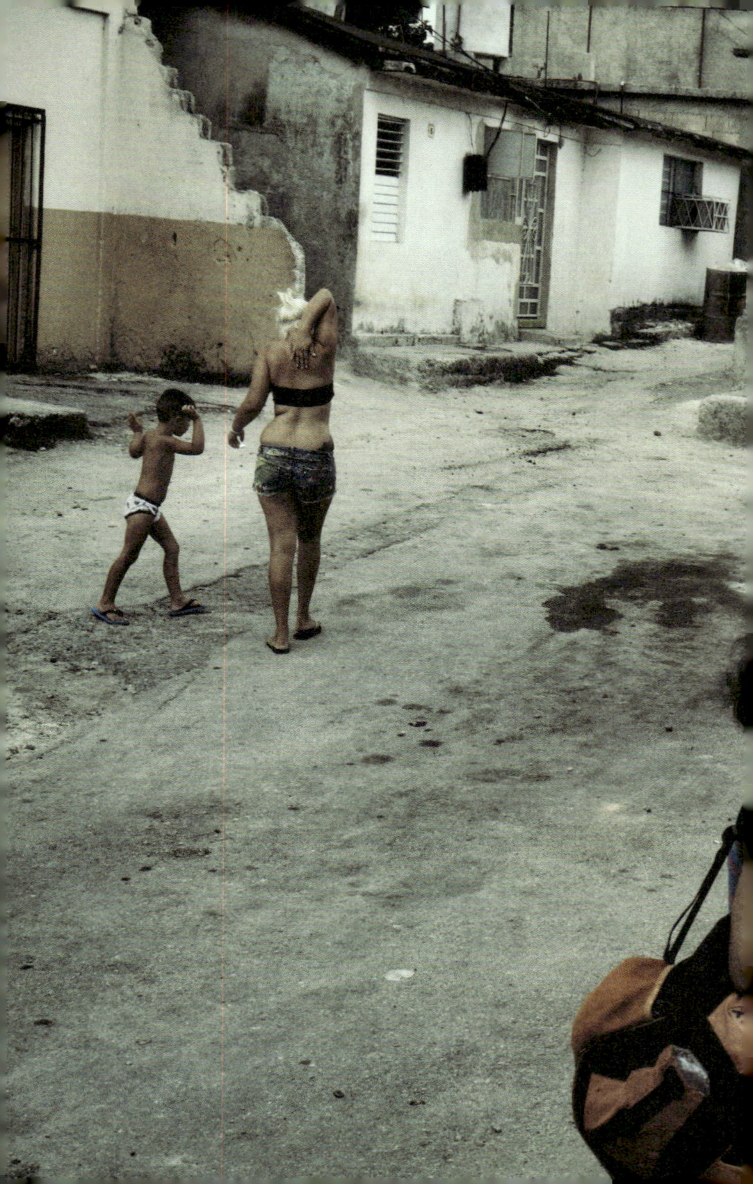

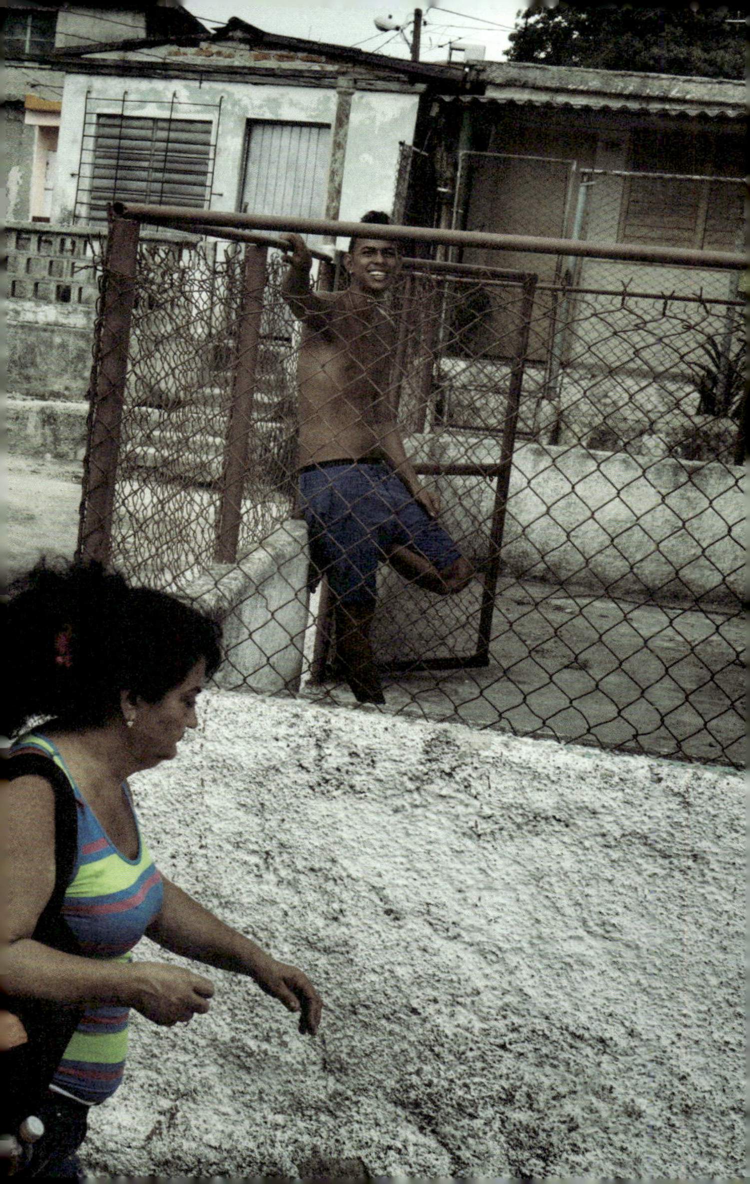

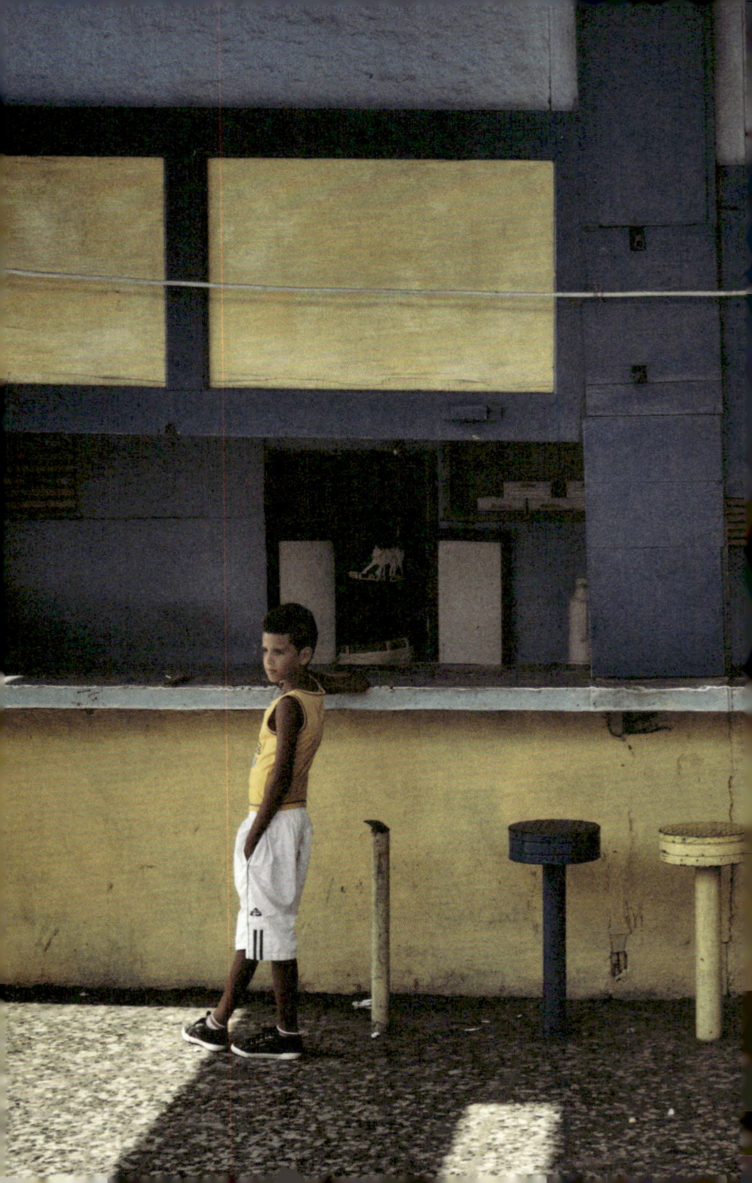

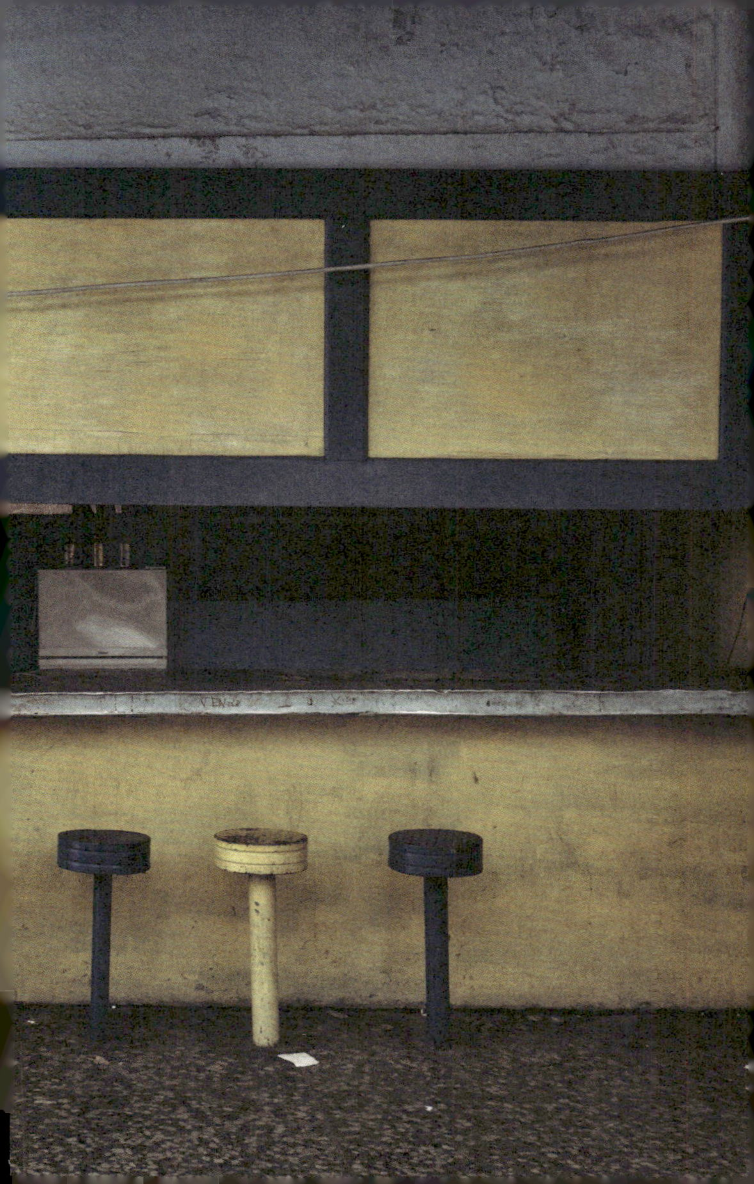

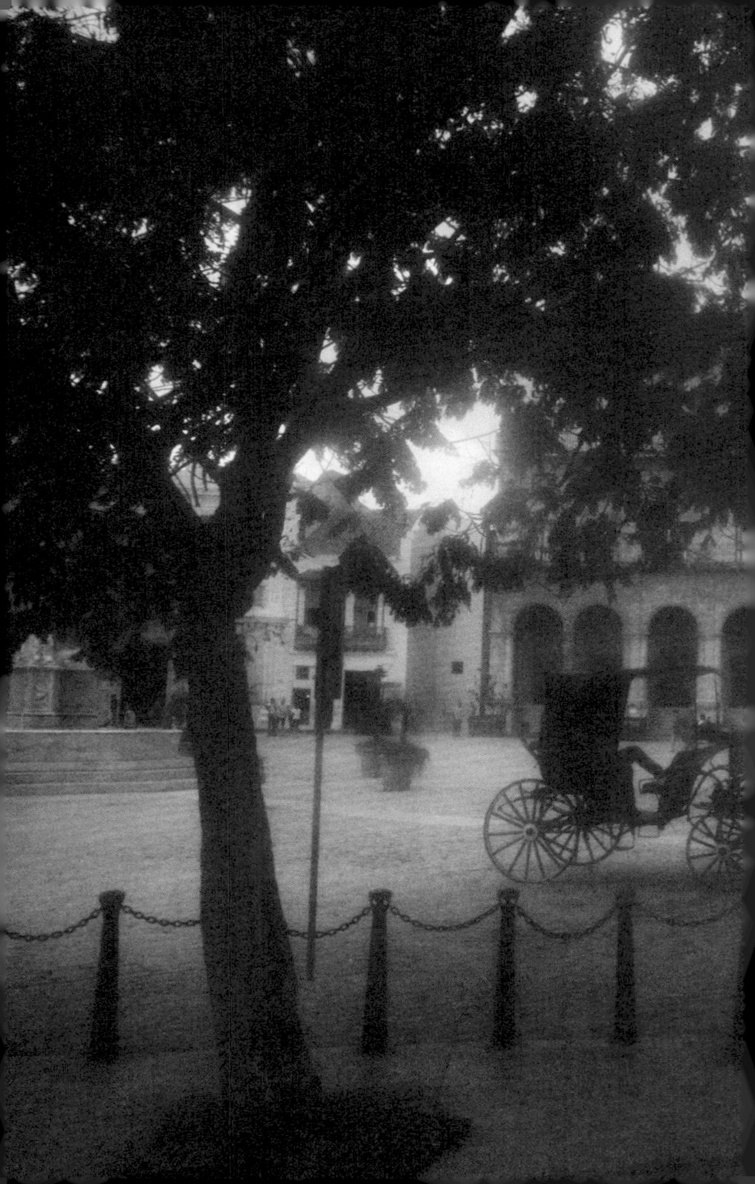

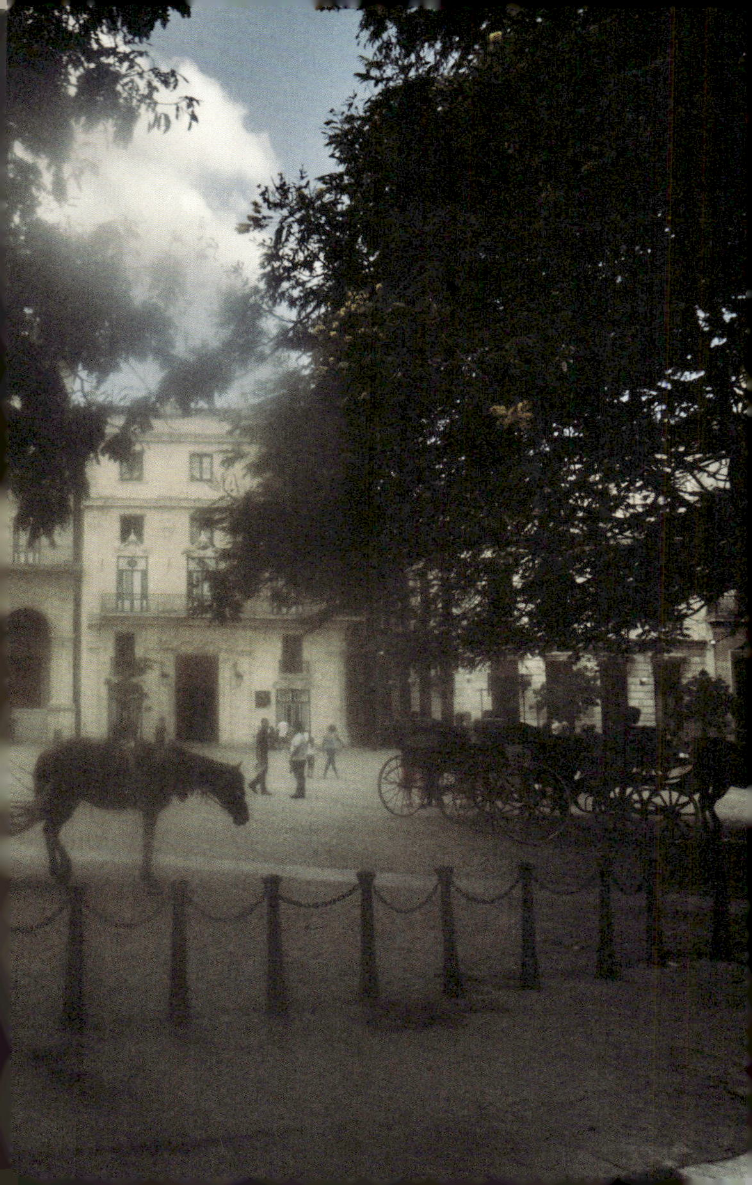

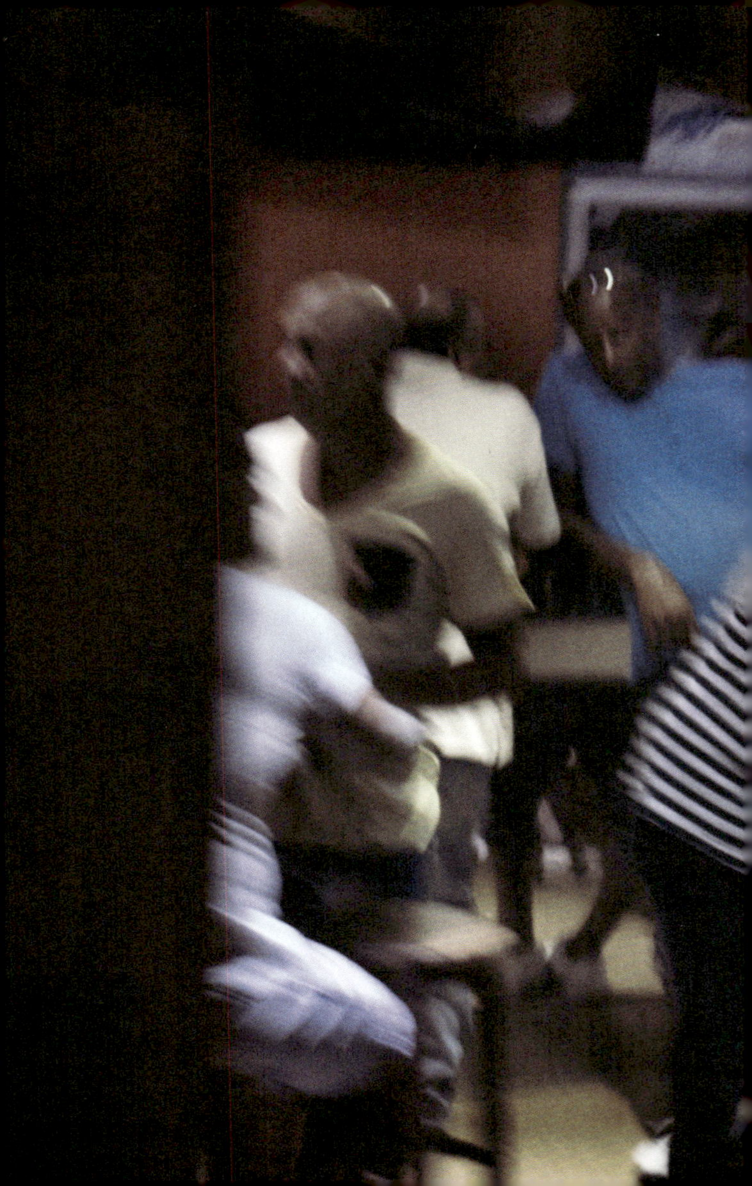

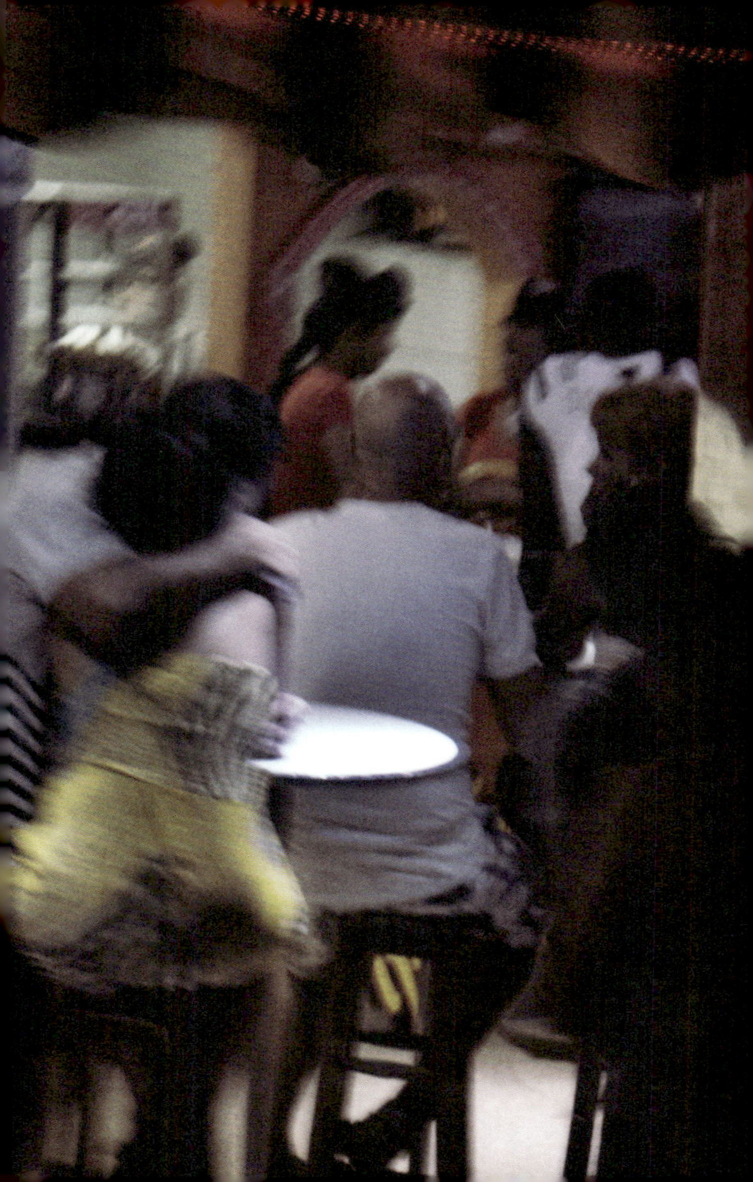

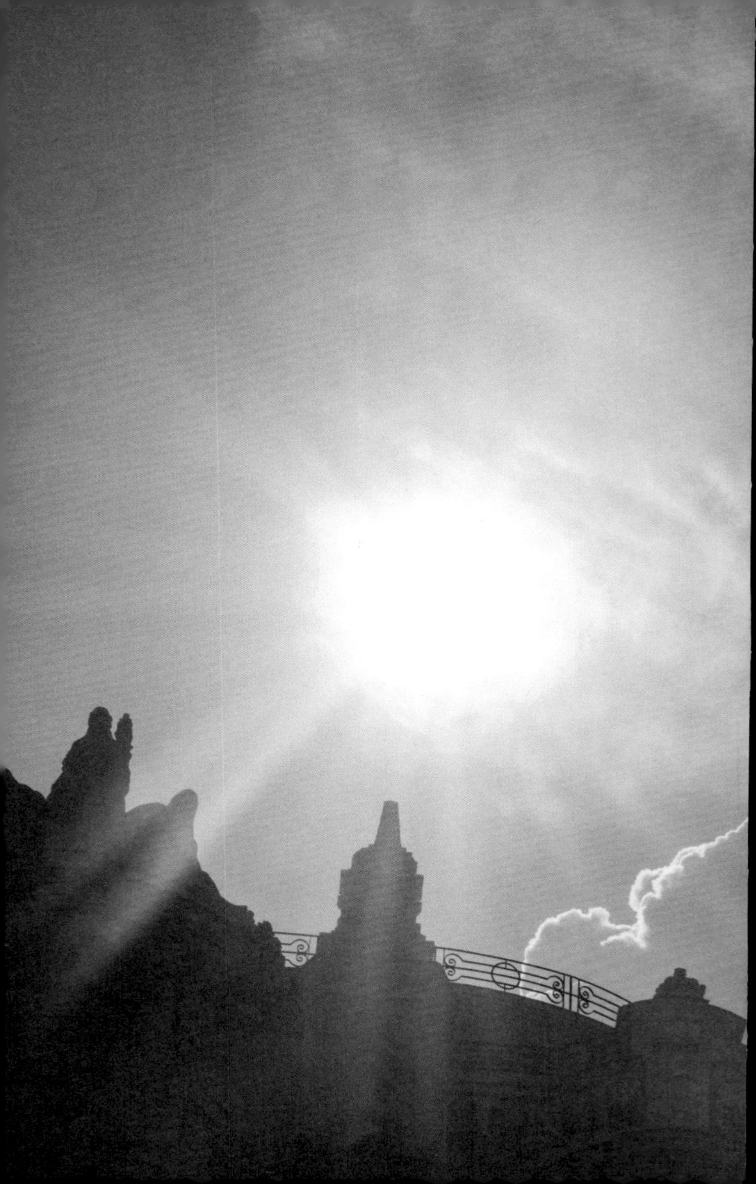

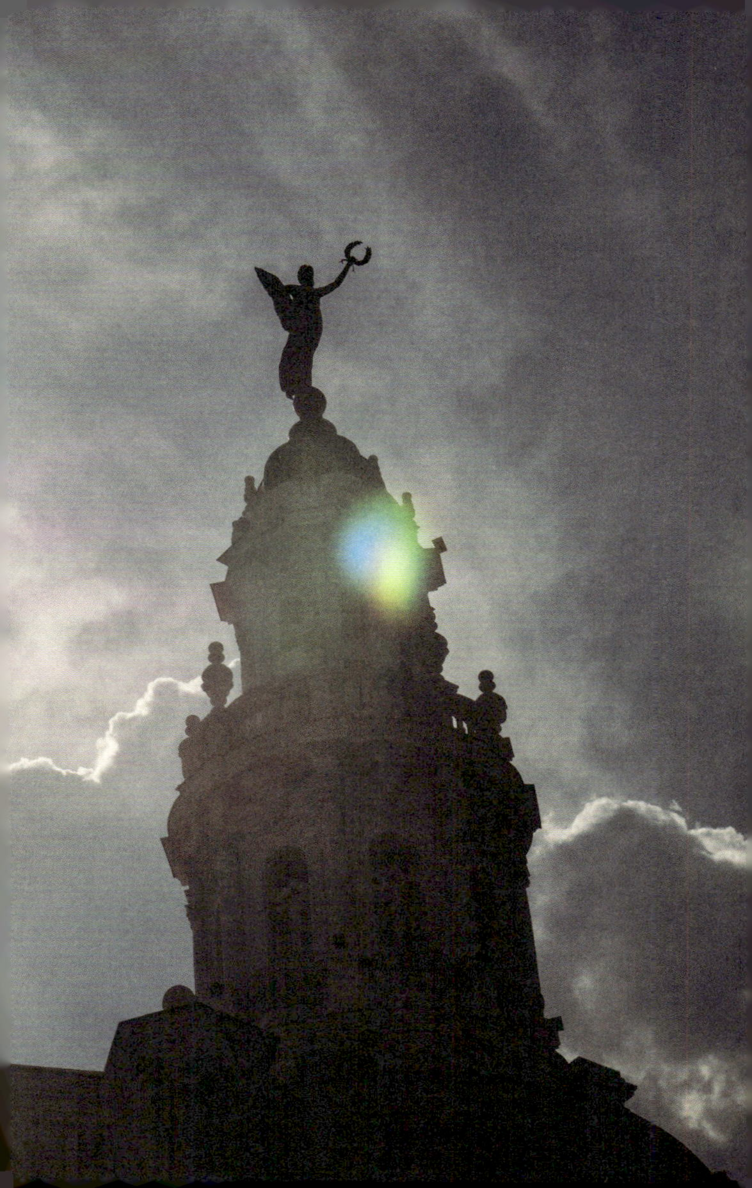

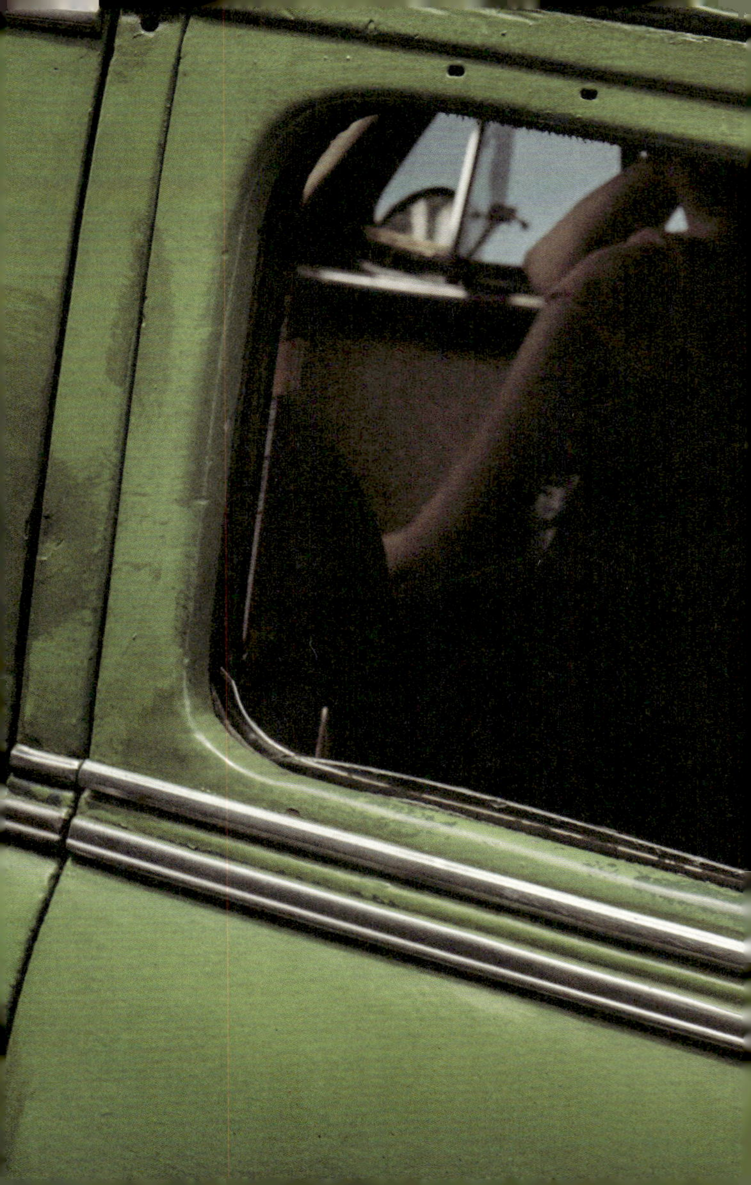

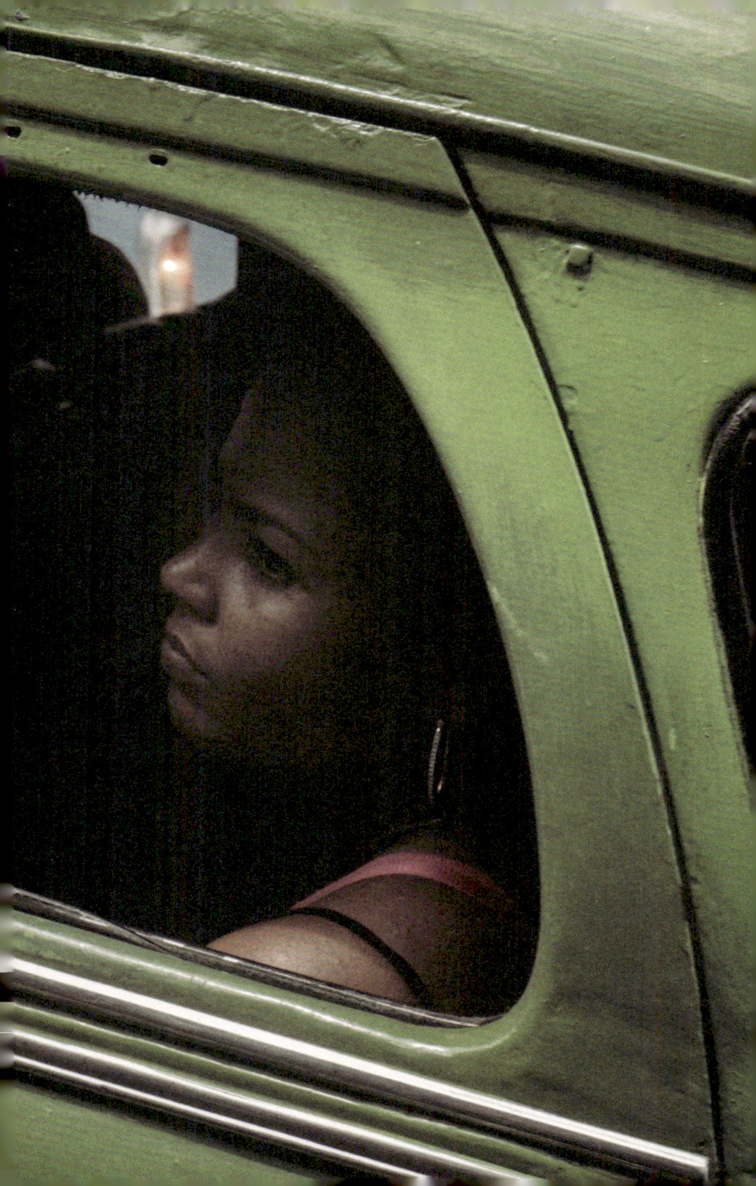

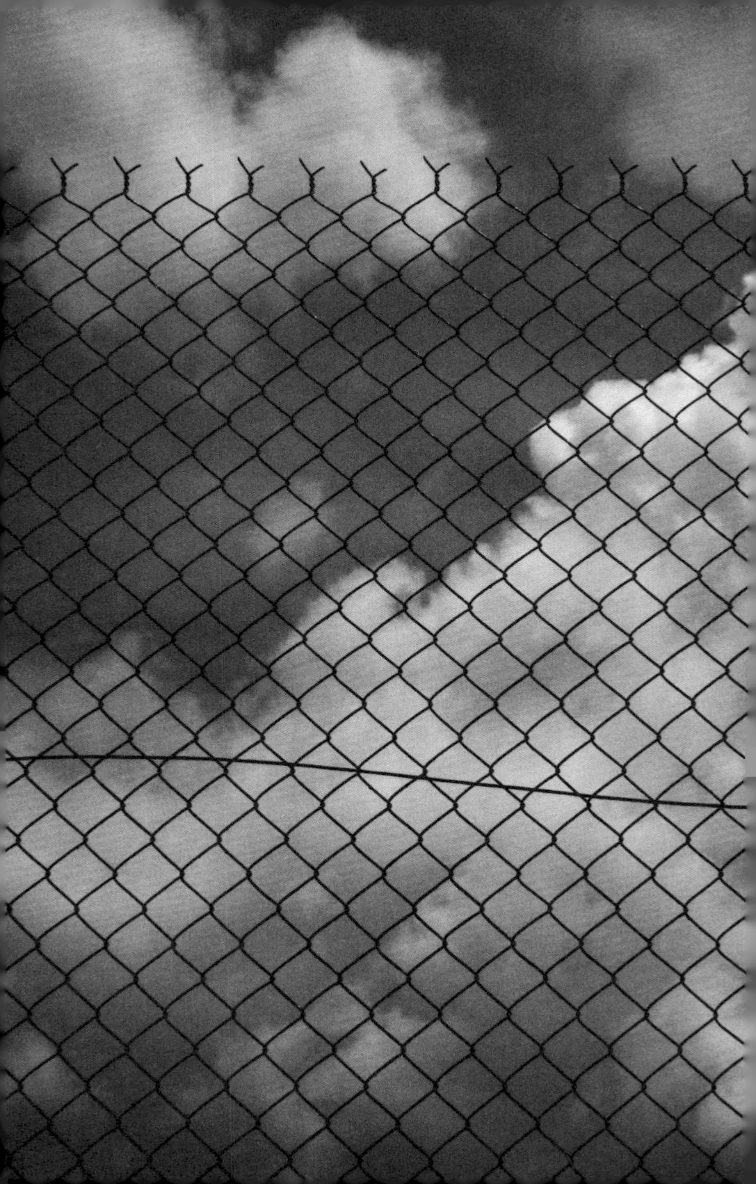

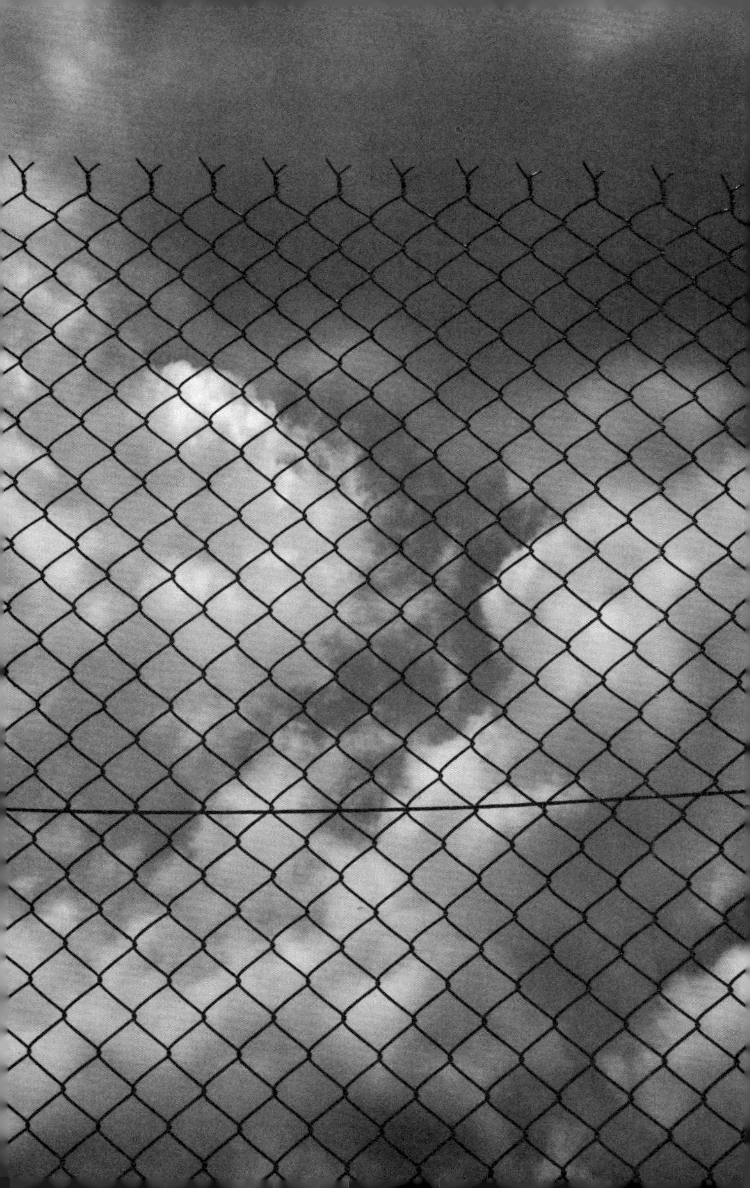

HAVANA: REAL LIFE IS (ALWAYS) SOMEWHERE ELSE

ABEL FERNÁNDEZ - LARREA

Havana is not a city.
It is a state of mind, a blessing, and a curse.
It's a decaying garden of stone full of ants. A Roman ruin.
Havana is not the pale reflection of a city that you see when you walk around its streets.
Havana is in the eyes of its people. In their memories.
Our memories.
Havana looks like a war zone. Sarajevo. Rome after the war, after the invasion of Barbarians.
But there was never a war. It was an inner struggle, a silent fight.
Against time. Against oblivion.
Long ago, I used to like imagining Havana was a different place, far away.
Like Rimbaud said: "la vrai vie est ailleurs." Real life is somewhere else. Always.
Squinting, a totally alien city appeared to my eyes.
Suddenly, I was in Moscow, Wien, Paris, Prague, New York.
Later, I realized Havana is all those cities, somehow.
Because Havana is many cities at a time.
Havana is like an onion. The Onion City.
Makes you cry.

Strudel City. Sweet and sour.
Havana is a colorful city of contrasts. Humid ochre walls of urine, green streets of vomit, dark corners of feces, stained pools of semen, washed sidewalks of sweat.
And the people, the people in Havana, are a mixture of gods and beasts, angels and demons, dii superii and dii inferii.
For Havana is the crossroad, the midpoint between heaven and hell.
The cemetery.
The pantheon.
The battlefield populated by worms and crows.
The spoils.
People in Havana seem to walk dressed in rags, but they are actually dancing, naked, a frenetic dance of maenads.
A bacchanal.
Havana is the place where all the races mingle, where all the creeds, all the languages mix up.
The Tower of Babel.
Babylonia.
The sacred whore of yore.
Havana is not a city. It is not even of this world.
It is a ghost, an echo.
A lament carved on a tombstone urinated by the dogs.
Havana is Antigone weltering among her siblings corrupted flesh. Antigone bathed in the dried blood of Polynices, rubbed by the putrid flesh of Eteocles.
Havana is a Greek tragedy, a mythical polis that never existed.
A polis cursed by the falling sphinx, by the sin of Oedipus.
The ruin of an ancient theater haunted by the souls of seven sinful kings.
Havana is a masquerade, a carnival in the middle of the lent.
The mask of a city, the empty disguise of a city.
A beautiful ruin. A nacred empty shell.
People in Havana seem to live in a frenetic dance of the possessed, but they are shadows, the tormented shadows of men, wandering by the riverbanks of Styx.
Never eat the pomegranate in Havana, or you'll never find the gates back to the earth.
Now I squint and I see Havana instead. When I was there, I was not, and now that I am not, sometimes I wish I was.

I'm doomed. I ate the pomegranate.
I'm sick for I carry the poison of Havana in the veins.
Urine and feces.
Vomit and sweat.
I am no longer, no matter where I go.
I'm always in Havana, that state of mind.
Real life is always somewhere else.

Abel Fernández-Larrea is a writer, editor, and translator born in Havana, Cuba. He has been a professor of literature at the University of Havana and is author of the collections of short stories *Absolut Rontgen* (Caja China, 2009), *Berlineses* (Ediciones Matanzas, 2013, and Casa Vacia, 2016), *Los heroes de la clase obrera* (Union, 2013), *Trilogia sucia de Manhattan* (Abril, 2015), and *Los macabeos* (Ediciones La Luz, 2015); and the novels *Buenos dias, Sarajevo* (Bokeh, 2015), *El fin de la inocencia* (Bokeh, 2015), and *Shlemiel* (Editions Fra, 2016).
In 2016, he received the Premio Novelas de Gaveta Franz Kafka for his novel "Shlemiel".
Abel currently lives in Miami Beach.

GAIA LIGHT

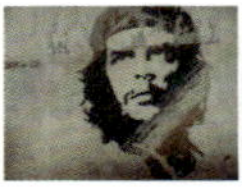
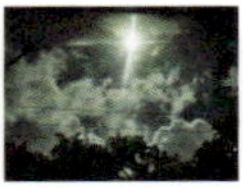
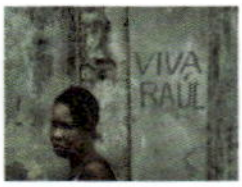

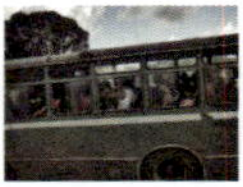
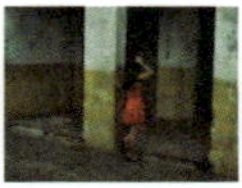
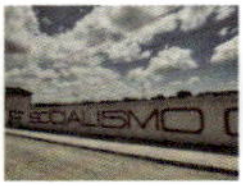
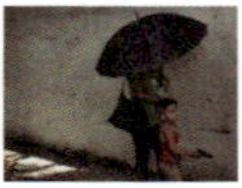
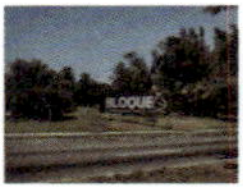
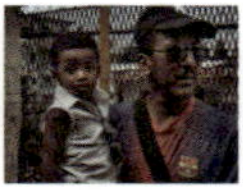
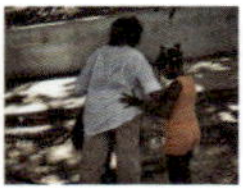
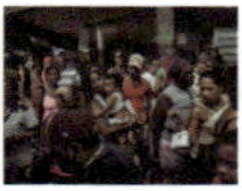
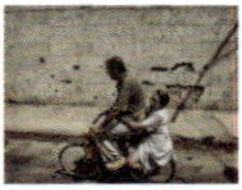
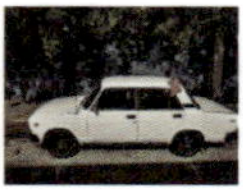
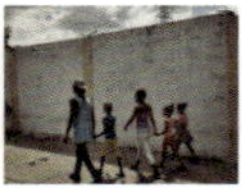
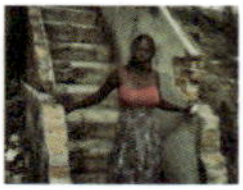

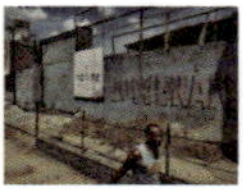
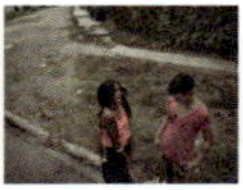
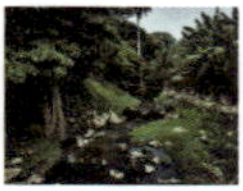
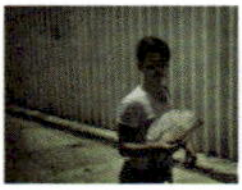
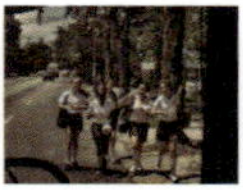
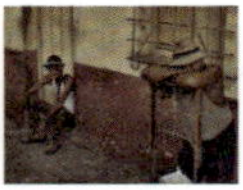
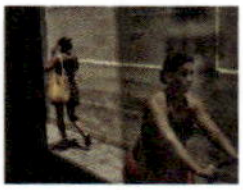
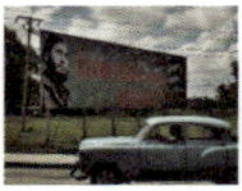
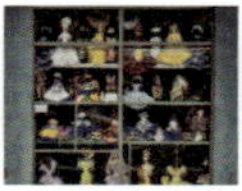
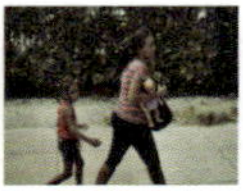
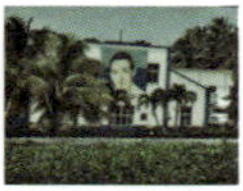
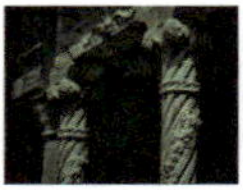
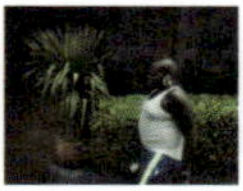
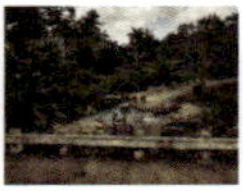
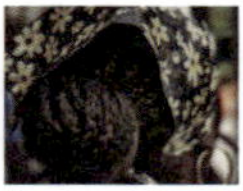

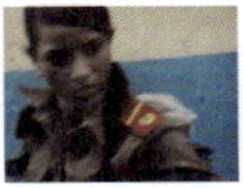
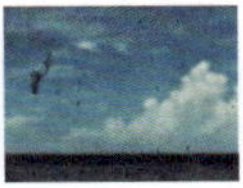
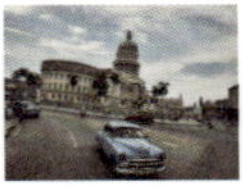
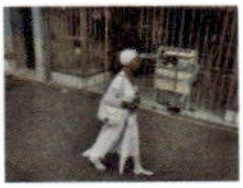
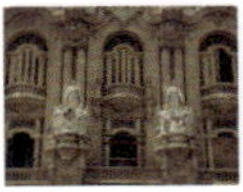
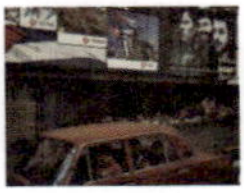
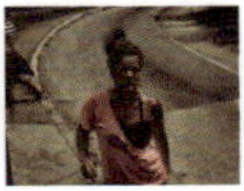
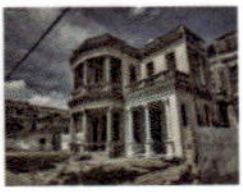
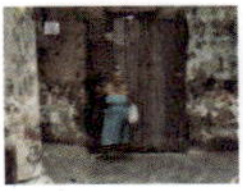
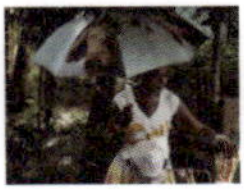
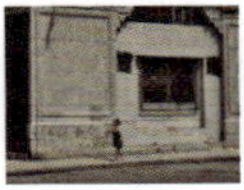
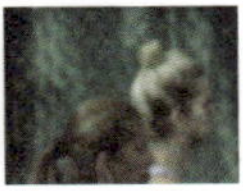
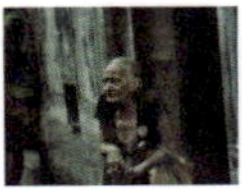
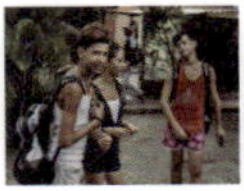
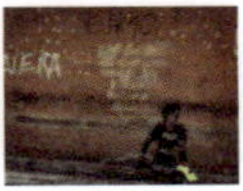
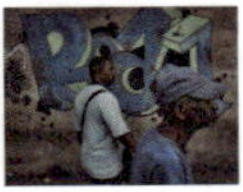
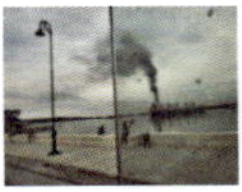
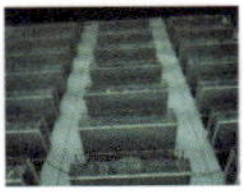
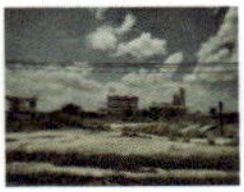
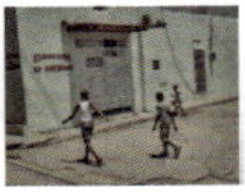
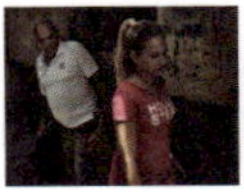
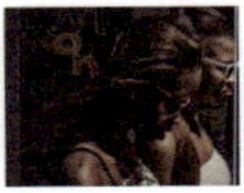
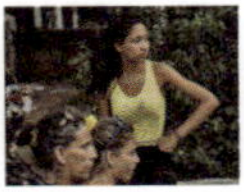
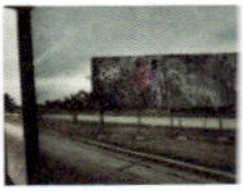
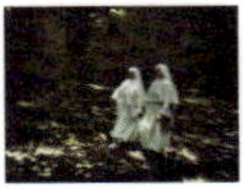
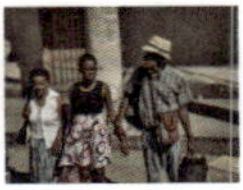
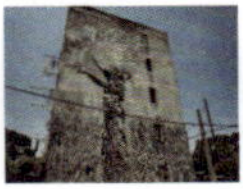
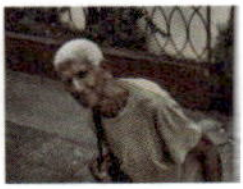
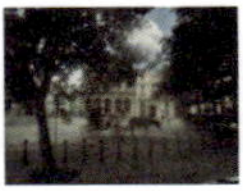
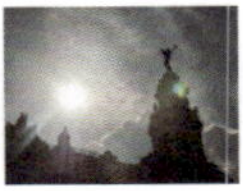
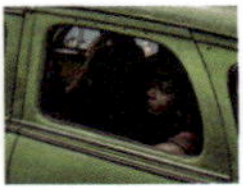
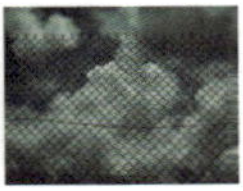

ALESSANDRO COSMELLI

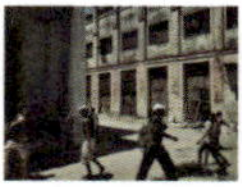
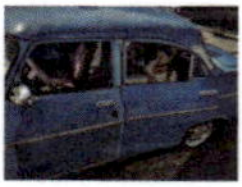
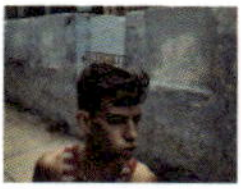
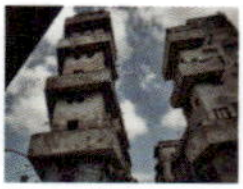
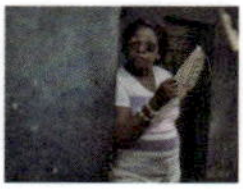
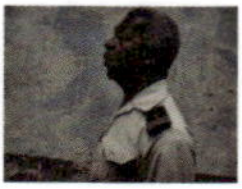
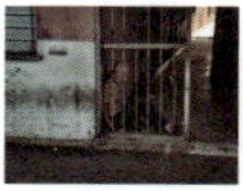
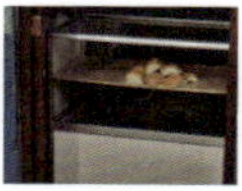
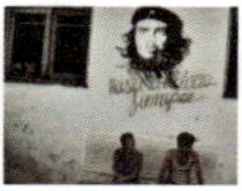
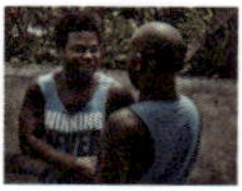
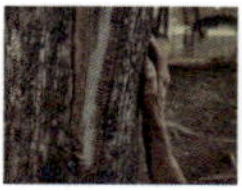
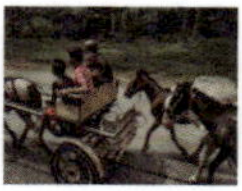
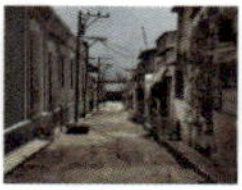
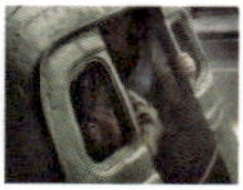
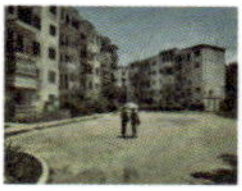
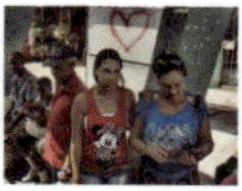
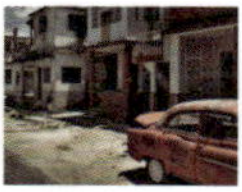
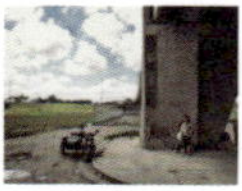
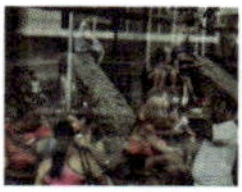
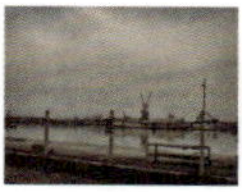
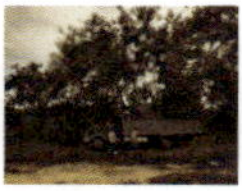
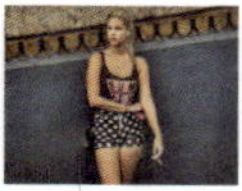
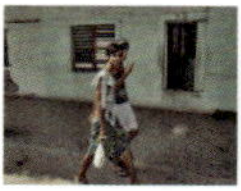
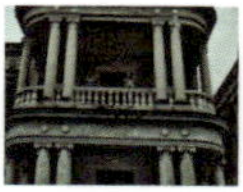
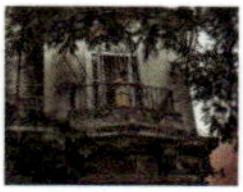
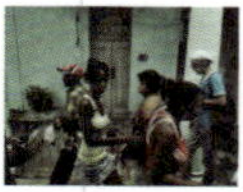
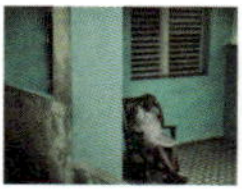
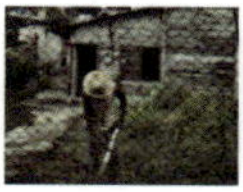
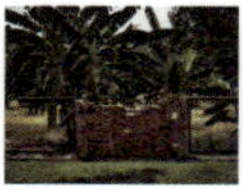
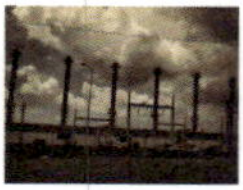

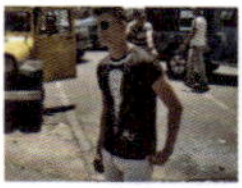
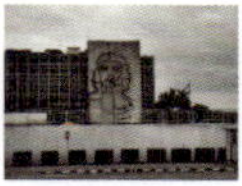
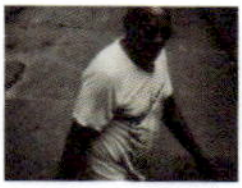
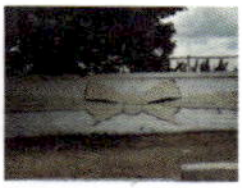
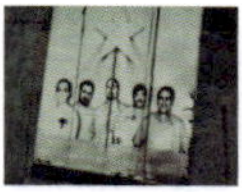
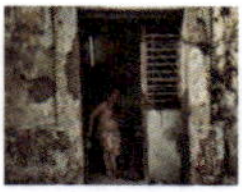
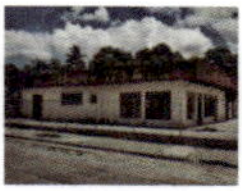
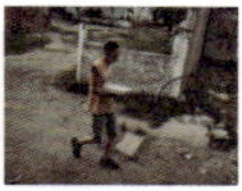
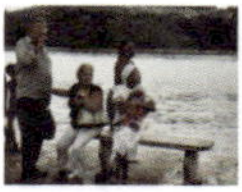
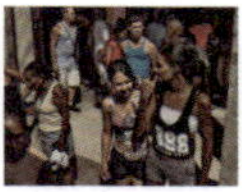
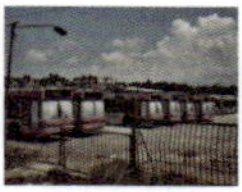
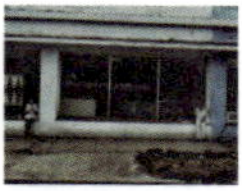
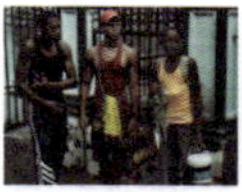
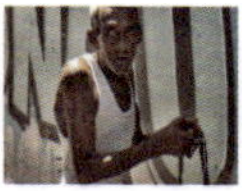
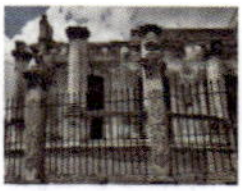
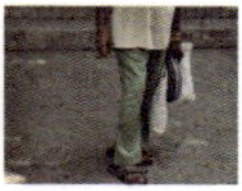
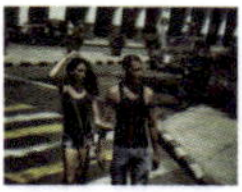
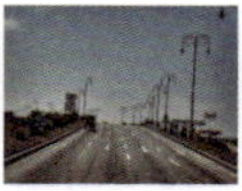
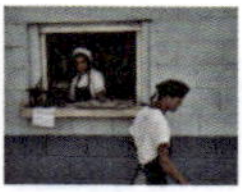
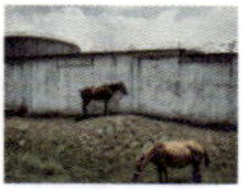
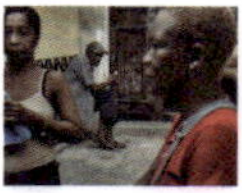
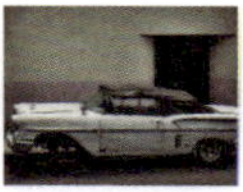
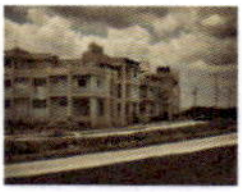
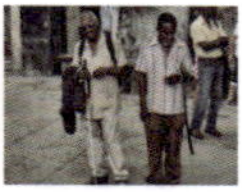
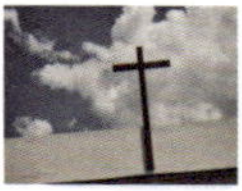
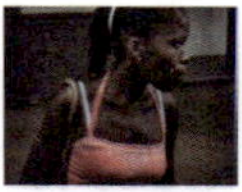
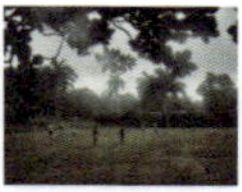
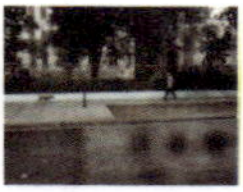
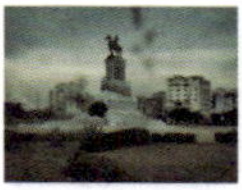
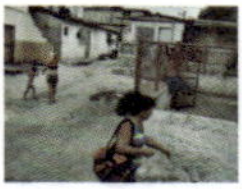
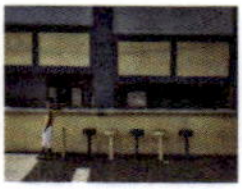
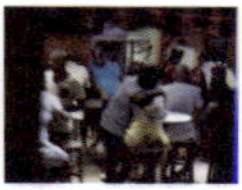

ACKNOWLEDGMENTS

Andrea Albertini, Eleonora Pasqui, Claudio Palmisano, Abel Fernández-Larrea, Lorenzo Tugnoli, Enrico Farinazzo, All the Staff at Damiani, Anna Lombardi, Angelo Aquaro, Roberto Saviano, Valentina Tordoni, Richard Slade, Michela Battaglia, Gavin Keeney, Casa Sofia, Rolando Esquinita, Angela Nocioni, Maurizio Longobardi, Sergio Vallesi, Tiziana Faraoni, Daniele Zendroni, Stefano De Luigi, Tiziana Gazzini, Piero Spila, M.C., Jamie Wellford, Cristiana Falcone, Melissa Pallini, Fabrizio Lazzeretti, Emilio D'Itri, Officine Fotografiche, Chiara Oggioni Tiepolo, Kelli Grant, Nadia Berardi, Silvia Albini, Silvia & Massimo Cosmelli, Alberto Cosmelli, Massimo Gattabrusi, Paola Gattabrusi, David Curzi, Venus, Marco Carnevali, Chica Lenzi, Roberto Sbolci, Federica De Paolis, Bruna & Giancarlo, Luise Hiesinger, Luca, Liz, Roman, Sara Rosen, Roberto Cozzi, Anthony Bellini, Linosa, Gianfranco Gasparro, Theresa Coffino, Carmen Andronache, Kathy Hiesinger, Ulrich Hiesinger, Judy & Ray McGuire, Aislinn & Ruadh McGuire, Yoani Sánchez, Mark Morris, Larry Jones, Tony, Mila Lake, Nicole Gagne, Frederic Fasano, Sebene Selassie, Suki, Nicola Guarneri, Gillian Arthur, Stephen Chu, Cristina Ottolini, Edoardo & Siena Chu, Ulle & Gino, Lapo, Giulietta, Brooklyn, New York, Sampa, Milan, Istanbul, Mumbai, Mexico City, The Buzz Project, Light TV.

Havana and its People.

Havana Buzz
Alessandro Cosmelli | Gaia Light

Editing by
Gaia Light

Book Design by
Alessandro Cosmelli

Image Toning by
Claudio Palmisano

Published by
Damiani
info@damianieditore.com
www.damianieditore.com

Havana Buzz is part of *The Buzz Project*, a multi-city photo-reconnaissance project inaugurated in 2010.

www.buzzproject.org

www.alessandrocosmelli.com
www.gaialight.com

Printed in June 2017 by Grafiche Damiani – Faenza Group SpA, Italy.

ISBN 978-88-6208-560-1